Map coding:

- - - - Boundaries of wards
.... Boundaries of polling districts
(Fc, Fd, etc.) Each polling district identified by letter
〰〰〰 Walk as described in Chapter 1
● Polling Place (1964)
■ Conservative Committee Room (1964)
▲ Labour Committee Room (1964)
⬛ Conservative Headquarters
▲ Labour Headquarters

Political Parties in Action

Ivor S. Richard *Labour*

William Compton Carr *Conservative*

THE CANDIDATES

Political Parties in Action *The Battle of Barons Court*

by Robert T. Holt and
John E. Turner

*A Study from The Center for Comparative Political Analysis,
Department of Political Science, University of Minnesota*

THE FREE PRESS, NEW YORK
COLLIER-MACMILLAN LIMITED, LONDON

To the Agents

Mrs. Patricia Bowman, Conservative,
Mr. Alan F. Clarke, Labour,

who represent the most skilled and dedicated of their profession,

and

To the Candidates

Mr. William Compton Carr, Conservative,
Mr. Ivor S. Richard, Labour,

who honor their parties, as well as their country—

This book is gratefully and humbly dedicated.

Preface

The investigation of two political organizations as they struggled for the marginal seat in Barons Court was both a demanding and a rewarding experience. The pace turned out to be much more hectic than we had bargained for, and, more often than not, we found ourselves having our evening meal at 2:00 A.M. in the Wimpey's bar on Queensway after the day's canvassing returns had been tabulated and interviews with party workers had been completed. But as we sat munching dry hamgurgers and drinking the cool hot-chocolate, we realized that the opportunity which had come our way was a rare one. We were being permitted to examine simultaneously two competing parties from the "inside" as they fought over an important prize. The privilege we had been accorded would not only give us a close view of British politics at the "grass roots," but would also enable us to study the battle from both sides, rather than from one side alone. Securing permission to have one researcher attached to each party headquarters was in itself an unusual achievement, and from these vantage points we were able to draw upon materials that, so far as we know, have not yet been used in studies of political behavior in Britain. We have, for example, been able to break down our data to the polling-district level, and we have managed to analyze a sample of canvassing cards from both the Labour and Conservative files. Even more important, we have addressed ourselves to the question of how the "reward systems" operated in the two parties.

The number of debts incurred in a study of this sort is understandably large. In order to collect the data, we needed to have the full cooperation of the officials and workers in the Labour Party and in the Conservative Association in Barons Court. The degree of cooperation we received was indeed exceptional, and we are greatly indebted to the people who were so generous with their time and were so willing to share their knowledge with us.

Three officials from the Conservative organization were particularly helpful. Mr. John Putnam, Mr. Edward O'Neil, and Mr. T. Gordon Hemming not only spoke freely about their respective roles in the campaign but also devoted long hours to discussions about the substantive issues raised in this book. Their enormous fund of knowledge about the Conservative Party made their contributions invaluable. We also interviewed a large number of other Conservative campaign workers to whom we owe thanks. However, since it is impossible to list them all, we shall not make invidious distinctions by mentioning a few.

On the Labour side, we benefitted greatly from the enlightenment provided by Mr. Tom Cox, Mr. Nigel Spearing, Mr. Donald Harker, Mr. George Simpson, and Mr. James Beckett. Other officials and workers in the Barons Court Labour Party—again too many to list in a short preface—willingly contributed valuable time for interviews and other assistance. Beyond the boundaries of Barons Court, special commendation must be given to Mr. Leslie H. Hilliard, C.B.E., and to Mr. Clifford Tucker. During the past decade these two knowledgeable people have spent countless hours discussing British politics with one of the authors, and they have opened many doors to him. Needless to say, their contribution is reflected in the present study.

Our major debt for this book is owed to four people—the Conservative agent, Mrs. Patricia Bowman; the Conservative candidate, Mr. William Compton Carr; the Labour agent, Mr. Alan F. Clarke; and the Labour candidate, Mr. Ivor S. Richard. Without their wholehearted support, this study could not have been carried out. The dedication of the volume to them is but a small token of our appreciation.

Nearly all of the individuals mentioned thus far appear as participants in the Battle of Barons Court. We have decided, however, to use pseudonyms for all of the people involved except the agents and the candidates who can be readily identified publicly.

Without the resources and advice provided by several other people who were not associated with Barons Court, this book would not have included some of the information it now provides. Since their office could no longer supply the census tabulations for the constituency, Miss R. Tallantvie and Mrs. F. Bowker of the Census Branch of the General Register Office went out of their way to secure the socio-economic data for us. Mr. B. J. Collins, C.B.E., Director of Planning for the Greater London Council, kindly provided the information on a ward basis. When we decided to use, in addition, certain data by enumeration districts, these tabulations were made available by Mrs. Ruth Glass, Director of Research for the Centre for Urban Studies at University College, London. The tables presented in Chapter 2 were compiled from computer runs of data which came originally from the Planning Office of the GLC and from the Centre for Urban Studies. While we were conducting the research, we were privileged to have several conversations with Dr. Mark Abrams who offered valuable suggestions and gave us some profiles of marginal constitutencies in the London area. Dr. Henry Durant, Director of the Gallup Poll, has kindly granted us permission to cite the public opinion data which are used in Chapter 2. To all of these people, we extend our sincere thanks.

We also incurred a number of obligations on the Minnesota

scene. Special acknowledgement is due to Professor William H. Flanigan of the Department of Political Science at the University, who translated our data requests into computer print-offs. Also assisting us in various research tasks were Mrs. Patricia Hayman-Chaffey, Miss Diane Johnson, Mrs. Diana Rigelman, and Miss Mary Heinz.

While we commend all of these people for the contributions they have made to this effort, we hasten to point out, in accordance with a tribal custom in academe, that we alone are responsible for any errors of fact or interpretation.

In line with another custom, we should also pay tribute to our wives and children who cheerfully kept the embers glowing in the domestic fireplaces while we were abroad. As we often promise, for reasons of domestic tranquility, we hope next time to take them with us.

One day, as we were checking the accuracy of punched IBM cards, we wondered whether it would be worthwhile to indicate in the preface of publications the expenses that were incurred in doing this research. This would make possible a cost-benefit analysis which might be useful to those who are called upon to allocate resources for research projects in the future. The total direct cost of this study was about $4,800.00.

For making grants available to support our research, we extend our sincere thanks to the Office of International Programs and to the Graduate School of the University of Minnesota; to the patrons of the Winton Fund; and to Mr. Frank M. Rarig, Jr., and Mr. Walter S. Rosenberry III, who were instrumental in providing funds from the Charles A. Weyerhauser Memorial Foundation.

ROBERT T. HOLT

Minneapolis, Minn.   JOHN E. TURNER

Contents

Prologue

Polling day in Britain is the climax of a drama. The directors (party agents) busily prepare for the engagement by grooming the star performers, planning their roles, selecting and training the key stagehands, and recruiting workers for the important but unspectacular tasks which must be carried out behind the scenes. Technically, of course, the drama is not even listed on the billboards until the monarch dissolves the old parliament, which is the signal for the curtain to rise and the campaign formally to get underway. As the campaign develops, the spectators view the head-on clash of protagonists, with intervals of pomp and ceremony which are a conspicuous feature of British politics. The leading actors (candidates) ride through the streets in sound cars, speaking their lines through loudspeakers. They stop to chat with local citizens and answer their questions, while campaign workers saturate the neighborhood with handbills. The candidates also take to the "stump" in the marketplace, on the street corner, and at the factory gate, attempting to get a hearing from potential voters as they pass by. In the evenings, they address indoor gatherings or appear with their opponents before groups of interested citizens who wish to see all the candidates in action. At most of their public appearances, the candidates are forced to cope with merciless hecklers who infiltrate the crowds and ask embarrassing questions or disrupt the proceedings with clever retorts—behavior reminiscent of an episode in a play where selected members of the audience toss barbs at the performers in order to throw them off the set script.

The drama itself is tragic or comic, depending upon the outcome and the political loyalties of the people involved. Similarly, a political personality will be hero or villain, according to the party allegiance of the partisans who are making the judgment. To the dedicated Labour organizer, a Quintin Hogg will probably be cast in the role of a knave who epitomizes Conservative privilege and aristocracy, the feeling of moral superiority which implies that the Tories by birth and training have a special claim to govern the country. To many a Conservative zealot, on the other hand, Quintin Hogg makes his entrance as a hero—an organizing genius who was largely responsible for rebuilding the party machine and who was willing to surrender his aristocratic birthright so that he could offer his services to the party as its leader. In a similar fashion, all of the party leaders—the Harold Wilsons, the Alec Douglas-Homes, the Edward Heaths, and the George Browns—are emotionally viewed in the dramatis personae as rascals or as men of mark, depending upon the political outlook of those actively participating in the drama.

While the party leaders command the billboards and the headlines, the main work of the campaign production takes place behind the scenes. Armies of volunteer workers deliver handbills, stuff envelopes, distribute literature, and perform other clerical and doorstep tasks. Even more important, teams of canvassers visit with as many voters as possible in order to gauge their political inclinations, and they relay this information to designated officials who compile lists of sympathetic electors. These lists become the basis for the party's activities on polling day, when workers swarm upon the doorsteps of favorably inclined voters, urging them to go to the polls.

While the pace is frantic, the formal campaign production in Britain is distinctively brief when measured by American standards. Eight days after the royal proclamation of dissolution (not including Sundays and holidays), the candidates and their agents journey to the local government hall to pay the filing deposits of £150 and to present ceremoniously their nomination papers to the "returning officer," usually the sheriff in a county, the council chairman in an urban district, and the mayor in a borough. The election is held nine days after the nominations have been filed, Sundays and holidays again excepted. After the polls have been officially closed at 9:00 on election night, policemen seal the ballot boxes at the numerous polling stations and carry them to a large room in the local government hall, where they are all opened and counted by a small regiment of clerks. As the ballot-counting slowly gets underway, the big room takes on a festive and ceremonial air. If the count is taking place in a borough, the mayor is present with his emblem of office in prominent display. The town clerk, bedecked in gray wig, governs the proceedings with stern impartiality. The candidates and their wives, along with their agents, pace among the long rows of tables with nervous smiles on their faces. Scrutineers from each political camp keep a watchful eye on the clerks as they tally the votes to make sure that no irregularities creep in. As they count the ballots, the clerks stack them in neat little bundles and tie them with bright ribbons. When the last ribbon is tied and the final result tabulated, the returning officer summons the candidates before him and announces the outcome. Amid jubilant cries from his supporters, the winner steps before the microphone to issue a brief victory statement and to thank the people who have helped him win. The victor's remarks are followed by a short message from one of the losing candidates who, in customary British fashion, moves a vote of thanks to the returning officer and the town clerk for their judicious supervision of the ballot-counting. As the curtain closes on the final act, the partisans exhibit fitting emotions of joy or sadness as they quickly disperse to listen to returns from other parts of the country, to celebrate the local result with appropriate libation, or to hold a somber "wake."

The ordinary British citizen participates in this electoral pageant both as bit-actor and as spectator. For the most part he is a spectator who might attend one of the public rallies or listen to the candidates at an outdoor meeting in a nearby park. During the campaign he can hardly avoid some of the political broadcasts when he turns on the wireless or "telly," and on election night he probably listens to the returns as they pour in from the marginal constituencies, where the question of whether Labour or the Conservatives will form the new government will be answered. His role as bit-actor is played on election day when he appears briefly on the political stage to cast his vote for a candidate to represent his constituency in the new parliament.

For the vast majority of the voters, the national contest holds greater interest than the local struggles. When a voter marks an "X" in front of the name of candidate John Doe, he is doing much more than voting to send an individual M.P. to Westminster; he is making a choice between the political parties, and indicating which party leader he prefers to have as prime minister. Strictly speaking, however, there is no election at the national level, for even the potential occupants of No. 10 Downing Street stand (no respectable British politician "runs") for parliament in their respective local bailiwicks. In other words, instead of voting for the prime minister directly, eligible citizens in 630 different constituencies use their franchise to elect local members of parliament, and the party that can control the House of Commons wins the right to have its leader installed as prime minister.

While each constituency has only one member of parliament, these parliamentary districts are not of equal importance when it comes to deciding which party is the winner in a national election. In many rural areas and in some urban residential districts, the

Conservatives attract such enormous majorities that the election outcome is never in doubt. By the same token, the Labour Party commands overwhelming support in mining areas and in the working-class sections of the industrial cities. When the election results were recorded in 1959, for example, Labour had accumulated 60 per cent or more of the votes in 96 constituencies and the Conservatives had garnered a similar vote in 101 districts. Nearly one-third of all the constituencies in the country were carried by these overwhelming majorities. It is sometimes said that in these "safe" districts the tellers need not bother to count the vote—they simply have to weigh them! At the opposite end of the spectrum, however, the 1959 election disclosed a large number of marginal seats. Forty-three members of parliament held seats with a plurality of 1,000 or less (twelve of them by less than 200 votes), and the pluralities in 82 other constituencies ranged between 1,000 and 3,000 votes. Even though the Conservatives won a heavy majority of 100 seats in the 1959 parliament, the Labour Party could have emerged as the victor simply by converting an average of about 850 voters from Conservative to Labour in each of 58 constituencies. The situation was essentially the same after the 1964 and 1966 elections. After the ballots were sorted in 1964, 40 seats were held with pluralities of 1,000 or less, and in 1966 the comparable figure was 46. Thus, to a considerable extent the fate of the contending parties in almost any election rests in the hands of a relatively few political leaders who are responsible for planning and executing the campaign in these vulnerable marginal constituencies.

This study is concerned with the contest between the Conservative and Labour parties in one of these key marginal areas in the 1964 election campaign. The constituency, which is called Barons Court, is located in a heterogeneous residential district in West London. Our study does not focus primarily upon the dramatic campaign issues, or on the personalities of the key actors, or even upon the rank-and-file voters, who are so frequently the major concern of recent electoral studies. Our attention, rather, is concentrated upon the two major parties *as organizations*. We are interested in how the major parties in a marginal constituency plan, organize, and carry out their campaign activities. Our concern is with the formation of strategy, the mobilization of resources, and the organization and direction of effort. The clash of personalities and issues is relevant only as it sheds light upon how the party's organizational machinery operated.

Politicians and journalists frequently write about a political contest by drawing an analogy between an election campaign and a military battle. In September 1964, for example, shortly before the Prime Minister journeyed to Balmoral Castle to advise the Queen to dissolve parliament, a headquarters official of one of the major parties noted the approach of the formal campaign. "Although both sides have been skirmishing for several months," he said, "the battle will now begin in earnest. This afternoon I shall take over the new post to which I have been assigned. Within a very few days, we shall all be on the barricades manning our battle stations!"

Once an election has passed into history, utterances like these sound melodramatic and the analogy appears to be forced or contrived. But at the time—just a few hours before the royal proclamation was issued—the statement seemed appropriate to those who had been working hard for many months preparing for an election they knew would be hard-fought. The analogy with military combat did catch some of the tension and resolution which at that exciting moment pervaded the atmosphere of politics. For dedicated political activists, the battle was indeed approaching, and it had to be won.

The analogy between political and military effort, of course, may be extended beyond a mere comparison of precipitated tension and strong resolution to win. In most political campaigns and military encounters, there is a specific and exclusive objective: victory. Both types of struggle rarely end in a draw, and there can never be two winners in the same contest. In a more formal sense, both encounters may be looked upon as a *zero-sum game*—what one side gains the opposing camp will surely lose. In political and military struggles, the specific and singular nature of the objective enables the leaders in both types of organizations to design specific, relatively simple strategies with an aim toward victory, and then pour their resources into the execution of their plans.

While the analogy between an election contest and a military encounter may be appropriate in characterizing the setting and the singularity of objective, it breaks down when we try to compare a political party and an army as *organizations*. In design and structure, an army is probably the most bureaucratized of organizations. It has a specified chain of command, an unambiguous ordering of ranks and offices, and clear-cut duties and patterns of authority attached to each office. Moreover, each "member" of the military organization is bound by law to serve in his unit and to obey the commands of his superiors. Army officials in authoritative positions have at their disposal a variety of sanctions which may be employed against subordinates who violate the regulations or refuse to carry out orders.

In sharp contrast, a political party—and especially a party at the constituency level—lacks the essential features of a highly bureaucratized organization. The constituency party, to be sure, may have a fairly well specified chain of command and there may be a distinct ordering of ranks and offices, with clearly defined duties and well-marked patterns of jurisdiction residing in each office. But the party breaks away from the bureaucratic model when we look at the method of recruiting officers and rank-and-file workers and at the procedures for subjecting them to discipline.

Any party which entertains hopes of winning the seat in a marginal constituency requires a core of loyal activists to serve as specialized officers in the campaign, taking their orders from the agent and, in turn, issuing orders to workers under their control. Besides the core of administrative personnel, large numbers of rank-and-file volunteers are needed for several hours each day to handle clerical and doorstep assignments. Needless to say, some of the tasks that these ordinary volunteers are requested to perform are repetitive and boring—humdrum work which must nevertheless be done if the campaign is to be effective. Thousands of envelopes have to be filled with literature and addressed by hand; piles of window bills, newspapers, and propaganda leaflets must be distributed throughout the constituency; from 30,000 to 60,000 voters need to be canvassed so that the party officials will know where their support lies; the canvassing results have to be carefully recorded; voters who have changed residence must be traced and the necessary postal or proxy forms processed; committee rooms in the several polling districts have to be staffed more or less on a full-time basis. The manpower requirements on polling day place an even greater burden upon the organization. Clerks are needed for each committee room; from 50 to 100 cars with drivers have to be lined up to transport voters to the polls; number-takers need to be scheduled for duty at each polling station; messengers are required to relay information at periodic intervals to the committee rooms; bands of workers must be recruited to knock on the doors of party supporters who have not as yet voted. To provide direction and continuity in the performance of these tasks, some dedicated partisans sacrifice their annual holidays by taking time off from work during the campaign so that they can be with the organization full time. In addition, some housewives or retired ladies will spend ten or twelve hours each day working at the central headquarters in the constituency or in one of the ward committee rooms. Without the aid of these "full-time" volunteers, the campaign machine is likely to do little more than sputter.

Such varied campaign activities directed by a handful of key supervisors and carried out by from 200 to 500 rank-and-file workers, who appear for duty as their schedules permit, require masterful direction and coordination. If the effort is to be successful, the organization must break down its workload into specialized tasks, which have to be delegated to responsible administrators and geared into a clear-cut hierarchy of command. In other words, the organization has to be fashioned into an integrated unit which provides at the same time for functional specialization; those in charge of managing the campaign must necessarily issue directives to key officials who in turn give orders to rank-and-file subordinates within their command It is essential, then, that individuals in the several echelons of the organizational hierarchy be willing and able to accept orders and to carry them out with dispatch.

But the people in authoritative positions cannot perform as first sergeants, barking out commands without fear of dissent and threatening company punishment or worse for those who fail to comply. Except for one or two paid employees, the workers in a constituency party—key officials and rank-and-file workers alike— are volunteers who offer their services at the sacrifice of their own leisure. Whenever they become dissatisfied, they are free to withdraw from the organization without fear of being subjected to coercive sanctions or suffering loss of income. This means that the officials who direct the party campaign must be able to perceive and to deal with personal sensitivities. Irritations have to be detected and taken care of; minor frictions must be located and then lubricated quickly. If such deficiencies are not discerned and hence permitted to grow, the organizational machine will operate far below the level of optimal efficiency. If personal annoyances and grievances erode the morale of the party, the number of volunteer workers who appear for duty will soon begin to diminish, and before very long the organization will find itself without enough manpower to handle its essential tasks.

But, despite the lack of obvious negative sanctions that are available in an army and other highly bureaucratic structures, party organizations in many marginal constituencies appear to be fairly cohesive and are able to maintain themselves during periods of stress without the control mechanisms which are noticeably present in most organizations. This suggests that some type of sanctioning system, not readily apparent, must nevertheless be operating within the party structure. One of the purposes of this study is to determine what holds the constituency organization together and to explore how the system operates.

Apart from maintaining cohesion and discipline within its ranks, a political party at the constituency level faces other difficult problems in the course of planning and executing a successful campaign. It must, for example, secure vital information about the setting in which it is forced to operate. This information concerning its environment has to be processed, stored, and retrieved at the appropriate time. On the basis of the information they have managed to pull together, the people in charge of the campaign have to plan their strategy. During the campaign additional information about voter intent must be gathered, analyzed, stored, and made available for immediate recall if the strategy is to be properly executed.

There have been no detailed "inside" studies of constituency parties as organizations. The people who have the most information about how parties are mobilized for campaign action are the agents, the candidates, and other officials, but these "insiders" could hardly be expected to present an objective account, even if they had the time to attempt it. Indeed, the local political leaders are not in a position to paint the complete picture, for each party group is familiar with only half the organizational scene. In order for an outsider to examine the constituency parties as organizations and to study how they plan their maneuvers, mobilize their resources, and reward their activists, he must work his way into the organizations so as to obtain a penetrating view from the "inside." To request that one be permitted to engage in such sensitive research at a time when the demands of a political campaign are the most pressing is asking a great deal of political leaders, especially when they are fighting for big stakes in a marginal constituency. To have his request granted and to be given unrestricted access to the information he needs, the researcher must gain the confidence of the agent, the candidate, and the members of their working force. The "outsider" has to be in a position to observe day by day—

and in periods of crisis, more closely—the behavior of the people who are deeply engrossed in an election campaign whose outcome is in doubt.

The splendid cooperation of the Labour and Conservative parties in the marginal constituency of Barons Court enabled us to operate freely within each organization in our search for the data used in this study. Turner attached himself to the Labour Party, while Holt worked inside the organization of the Conservative Party, and each of them followed the campaign day by day— at times, hour by hour. Before commencing with the field research, we formulated a set of questions which we tried to answer as we observed the party machines in operation. Although we revised and elaborated these questions as the campaign progressed, we did not compare notes or discuss our findings until after polling day. Only three or four of the top leaders in each organization knew about the total project and were aware of the fact that an American professor was attached to each of the opposing camps. While in the constituency we studiously avoided being seen together lest we unwittingly arouse the suspicions of partisans who did not know the nature of the study. Needless to say, we feel deeply indebted to the leaders of the two parties for their assistance, their patience, and especially for their trust.

After the 1964 campaign, we had a good idea of how campaign strategies were devised and executed, and we obtained insights into the kinds of problems the parties faced and how they sought to master them. We were amazed at the hundreds of people who were involved in the campaign, and we noted that many of them were working eight, ten, and even twelve hours a day at great personal sacrifice. But we were at a loss to explain why these people were willing to make such an effort. We paged through reams of notes we had collected in 1964 to try to uncover some clues that would indicate the nature of the incentive system which appeared to be operating. We were about to throw our hands up in despair when Mr. Wilson conveniently called another general election in March

1966—at a time when we could break away from our regular duties for a three-week period. So we hurriedly packed our bags and flew again to London, determined to get information about the system of incentives in the two parties at the constituency level.

In 1966 we did not attempt to follow the campaign in Barons Court (or in any other constituency) in as much detail as we had done in 1964. Instead, we sought to establish contacts in a number of districts in the London area, talking to many leaders and rank-and-file workers in an effort to discover how the system of "rewards" and "punishments" operated. Thus, much of our explanation of how the organizations operated in 1964 is also based upon research done in 1966.

This book is essentially a comparative study of the Labour and Conservative parties in Barons Court. It presents a case history of the 1964 contest and then analyzes the two organizations along certain dimensions in the context of other constituency parties in the London region. But before we raise the curtain on the parties and the campaign in Barons Court, we need to describe in some detail the stage setting within which the contest took place. This can be done by discussing the nature of the constituency, the personalities and experiences of the leading actors, and the salience of national issues, all of which will prepare us for a view of the struggle between the Labour and Conservative forces for the marginal seat in Barons Court.

CHAPTER I

The Setting

T he next time you visit London, take
a trip to the parliamentary constituency of Barons Court. Carved
out of the center of the new Borough of Hammersmith, it is
bounded on the west by a meander in the Thames River, and on the
north and northwest by Goldhawk Road. Its eastern boundary,
which runs along railway and underground tracks, is punctuated
by the Great Exhibition Hall at Earls Court and by the new Empress
State Building. The District or Piccadilly lines of the "tube" will
take you to the heart of the constituency. You may get off at any
of a number of stations—Fulham Broadway, Hammersmith Broadway, Ravenscourt Park, Barons Court, or West Kensington—and
when you emerge from the underground, you are in a position to
walk along the streets of the parliamentary district.

If you are a stranger to London, you will at first be puzzled and
then perhaps annoyed by our advice. Your *Baedeker's* (or any other
guidebook that is in vogue these days) will call your attention to few
tourist attractions in the area; there is nothing comparable to the
great sights of historical interest which you will find in many other
parts of London. If you are lucky and arrive on a certain Saturday

early in the spring, you may see *the* boat race of the year from a charming "pub" on the banks of the Thames. But the odds are that you will not be in the district at that time, and in any event the boat race is not the reason why we are calling your attention to Barons Court.

After wandering through the streets, you may return to the familiar tourist haunts of Piccadilly, Westminster, and the Tower, thinking that we have sent you to Barons Court merely to get a picture of a "typical" residential district in London. Nothing could be farther from our intention. Indeed, it would be difficult to find any single locale in this huge and diverse capital that could be regarded as typical. In any case, we recommended your trip to Barons Court for precisely the opposite reason—because it is *atypical* in a very important respect. So let us direct you into the constituency again so that we can take you on a special type of guided tour, one that no publisher would ever include in an ordinary tour book.

As you come out of the Barons Court tube station, just a long block west of the Conservative headquarters (see endpapers), turn to your left and look across the major thoroughfare, which is called West Cromwell Road. Here you will see a large block of modern flats set some distance from the street and framed by an impressive strip of green grass. A private drive large enough to accommodate the biggest cars allows easy access to its entrances. This housing estate is known as Barons Keep. Few, if any, Labour supporters reside behind its brick walls. But even if all of the residents cast their votes for the Conservatives, it is not a hot bed of Tory activity. Even Conservative Party workers have to invent some ruse in order to get through the entrance to canvass their supporters. The Tories in Barons Keep are comfortable.

After a lingering gaze at Barons Keep, turn around and walk in the opposite direction toward the south. The politically minded tour leader can hardly resist pointing to a third-story window in a block of flats on Barons Court Road to your left, and mentioning the rumor that a certain nobleman had paid the rent on the dwelling for a young "model," Miss Christine Keeler. (The story would be better if she had been "kept" in Barons Keep!)

As you keep walking through respectable but undistinguished residential streets, you will soon come to a large block of flats built in an impressive, late-Victorian style; these residences surround a small park, which serves as a central courtyard. The area is known as Queens Club Gardens, another Tory stronghold. But if you visit the gardens during an election campaign, you will observe that some windows are adorned with the Labour red.

As you move south and east, the building pattern gradually changes; attached houses begin to displace the blocks of flats, and the cars parked on the street are smaller and older. As you turn a corner into Normand Road, however, this setting changes abruptly. Across Normand Park you are confronted by a large, modern housing complex, which is made up of three high-rise buildings and large, rectangular blocks of flats. This is Clem Attlee Court, one of the most impressive examples of public housing in the entire constituency. Its name not only indicates the party auspices under which it was constructed, but also the political loyalties of the vast majority of its inhabitants. The Tory canvassers are pleased if they can get 30 per cent of the residents to indicate support of the Conservative candidate.

Your walk along the streets of Barons Court has taken less than fifteen minutes. At the outset, when you were looking at Barons Keep, you were examining a part of Avonmore Ward, where the core of the Conservatives' strength lies. If they cannot run up overwhelming margins in this ward, they cannot win the seat. As you walked from the tube stop to Queens Club Gardens, you were crossing Gibbs Green Ward, a "mixed-bag" area in which any winning party must at least break even. The visit to Clem Attlee Court took you to Halford Ward, a district that leaned toward Labour even before the construction of this massive public-housing scheme put it safely into the Socialist column.

By now you should be aware of why we sent you to Barons

Court. During little more than a half-mile walk, you have seen three wards—one Tory, one marginal, and one Labour. You have also seen a cross section of the constituency. We could have directed you to almost any tube station and in a fifteen-minute walk you would go through wards with similarly contrasting shades of political coloration.

It is unusual to find such a diverse mixture within just a few thousand acres in the heart of a large city. Most areas of this size are more homogeneous, and for this reason tend to be safe districts for one party or another. But the constituency of Barons Court is impressively marginal. Except for the 1955 election—the first contest for the then recently created seat, which Labour won by the slender margin of 125 votes—Barons Court has been represented only by the party that has won the national election. In other words, the party that loses Barons Court is not likely to gain a majority of the seats in the House of Commons. There are fewer than a hundred of these marginal constituencies in all of Britain (about one-sixth of the total number), and it is in these districts that the outcome of a national election is determined. The Conservatives could easily afford to swap ten votes in South Kensington for one in Barons Court, while Labour could advantageously make a similar trade from their voting reserves in North Hammersmith.

The political marginality of Barons Court reflects the heterogeneous social composition of the area. Indeed, one might expect to find that this small segment of West London approximates in microcosm a cross section of the entire nation, both in socio-economic and political features. The short visit to Barons Court gave us a visual impression of its wide diversity. A closer examination of the constituency through the use of census data at the polling-district (precinct) and ward levels will point up the socio-economic differences and help to indicate the reasons why the constituency is marginal politically, and hence a coveted prize for the two major parties.

Socio-economic Features of Barons Court

Although by walking through the constituency one can get an impression of residential, commercial, and industrial patterns, as well as a "feel" for the levels of living in the various sections, this is hardly sufficient for our purpose. Great diversity may be hidden behind the walls of the houses and blocks of flats, which from the outside seem quite similar in appearance. More detailed and precise data are needed if we are to obtain an accurate picture of the socio-economic composition of Barons Court. Since much of the political activity, especially at election time, is organized at the ward and polling-district levels, the most politically relevant way to examine the makeup of the constituency is by drawing socio-economic profiles of selected wards and polling districts. But before we can do this, it will be useful to identify them.

In the northern sector of the constituency, there are seven polling districts which lie in four different wards. Polling districts Fc and Fd in the northwest corner are located in Starch Green Ward. (The other two polling districts in this ward—Fa and Fb—are in the parliamentary constituency of Hammersmith North. We shall soon see that five of the wards in Barons Court have one or more polling districts in other constituencies—a fact that creates some organizational problems.) To the east of Fc and Fd is Grove Ward, which embraces three polling districts, Ga, Gb, and Gc. Of the other two polling districts on the northern boundary, Hᴜ and Ic, the former is in Addison Ward and the latter in Brook Green. Both of these wards include polling districts that are located in Hammersmith North.

Broadway Ward, the largest unit in the constituency, extends from the western boundary almost to the eastern end and encompasses the main commercial district of the old Hammersmith borough. This ward includes six polling districts: Ja, Jb, Jc, Jd, Je, and Jf. To the east of Broadway lies Avonmore Ward, with polling districts Ka and Kb. Polling districts La and Lb are part of Margravine Ward (Lc is in the Fulham constituency). Polling district Oa in the southeastern corner used to be a part of Margravine before the ward boundaries were redrawn. The readjustment of the ward map made it a part of Crabtree, which has two other districts in Fulham. Gibbs Green Ward with Ma, Mb, and Mc, and Halford Ward with Na, Nb, and Nc are also located in the southeastern corner of Barons Court (Nd is located in Fulham). The wards and polling districts are shown on the map on the endpapers.

Barons Court—a "naughty" district in Edwardian times, little more than a "stop" on the tube line in the 1930s, and a parliamentary constituency since 1954—can best be characterized today as a "mixed bag" of socio-economic elements. Industrial development, for example, is quite pronounced in some polling districts of Broadway Ward, while the districts in Starch Green are almost exclusively residential. In polling district Oa, 28 per cent of the households are owners-occupiers, but in Jb the figure is only 2 per cent. Whereas nearly 60 per cent of the households in Jc are comprised of people living in council property, there are virtually no council tenants in Fd. By the same token, 92 per cent of the households in Fd rent their living quarters from private landlords, but private rentals dwindle to 39 per cent in Jc. This slice of West London accommodates natives and immigrants, doctors and dockers, teachers and toolmakers, and clerks and carpenters.

Although the smokestacks of huge factories are rare sights, Barons Court does have a substantial amount of light industry, especially in Broadway and Margravine wards (which lie along the Thames River) and in Brook Green Ward. Here can be found electrical works, distilleries, engineering establishments, scaffolding mills, oil depots, joineries, coal stations, and repair shops, as well as the J. Lyons Company, a huge catering and food-processing firm.

The constituency has two main shopping centers, one around Hammersmith Broadway and the other along North End Road, at the lower end of which is located an open-air street market. As the visitor strolls along the sidewalks, he observes a wide range of commercial establishments, from food and furniture stores to real estate offices and betting shops, with an occasional pub of Edwardian design featuring spirited "rock and roll," or a cinema converted into a bingo den.

But, for the most part, Barons Court is a residential district for people who hold jobs in other parts of London. About two-thirds of the inhabitants leave the constituency each morning, usually by tube or bus, for their places of outside employment, streaming back into Barons Court in the evening after their day's work on the assembly line or at the warehouse or office. This is especially true of the people who reside in the strong Tory districts, where 74 per cent of the gainfully employed are commuters. We can probably obtain a better view of the constituency by examining it in terms of social class; distribution by age, sex, and marital status; nationality groupings; and housing arrangements. At the same time it will be useful to note the areas of Labour and Conservative strength with respect to these categories.

Social Class

Income, occupation, and education are generally considered to be fairly sensitive objective indicators of social class. The British census, however, does not include any information about personal income, and for this reason we shall have to be content with just two indices of social class: (1) occupation of employed and retired males, and (2) education. On occupation, the census provides data for the following groupings: (1) Professional Workers; (2) Employers and Managers; (3) Nonmanual (Clerical) Workers; (4) Skilled Manual Workers; and (5) Lesser-Skilled Manual Workers.[1]

---

1. The census divides what we have called the "lesser skilled" into two groups: "semiskilled" and "unskilled." We have treated these two groups as a single category. In the case of retired persons, we have listed them according to the occupations in which they were engaged prior to retirement, and hence the term "gainfully employed males" includes them.

In this breakdown, groups 1, 2, and 3 in effect represent "middle-class" occupations, with group 3 embracing lower-grade office workers of various sorts, while categories 4 and 5 represent a spectrum of manual workers with differing degrees of skill. Table 1.1 presents an occupational analysis of gainfully employed males for the constituency as a whole, as well as for the strongest Labour and strongest Tory districts and a group of the most marginal polling districts.[2]

Here one can see that the strong Conservative districts contain a high component of professional and managerial personnel, as well as people engaged in ordinary clerical work. The Labour districts, on the other hand, have a high listing in the manual categories, which total 73 per cent when the skilled and lesser-skilled groups are combined. Moreover, nearly half of the employed population in the strong Labour polling districts work in production (as op-

Table 1.1—Occupations of Employed Males

(in percentages)

Area	Professional/ Managerial Workers	Non- manual Workers	Skilled manual Workers	Lesser- Skilled Workers
London	12.6	21.3	34.3	31.9
Constituency	12.3	22.9	35.3	28.6
Strong Labour PDs	5.9	18.5	38.7	35.9
Strong Tory PDs	23.1	29.8	27.6	18.5
Marginal PDs	9.8	21.9	36.5	30.8

2. The polling-district data have been compiled from census reports by enumeration districts. In some cases, the enumeration districts overlapped the boundaries of polling districts; when this happened, we estimated as best we could the proportion that fell within a given area. The strong Labour, strong Tory, and marginal polling districts were selected on the basis of a detailed analysis of Labour and Conservative canvassing returns for the 1964 and 1966 general elections. This breakdown coincides with the evaluation of the agents.

posed to service) enterprises, while the corresponding figure on the Tory side is only 28 per cent.

Education as an indicator of social class is measured in terms of the age at which people left school. The data on the educational level of the Barons Court population are compiled in Table 1.2. From even a glance at this table, one can see the extremely high proportion of individuals with only elementary education in the Labour districts—a sharp contrast with the Tory areas with high percentages in the sixteen-to-nineteen bracket (in effect, secondary education) and in the "at age twenty or later" column (university or college training).

Distribution by Age, Sex, and Marital Status

In terms of age structure, Barons Court registers below the London average on the number of children under the age of fifteen, but in the other age categories it corresponds closely to the London pattern. A comparison between the strong Labour and Conservative districts, however, reveals in the latter a disproportionately low number of children, a slightly higher proportion of adults in the fifteen-to-twenty-four age bracket; and a slightly lower proportion

Table 1.2—Age at Termination of Formal Education

(in percentages)

Area	Left School at Age 15 or Under	Left School at Age 16–19	Left School at Age 20 or Later	Current Students
London	78.1	16.8	4.6	0.5
Constituency	67.5	23.7	5.1	2.9
Strong Labour PDs	80.7	14.6	1.6	2.3
Strong Tory PDs	41.8	41.9	11.6	3.8
Marginal PDs	71.7	20.2	4.3	3.0

of people over the age of sixty-five. These comparisons can be seen in Table 1.3.

The relatively small number of children in the Tory polling districts is a reflection of the low proportion of married people in these areas. Whereas the percentage of married people in the constituency as a whole is 57.8 per cent, the figure drops to 50 per cent in the areas of Conservative strength and rises to 61.7 per cent in the Labour polling districts. In two polling districts—Kb in Avonmore and Ma in Gibbs Green—single persons comprise 43 per cent of the adult population.

In the distribution of males and females of working age, Barons Court again follows the London norm, with a male population of 46.8 per cent. In the Labour areas, however, the percentage is higher—47.4 per cent, compared with 44.0 per cent in the Conservative districts. The pattern takes on added interest when we examine the figures for unmarried people. It soon becomes obvious that parts of the constituency are a veritable haven for single females. In polling district Fc of Starch Green Ward, for example, there are 159 single women for every 100 single males. The same pattern unfolds in Ic of Brook Green Ward, where the ratio is 152 to 100. Of course,

Table 1.3—Age Distribution*

(in percentages)

Area	Children Under Age 15	Adults 15–24	Adults 25–44	Adults 45–64	Adults 65 and Over
London	19.4	18.2	34.8	32.4	14.7
Constituency	17.0	18.3	34.6	32.8	14.8
Strong Labour PDs	19.0	18.0	33.2	33.1	15.6
Strong Tory PDs	13.1	19.0	33.7	33.0	14.1
Marginal PDs	17.2	17.3	35.0	32.3	15.0

* The proportion of children under age fifteen is based on the entire population, while the distribution in the other age categories is on the total number of people above age fifteen. For this reason the totals are in excess of 100 per cent.

in some Labour sections of the constituency the distribution between single females and single males is reversed. This is true, for example, in a part of Broadway and a part of Grove wards, where in each instance there are about 150 single males for every 100 single females. The overall picture is presented in Table 1.4. As we shall soon note, certain districts in Barons Court are characterized by large numbers of these young unmarrieds who live in multioccupied dwellings, usually in single rooms or "bed-sitter" units.

Nationality Groupings

Census breakdowns on national origin do not enable us to be very precise on this dimension, since they are based entirely upon birthplace statistics, thus accounting only for first-generation people born in other lands. Using these crude data, however, it is possible to make a few rough estimates by separating the countries of origin into two groups—the predominantly "colored" and the predominantly "white." This enables us to compare in a general way the relative distribution of colored immigrants, as well as a wider group of foreign born which we shall designate as "other."

Table 1.4—Distribution by Sex and Marital Status*

(in percentages)

Area	Married Persons	Total Single Persons	Single Males	Single Females
London	55.8	29.8	14.7	15.1
Constituency	57.8	31.1	15.7	15.4
Strong Labour PDs	61.7	27.2	14.5	12.6
Strong Tory PDs	50.0	38.8	17.3	21.5
Marginal PDs	58.8	29.7	15.4	14.3

* This table does not include the category of "Others" (divorced persons). The distribution is by individuals fifteen years of age and older.

Although the number of colored people in Barons Court is only about 3.7 per cent of the total population, close to the average for all of London, the patterns of residence are uneven. In parts of Gibbs Green Ward, the proportion of colored people varies from 5 per cent to more than 9 per cent, and in parts of Grove Ward and a segment of Avonmore, the figure is close to 5 per cent. It is interesting to note, however, that there is no sharp distinction between strong Labour and strong Tory areas in the distribution of colored immigrants; in the Labour districts the proportion is 3.2 per cent, while in the Conservative districts it is 3.8 per cent.

About 7 per cent of the Barons Court population was born in other lands of predominantly white stock. The distribution of this group is most noticeable in some of the Tory and marginal districts —Avonmore Ward, a large part of Gibbs Green, a sector of Starch Green, and polling district Ic in Brook Green—where the proportion ranges from 11 to more than 17 per cent of the total population. This is reflected in the comparative figures for the Labour and Tory strongholds: Labour, 3.9 per cent; Conservative, 13.3 per cent. The Labour districts with the highest proportion of noncolored foreign born are in the Hammersmith end of the constituency— especially in parts of Broadway Ward and a nibble of Brook Green Ward—where there is a heavy concentration of Irish folk.

Housing Arrangements

The housing picture in Barons Court is extremely spotted. It contains some of the most luxurious flats in West London (e.g., Barons Keep), as well as some of the poorest slum dwellings. Although the proportion of public housing was not markedly high in 1961—about 10 per cent of the households lived in such accommodations—the council estates erected in the immediate postwar years are comfortable, and the more recent ones of contemporary design are among the nicest to be found in London. But most of the dwellings in Barons Court are structures of nineteenth-century vintage, many of which have been chopped up into single rooms and dismal "flatlets" and let for exorbitant rents. As one travels about the constituency, he sees dreary streets of small semidetached and terraced houses occupied by single families, as well as two- and three-story dwellings of Victorian design which a century ago were occupied by families that employed servants. These larger buildings have been remodeled to accommodate a dozen or more tenants each in a single room or to house "two families up" and "two families down" (in the basement). Many of the people living in the multioccupied dwellings enjoy few amenities.

Only about 12 per cent of the households in Barons Court are owner-occupied. Since the decontrolling of property under the Rent Act, many people have moved back into the constituency and taken up residence in their own homes. While some of those living in their own homes, especially in places like Starch Green Ward, inhabit high-class quarters, most of them live in modest surroundings. The highest incidence of home ownership is to be found in strong Labour districts, especially Margravine Ward and parts of Grove Ward, where lower-middle-class workers and skilled laborers managed to purchase their dwellings before the war, or where they have been forced to buy their homes in recent years in order to

Table 1.5—Types of Tenure by Households

(in percentages)

Area	Owners-Occupiers	Council Tenants	Private* Rentors
London	15.6	21.2	59.8
Constituency	11.8	10.6	77.5
Strong Labour PDs	12.2	13.4	74.4
Strong Tory PDs	7.0	6.1	86.8
Marginal PDs	14.0	5.8	80.1

* Does not include people whose accommodation was provided in connection with employment.

forestall eviction. These people take pride in improving their property, fixing the gates and painting the doors and window sills, usually in deep red, yellow, or blue. Data on overall housing tenure are presented in Table 1.5.

The proportion of multioccupied dwellings is high in several Conservative areas, especially in Avonmore, Brook Green, and Gibbs Green wards, where the range of "no family" households is from 40 to 52 per cent of the population. It is here that a large number of the larger homes have been split up into small units and rented as "bed-sitters" to single persons. Although the incidence of single-room accommodation is high in the constituency as a whole, it is more marked in the areas of Tory strength, as can be seen in Table 1.6.

Areas of high single-room occupancy are characterized by high mobility, making it difficult for both parties to trace their potential support. In five polling districts of Barons Court—Ka and Kb (Avonmore), Ic (Brook Green), Fc (Starch Green), and Ma (Gibbs Green), the proportion of adult inhabitants who have moved from their residence within the previous year ranged from 20 to 23 per cent. More complete data on the mobility of the Barons Court population are presented in Table 1.7.

The fact that the Tory districts are characterized by a large

Table 1.6—Single Room Occupancy by Households

(in percentages)

Area	One-Person Households in One Room	Total Households in One Room	No Family Households
London	7.4	10.8	28.0
Constituency	12.8	13.6	34.5
Strong Labour PDs	8.8	12.8	31.0
Strong Tory PDs	22.4	20.8	43.5
Marginal PDs	8.2	10.6	32.3

proportion of adult movers, many of them new to the area, does not mean that the Tory Party is necessarily more affected than its opposition. A sizable percentage of these mobile people, especially those who reside in bed-sitter units, are working-class people or lower-grade clerks who have moved from heavily Labour areas and who have some sympathy for the Labour cause. Thus, the problem of tracing shifts in residence in these highly mobile areas is one that concerns both parties.

The housing situation in Broadway Ward merits special attention, for it harbors unique problems which challenge the ingenuity of the party activists on both sides. About 27 per cent of the households in polling district Je live in their own premises, while in Jc nearly 60 per cent are council tenants. Many of the people who live in tenanted properties are in huge blocks of flats, like the Peabody Trust and the Guinness Trust, which accommodate working-class families. In addition, the ward has a large convent, several quarters for nurses, and a huge lodging house for "floating" Irish workers. Polling district Ja, which includes the convent and the lodging house, has a high population turnover, nearly one-fourth of the residents having moved there within the previous twelve

Table 1.7—Shifts in Residence for Adults

(in percentages)

Area	Total Movers	Moved inside the Borough	Moved from outside the Borough
London*	12.9	8.1	4.8
Constituency	13.8	5.1	8.5
Strong Labour PDs	12.0	5.4	6.4
Strong Tory PDs	19.4	5.4	14.0
Marginal PDs	12.2	4.7	7.4

* The London figures are not strictly comparable, since they include people below the age of fifteen.

months. Party workers find it difficult, if not impossible, to canvass their potential supporters in these huge rooming houses and religious establishments.

Although the strong Conservative polling districts have higher single-room occupancy and are more mobile than the Labour districts, the latter have more crowded living conditions. This can be seen from the data in Table 1.8, which compares the two groups with respect to density of room occupancy and the sharing of dwellings and certain facilities.

In light of the housing situation in Barons Court, it is small wonder that voters are concerned about such problems as crowded living quarters, influx of colored immigrants, lack of council-housing in some districts, high rents demanded by private land-lords, and increased rents levied by the borough councils on council properties. In a real sense, these day-to-day issues loom larger for many people than rebellion in the Congo or colonialism in Goa.

Table 1.8—Housing Conditions by Households

DENSITY OF ROOM OCCUPANCY

Area	Average No. of Persons per Room	More than 1.5 Persons per Room	1–2 Person House-holds in Five or More Rooms	House-holds Sharing Dwellings	House-holds Sharing Water Closets
London	0.77	7.2%	7.0%	29.9%	30.2%
Constituency	0.78	7.9	6.2	33.3	20.5
Strong Labour PDs	0.82	8.7	5.0	43.7	27.5
Strong Tory Pds	0.73	6.6	10.2	25.4	19.0
Marginal PDs	0.76	6.6	5.0	28.9	12.9

The Party Organizations in Barons Court

The physical setting of what is now Barons Court is the product of the development of Fulham and Hammersmith in the nineteenth and early twentieth centuries. During that period, the industrial and residential patterns were largely set, and there has been little change in the social composition of the population since the end of World War II, except for the movement of tenants into the area from the high-rent districts in other parts of London and the return of some property owners to take up residence in accommodations which they had previously rented to other people.

But the constituency of Barons Court—and hence its political organization—is of much more recent vintage, having been created in the parliamentary redistribution (reapportionment) of 1954. While at the present time it is one of three constituencies in the Borough of Hammersmith, this situation has prevailed only since 1963, when an act of parliament reorganized London government, changing the existing boroughs and bringing a number of wealthy suburbs under the umbrella of the Greater London Council. When Barons Court was established in 1954, it was made up of parts of two old boroughs, Fulham and Hammersmith. This was the situation at the time of the 1964 election.

The fact that the constituency of Barons Court embraces parts of two long-established units of local government has given rise to a number of organizational problems. In general elections, of course, both the Conservative and Labour parties focus their attention upon the singular objective of electing a member of parliament from Barons Court. But prior to the recent reorganization the two parties were faced with a marked ambivalence when it came to running campaigns in borough council elections. The wards in one section of the constituency were concerned with the election of councillors to serve on the Hammersmith council, while the rest of the wards had to sponsor candidates for the borough council in Fulham. In these local elections, Barons Court was a political entity of no consequence; borough loyalties and concerns had to supersede those of the constituency itself. Paradoxically, this peculiar arrangement created the most serious headaches for the Labour organization, because both the Hammersmith and Fulham councils were safely under the domination of the Socialists. On some occasions the two Labour-controlled councils took different stands on crucial local issues. The two authorities, for example, established council-housing rents on opposite and virtually incompatible principles, and hence the Labour Party in Barons Court had to work out two different sets of campaign literature. Under these circumstances, the local Tories could have a field day attacking one Labour policy with the ammunition provided by an opposing Labour policy. But for both the Conservative and the Labour parties, the establishment of a new parliamentary constituency from segments of the party organizations in Hammersmith and Fulham laid the basis for potential factionalism in the new structure.

The restructuring of the wards as a result of the new Greater London scheme of local government shortly before the 1964 parliamentary election also created organizational problems for the two parties in Barons Court. When the ward boundaries were realigned, new ward organizations had to be set up in each party. Since some of the wards in Barons Court now lapped over into other parliamentary constituencies, the problem took on added complexity. For the Tories who experienced difficulty in securing a permanent agent to take the lead in building up the new ward organizations, the consequences of the change were particularly severe.

In light of the problems that the Conservative and Labour parties were compelled to wrestle with in the 1964 and 1966 elections, it will be instructive to examine the normal patterns of organization in each of these political structures.

The Conservative Association

In the summer of 1964, just a few months before the general election, the Conservative Association in Barons Court listed about

3,000 "card-carrying" members on its record books at the head-quarters at 84A North End Road.[3] However, only a small fraction of these people are even reasonably active; most of them simply pay their dues in order to give a modicum of support to the party of their preference. Once each year these dues-paying members are entitled to attend a general meeting of the association for the purpose of electing officers, as well as to hear reports about past and projected activities.

The organization of the Conservative Party in a constituency in some respects resembles the main patterns of British government nationally. There is a president who is chosen from among the most prestigious members of the association. Typically a peer, a well-placed businessman, or a notable personality in the community, the president plays no active role in the running of the organization. He is the symbolic leader who occupies the place of honor at the important meetings, gatherings, and fetes; he is, in a real sense, the monarch. The active figure in the executive of the organization—the "Prime Minister," so to speak—is the chairman of the association. As a rule he holds his post for a number of years, although he is technically elected at the annual meeting. In the period from 1954 to 1966 only two individuals served as chairman of the Conservative Association in Barons Court.

The Tory organization in the constituency also provides for two "general" vice-chairmen—one from the Fulham wing and the other from Hammersmith—and two "reserved" vice-chairmen, one of whom represents the Women's Branch and the other the Young Conservative groups. Included on the roster of officials are a treasurer and a secretary. As is usually the case with local parties in Britain, the position of secretary is held by the agent. These officers all serve on the party's Executive Committee (the "ministry"), which also includes at least two representatives from each ward, from the Women's Branch, and from the Young Conservatives. The wards and auxiliary bodies are entitled to an additional repre-

3. This description of the organization depicts the situation as it was in 1964. After the Conservative defeat, a major reorganization was undertaken.

31

sentative for each 250 members. The Executive Committee meets in plenary session each quarter to discuss the business of the association and to plan its activities.

The real leadership of the Conservative organization, however, rests with a smaller committee, the Finance and General Purposes Committee (the "cabinet"), which meets regularly once a month. It is made up of the officers of the association and one representative from each of the wards. Since the leading members of the Finance and General Purposes Committee also serve on the Executive Committee, there is little possibility of conflict arising between the two groups.

These two important committees are primarily concerned with problems of organization, membership, finance, and, when necessary, the selection of a prospective parliamentary candidate. As is typical of local Conservative party organizations, the members of these groups spend little time or energy at their meetings in discussing and debating policy alternatives. Policy matters, of course, do become relevant when the Executive Committee or a small special committee set about the task of choosing a candidate for a parliamentary election. But only when it is looking for a candidate or when it formulates an occasional resolution to be submitted to the annual conference of the national party does the association actively and deliberately attempt to influence policy stands of the national organization.

This brief discussion of the central organization of the local association will easily suffice for a book that focuses upon a specific campaign, because these committees as such become virtually irrelevant once the campaign gets underway. To be sure, if the committees have not done their work well between campaigns, the organization is not likely to be in good shape to contest the election. But as the campaign approaches, a special group—which will be described in the next chapter—is set up for the specific purpose of conducting the campaign.

Although the existing ward organizations are usually of greater importance in the campaign, this was not true of the Tory machine in Barons Court in 1964. The restructuring of the wards a year before the election had destroyed the territorial base of ward organizations which had existed for a decade, and in several wards new organizations hardly existed except on paper.

In terms of membership, the strongest Tory ward organization was Avonmore. It was also reasonably well organized, having survived the changes in ward boundaries without serious disruption. Although Starch Green, too, had a good organization, the Barons Court Tories suffered from the fact that its electorate was small and two of its polling districts were in North Hammersmith. The Conservatives treated polling districts Hb and Ic as a single unit, and, although these districts had good local organizations, their existence as fragments of wards that crossed constituency boundaries complicated the organization of a campaign. Gibbs Green Ward was considered by the Tories to be truly marginal, but only one of its three polling districts was well organized by the time of the election. Grove Ward was a real Labour stronghold, but the Tories who lived there were the old-time residents and were well organized. Although the Conservatives also regarded Halford Ward as being strongly Labour, they had some good workers who lived there. As we shall see, the organization of Halford was perceived by the center at the time of the election as being better than it really was. As the campaign drew near, Broadway and Margravine wards were probably in the worst shape in terms of organizational requirements. In spite of hard work by a few, the ward structure in both districts had not really taken form by the time of the election.

Each ward organization, which schedules regularly monthly meetings, has its affairs directed by two chief officers, the chairman and the secretary. In a well-run association, much of the detailed campaign work, such as canvassing and literature distribution, is handled through the wards. A special campaign organization would be established in advance in each of the units to handle these tasks under the supervision of the agent and perhaps the chief association officers. Prior to the 1964 campaign, however, only two Tory ward organizations were sufficiently well organized and staffed to handle the canvassing in their own areas, and two of the wards were not prepared as organizations to undertake any campaign work, although individuals from these wards worked hard before and during the campaign. In light of these organizational problems, the Tory campaign leaders were forced either to recruit outsiders to set up and man the committee rooms, or to handle all canvassing and literature distribution from the central headquarters. In the remaining three wards, at least half of the organizing and canvassing was done either by outsiders or directly from the center.

An adequate description of the Conservative organization must necessarily include reference to two "auxiliary" groups, the Women's Branch and the Young Conservatives. The Women's Branch had about ninety active members, and the attendance at monthly supper meetings averaged about fifty. To judge from the topics discussed and the conversations carried on at these meetings, one might gain the impression that the women's group is more of a social club than a political organization. But, quite apart from any recruitment and morale-building that grow out of social activities, the women make an important political contribution in the form of fund-raising. Their sponsorship of morning coffee parties, jumble sales, afternoon parties, and "good-as-new" sales brings useful financial resources into the local party. Even more important in terms of campaign work, the Women's Branch constitutes a reservoir of organizational and clerical talent which can be quickly tapped for the huge volume of work which has to be done just before and during the campaign: 45,000 envelopes to be addressed and stuffed, 4,000 canvass cards to be prepared, and hundreds of little, unanticipated jobs to be done. Many of the people who worked at 84A North End Road during the campaign had initially come to the Tories through the Women's Branch.

Two groups of Young Conservatives are involved in the Conservative Association at Barons Court, the Riverside Branch and the West Kensington Branch. A Young Conservative Branch, of course, can be different things to different people. For some of its members, it is perhaps little more than a clearing house for marriage; for others, it may be the first rung in a political ladder which hopefully will lead to the palace at Westminster or even to No. 10 Downing Street. From the viewpoint of the national party, the Young Conservatives are entrusted with the recruitment of each new generation of young people into Conservative ranks. But however the youth organization may be looked upon elsewhere, to the Barons Court Association facing the election, the two branches were an important political asset. Since the territorial basis of their membership is not tied to any specific ward, both branches were untroubled by organizational changes wrought by the redistricting of the wards, and the agent was able to employ them as reinforcements for weak ward organization. As we shall soon observe, the canvassing and literature distribution in two polling districts were handled by the Young Conservatives, who operated under the supervision of the central headquarters, and they manned two committee rooms on polling day.

The Labour Party

In its basic, formal structure, the Labour Party in Barons Court differs strikingly from the Conservative Association, but on several dimensions the differences begin to blur when one examines the two organizations in actual operation. Much of the difference in formal structure can be explained by the contrasting histories of the two parties. The Labour Party began as a federation of trade unions, socialist societies, and cooperative associations, and until 1918 individuals could become involved in the organization only through membership in one of these component groups. At the end of World War I, however, the party's constitution was changed so as to permit the enrollment of individuals. The several elements of the original federation can still be detected readily in the pattern of organization of most constituency Labour parties, including the one in Barons Court.

Under the constitution adopted in 1918, the Labour Party embraces two types of members: affiliated and individual members. An affiliated member is one who is associated with the organization as a result of having joined a trade union, a cooperative society or a branch of the Cooperative Party, a socialist society (like the Fabian Society or the Socialist Medical Association), or some other group which the national party recognizes as an "affiliate." An individual member, on the other hand, is one who joins the party directly by becoming a member of a ward group and by paying his subscription (dues) to the collectors at regular intervals. To be eligible, an individual must be a British citizen at least sixteen years of age and a resident of the ward or entitled to vote in one of the polling districts in the ward. (It should be pointed out that the Conservatives have no such residence requirement.) He must also sign a statement indicating that he endorses the constitution and policies of the Labour Party and does not belong to any organization that has been proscribed by the national party. The latter requirement has been specifically designed to keep extremist groups from infiltrating Labour at the grass roots. Needless to say, the individual members are much more interested in politics than are the affiliated members, and the party depends upon them for virtually all of its work.

Responsibility for handling the affairs of the party at the ward level resides with a group of officers who are elected for one-year terms at an annual meeting. The principal officials include the chairman, secretary, and treasurer. The main burden of organization typically falls upon the secretary. He keeps the membership records, schedules the meetings and sets the agenda, and is responsible for forwarding periodic reports to the officials at the constituency party level. In short, he is the chief link between the officers at the central echelon and the individual party members and supporters who reside in his ward.

At the time of the 1964 election, the ward membership in the Barons Court Labour Party ranged from 100 in the truncated Addison and Brook Green wards to 513 in Margravine, a Socialist stronghold. A total of 1,821 individual members was recorded for the constituency as a whole, about 11 per cent of those who vote Labour in a general election. If account is taken of the affiliated membership, however, the number of people associated directly and indirectly with the Barons Court party is somewhat higher. As is the case with the Tories, only a very small proportion of the members are really active in party affairs. Attendance at each of the monthly ward meetings ranges from ten to twenty, although a social event often brings out as many as ninety or a hundred.

The Labour organization in Barons Court responded more quickly than its Tory counterpart to the disruption caused by the redrawing of the ward boundaries, and most wards were in reasonably good shape to fight the borough council elections as a warm-up exercise in May 1964. In terms of voting strength, the bastions of Labour support were Margravine, Grove, and Halford wards. The Margravine and Grove areas were well organized, and Halford, with some supplementary assistance from the center, was capable of delivering its quota of Socialist votes. The organization in Broadway Ward, which was also responsible for two polling districts in Starch Green, was rated among the best, although the area could not be regarded as safely Labour. Gibbs Green Ward was marginal territory, but the organization was strengthened by the fact that a group of the party's leading activists resided there. Even Avonmore Ward, a Tory stronghold, had a viable organization which, with aid from the central headquarters, operated with surprising effectiveness. Polling districts Hb and Ic in Addison and Brook Green wards respectively had no regular Labour organization, and had to be worked from the center.

From this brief description, it is clear that the Labour organization had managed to adjust in more than a minimal way to the restructuring of the wards, and was on the whole in good shape to fight the campaign. Most of the Labour strongholds had good organizations, the marginal area was quite well covered, and one of the heavy Tory districts had a Labour cadre that was not willing to let the area go by default. It was only in the strong Tory wards which were split between the two constituencies of Barons Court and Hammersmith North that Labour lacked a significant organization. These two districts, it should be pointed out, were not only heavily Tory, but also had small electorates. Hence, in these polling districts even a strong Labour organization would probably not have been able to pull out very many additional votes.

The federational nature of the Labour Party is easily noticeable at the constituency level. Each of the organizational components is entitled to send delegates to the party's governing body, the General Management Committee (GMC), which meets at a regular time each month. In the Barons Court party, each ward is allowed four delegates, and one additional delegate for every hundred members (or part thereof) that it recruits over the initial hundred. Beside these elected representatives, the ward secretaries are ex-officio members of the GMC. Trade union branches that are affiliated with the local party can claim a delegate for every fifty members or part thereof, with a maximum of five from any single branch. Cooperative societies have a similar formula of representation based upon the size of their membership lists. Other party units, such as the Women's Section and the Young Socialists, are entitled to send two delegates.

In 1964 the GMC of the Barons Court Labour Party consisted of fifty-two members who represented the ward organizations and the various affiliated groups (trade unions, cooperative societies, Women's Section, etc.). The largest bloc of delegates—thirty-eight out of fifty-two—came from the wards. As is usual with constituency parties in urban centers, the trade unions were not conspicuously active on the GMC. While about twenty-five branches representing fourteen different unions were affiliated with the party, a number of them did not bother to appoint delegates.

At the time of the 1964 election, only eight trade union branches from six different unions were represented on the GMC, making a total of nine delegates in the trade union section. The relative weakness of the institutionalized union component in Barons Court arises partially from the fact that the branch offices of many unions are located within the constituencies of North Hammersmith or Fulham. Some of these unions, however, paid their affiliation fees according to the actual residence of their members, which gives them a nominal affiliation with the Barons Court party. But one must draw a distinction between the involvement of the trade unions and that of individual trade unionists. A number of the latter preferred to come on to the GMC through other routes than through the trade unions—for example, as delegates from a ward or from a cooperative society.

The cooperative movement is somewhat more active in the local party than the trade unions. The parliamentary candidate in the 1955 and 1959 elections had been sponsored by the Cooperative Party, and the Labour Party premises (Robert Owen House at 160 Shepherds Bush Road) are leased to the Socialists by this organization. It is not surprising, therefore, that four members of the GMC were from two cooperative societies, one from Fulham and the other from Hammersmith.

The main officers of the General Management Committee include a chairman, two vice-chairmen, a treasurer, and a financial secretary who are elected at its annual meeting. In addition to these main executive officials, the GMC elects a political education officer, two officers to supervise the Young Socialists, a delegate to the annual conference of the national party, a representative to the United Nations Association, a House Committee responsible for the party premises, a Bazaar Committee, and a delegate to serve on the Road Safety Committee. In 1964 all these posts but two were filled by representatives of the ward organizations.

The GMC also elects an Executive Committee from among its own members. Responsible to the GMC, this agency considers in a preliminary way the party's business and policy matters, including changes in the organization's rules and official positions the party may want to consider on important issues of the day. On these items it makes periodic reports and recommendations to the parent body. The chief party officials are members of the Executive Committee by virtue of their positions, while the remaining seats are occupied by representatives from the various components of the federation. In 1964 the Executive Committee was made up of the agent and five elected officials, ten delegates from the ward organizations, two from the trade unions, one from the cooperatives, one from the Women's Section, and one from the Young Socialists.

One of the big differences between the Conservative and Labour parties at the local level is that in the latter the activists spend considerable time in discussing policy issues. These discussions may occur obliquely at candidate selection conferences, but they become more direct at ward meetings and GMC meetings, usually as an outgrowth of particular resolutions which the activists in the ward organizations have sent forward in the hope that they will be transmitted to the national party. Many of the people who are active in local party affairs have a strong commitment to Socialist beliefs, and are very much interested in policy questions. This concern over issues, of course, often serves to make the meetings lively, but it can also generate ideological factions within the organization.

It should be clear from these descriptions of the Conservative and Labour organizations in Barons Court that, despite the important differences in formal structure, they exhibit in their practical workings certain patterns of similarity. The Labour Party's GMC, for example, is fairly comparable in structure and function to the Conservative Executive Committee, although it does devote more time to the treatment of policy issues. By the same token, Labour's Executive Committee has a close counterpart in the Tory Finance and General Purposes Committee. Another parallel lies in the fact that in neither party do the top policy and management committees as such play an active part in the campaign. Working with the agent, the committees in each organization are responsible for setting up another body which assumes primary responsibility for running the campaign. These special campaign agencies will be considered in the next chapter.

Crucial Party Roles

This description of the formal organization of the two constituency parties seriously underplays the importance of two roles which are of crucial importance between and during campaigns. The role of the agent and the role of the candidate, which have received bare mention up to this point, merit special consideration.

The Agent

Every parliamentary candidate, no matter what his party affiliation, must by law designate someone to serve as his agent during the campaign. The political parties go much farther than this. The Labour Party has full-time, professional organizers or agents in virtually all of the marginal constituencies, and in others that can hardly be considered anything but safe. The Tories have a full-time agent in almost every constituency.

The agent's legal duties and responsibilities are defined by the various Representation of the People Acts. Regulating campaign practices largely through the control of expenditures, these laws make illegal any expenditure or activity on behalf of a candidate without the approval of the agent, and the latter is entirely responsible before the law for anything he authorizes. The laws defining acceptable and illegal practices and expenditures in a campaign are not only tightly written, but they are also strictly enforced. An agent who is found guilty of violating the law, even if the transgression is accidental, is severely punished. When the laws are contravened, the agent and his candidate may be barred from officially participating in a campaign for at least five years, and the candidate, if he has won, must forfeit the election. Punishment may be inflicted upon the agent and the candidate if the former has unwittingly exceeded the expense limit by a pound or so because of a simple mistake in arithmetic while he was planning the campaign. Deliberate violations of the corrupt practices sections of the law can lead to fines and imprisonment for as long as two years.

A specific case will illustrate how closely the work of a party agent may be scrutinized. The law requires that every piece of campaign literature and every advertisement be plainly marked with the name of the printer and the name of the agent as publisher. In one postwar election, the agent of a prominent member of parliament prepared an election address in such a way that one corner could be torn off along perforations and used as a window bill. Although the election address carried the agent's mark, the part that could be torn off and pasted in a window did not carry a separate designation of printer and publisher. This oversight resulted in the filing of a petition which challenged the election of the victorious candidate. The judges denied the petition, but they indicated that the agent had been treading in a dangerous borderline area and should be reprimanded. The ruling suggested that if the window bill had been separated from the rest of the address prior to mailing, the law would have been clearly violated, the election voided, and the agent and candidate barred from participating in elections for five years, even though no illegal expenditures were involved.

Note that in this case the candidate would have been made to suffer even though he had no direct responsibility for the acts of his agent. The legal interpretations of the basic statutes recognize that the law defining the relationship between candidate and agent is harsh and stringent.[4] The candidate is responsible for all of the agent's acts, even those that have not been specifically authorized

4. For a review of the basic judicial decisions concerning the relationship between candidate and agent, see Alfred N. Schofield, *Local Government Elections* (London: Shaw & Shaw, 1962), pp. 138–144.

by him; indeed, the candidate is held responsible even when the agent is operating in direct violation of his specific orders. The judges have held that the relationship is one of master and servant and not one of principal and agent. The common law of agency which protects the principal against unauthorized acts of his agent does not apply. The basic law and its interpretations indicate that we do not speak figuratively when we say that the candidate places his political honor and his political career in the hands of the person he selects as his agent. The agent bears a grave responsibility.

While the agent's legal duties and responsibilities deal largely with the election campaign, he is a regular, full-time employee of the local party, and as such his responsibilities to the organization are continuous—some agents are even prepared to say "infinite." His major task is to build a strong and effective party machine in his area so that it can be put into full operation at election time. This means that he must initiate and supervise recruitment drives for new members, make sure that funds are available to support the organization, and see to it that the ward units and the central structure are in healthy condition. To achieve these objectives he must attract a core of loyal workers and keep them interested in party activities on a continuing basis. Since the agent cannot afford to have his party weakened by factional rivalries and personal feuds, he needs to be blessed with the skills of a diplomat, mediating conflicts and smoothing ruffled feathers when the need arises. The local party, of course, is a major point of contact between the voters and the national organization. It plays a major role in disseminating information about the party's stand on policies throughout the constituency. The planning and execution of these publicity drives rest with the agent, who needs to have a sense of public relations in performing this important function.

The Conservative agent in Barons Court was Mrs. Patricia Bowman, who came to the constituency a scant six months before the election. A university graduate with a degree in science, she became interested in politics through a debating society while at the university. Her love for political combat prompted her to become a party agent, and she had fought several elections before coming to Barons Court. Her most recent national contest had been a victory in Holborn and St. Pancras in 1959. As the story of the Tory campaign unfolds in subsequent chapters, we shall get a clear picture of how Mrs. Bowman approached the tasks of an agent. It will be sufficient at this point to indicate that, in her view, the agent's role was primarily one of responsibility for party organization and campaign strategy and tactics. Although she had personal convictions on issues of public policy, she rarely expressed these preferences publicly. Whenever she was asked for a public statement about a policy issue, she invariably deferred to the candidate. At the same time, she expected the other people in the organization, including the candidate, to respect her wishes on matters of organization and the conduct of the campaign. This did not mean she would not seek advice or listen to suggestions. But, after listening to the advice and studying the alternatives, she made many of the final decisions herself.

Mrs. Bowman's rigid distinction between policy matters and matters of campaign organization was based on more than a consideration of the relative expertise of the agent and the candidate. One of her main jobs was to keep the organization united. Since ideological and policy issues can easily split a constituency party, she felt that an effective agent cannot afford to be put in the uncomfortable position of having to take sides with one faction against another. By being publicly neutral on divisive questions, the agent is better equipped to keep potential factions working in common harness.

The Labour Party agent was Mr. Alan F. Clarke, who had more than a decade of experience with two different constituency parties before taking his post in Barons Court in 1961. Recognizing as his main objective the winning of elections, Clarke devoted his attention to strengthening the organization and recruiting effective workers and new members. Indeed, as one observes the two agents, he can detect great similarity between Mr. Clarke's conception of the agent's role and that of Mrs. Bowman. By not becoming openly and vociferously allied with any political faction, Clarke was in a strong position to attract party workers of all shades of opinion, and thus to minimize differences among rival groups by trying to direct their energies toward the single goal of victory. Since the Labour Party tends to be more subject to ideological splits than the Conservatives, this stance was probably of greater importance to Mr. Clarke than it was to Mrs. Bowman.

In contrast with Mrs. Bowman, however, the Labour agent did not impose restrictions upon himself when it came to meeting with reporters who wanted statements on policy issues. He and the candidate had come to Barons Court at about the same time. They knew each other's views, and they enjoyed a warm, personal relationship. Clarke knew that he could accurately reflect the candidate's position, and he felt no hesitation in making public statements about issues which were important to the voters in his constituency.

The two agents also differed in the way in which they responded to their duties. In managing her campaign, Mrs. Bowman was openly and obviously the central director. The directives that were needed to keep the efforts of several hundred volunteer workers integrated and effective were usually sent out from her office. She personally supervised the work in the ward committee rooms, visiting them frequently and discussing particular problems with the clerks in charge. Mr. Clarke, on the other hand, tended to work through his lieutenants, directing and supervising their activities but letting them deal directly with the active workers. The officer in charge of canvassing, for example, was largely responsible for managing the activities of the canvassers who worked out of the several committee rooms once the campaign got underway. Thus, the ward organizers and volunteers would have important contact with certain campaign officials who were responsible for supervising special aspects of the campaign. This arrangement relieved the agent of some of the supervisory work.

The Candidate

Before we turn to the planning of the campaign itself, we need to discuss briefly a second crucial role—that of the candidate. The candidate's role in the party organization is not so structured as the agent's, and hence we would expect that the personality and personal experiences of the two candidates would influence their approach to political activities and their role in the campaign. Striking contrasts existed between the two candidates, especially the way in which they were projected into the political limelight in Barons Court, and these help to account for the different roles they played in the election contest.

The Conservative candidate and a sitting member of parliament was William Compton Carr. Bill Carr, as he preferred to be called, had a long record of political and community activity in the Barons Court area even before he won the seat in 1959. He commenced his active political work in the early 1950s, and, beginning in 1953, he served as a ward officer and as a member of the Executive Committee in the old East Fulham constituency. In 1955 and again in 1958, he stood for the London County Council from Barons Court. He was also active in the Bow Group, a national organization of younger Conservative intellectuals.

In addition to his political work in the area, Carr engaged in a wide variety of community activities in Hammersmith and Barons Court. Deeply concerned about the problems of youth, education, and welfare, he served as a member of the Board of Governors of a secondary school in Fulham, and as a member of the Board of Managers of a group of special schools in Hammersmith. He was also a member of the West London Hospital House Committee, vice-chairman of the Deptford Old People's Welfare Association, vice-president of the Hammersmith District Society for Mentally Handicapped Children, and vice-president of both the Hammersmith and Fulham branches of the National Society for the Prevention of Cruelty to Children. Although this record of voluntary service to the community could be expanded, further elaboration is not necessary for the point to be made. Carr had worked hard for Hammersmith and Fulham, and he had expended great energy in behalf of the Conservative Party in this section of London. When the Tories needed a prospective candidate in 1958, Mr. Carr, was an impressive local contender, whose work could not be easily overlooked.

Mr. Ivor Richard, the Labour candidate, had taken a different route to the Barons Court arena. His active work in a local Labour party began in the nearby constituency of South Kensington, where in 1959 he was selected as the parliamentary candidate. In that district, which is a barren wilderness for Socialists, it is usually regarded as a victory for the Labour candidate when he saves his deposit. But the 1959 contest in South Kensington did provide Richard with valuable campaign experience. He also fought hopeless battles for the Kensington Borough Council and for the London County Council. Naturally, Mr. Richard's work in behalf of the South Kensington party brought him into contact with other Labour activists in West London, including some Labour people from Barons Court. Later in this study we shall describe the selection conference which brought him into formal relationship with the Barons Court party. But at this juncture it is sufficient to point out that, in sharp contrast with Mr. Carr, Ivor Richard was relatively unknown to the voters in the Barons Court community—he was much more of an "outsider" than his opponent. As an "insider," Carr had absorbed himself in the affairs of the constituency, which he knew very well. He had known many of the party workers as colleagues before he became their candidate and member of parliament.

The differing background and experiences of the two candidates help to explain why they were oriented toward their respective organizations and agents in quite different manners. With his long-time involvement in both local party organization and in community affairs, Carr was an expert on the constituency and conceived of himself as such. Although he accepted a division of labor based upon the organization-policy dichotomy between himself and the agent and essentially carved out his role in the campaign according to his agent's prescriptions, he was somewhat uneasy with the arrangement. His ideas about how his own time (and the time of his wife) might be used most effectively differed from Mrs. Bowman's, and they were reinforced by the fact that he had been permitted to carry out these ideas in the 1959 campaign when he won the seat.

Mr. Richard, by contrast, was a more willing servant of his agent on campaign matters. Although he frequently discussed his role with Mr. Clarke, he responded to the agent's requests, bowing to his detailed knowledge of the constituency and his reservoir of experience from previous campaigns. In other words, Richard tended to develop his role in accordance with the suggestions of his agent.

The two candidates also reacted differently to their own organizations and to the Barons Court electorate. His role as sitting M.P., combined with his involvement in so many nonpartisan educational and welfare activities in the community, prompted Mr. Carr to orient himself as much—or even more—toward the voters in the constituency than toward the core of workers in his party organization. According to his outlook, it was the duty of the party workers to throw themselves wholeheartedly into the campaign, and his task, so far as the key workers were concerned, was simply to demonstrate that he was working harder than anyone else. Mr. Richard, while not neglecting the constituency and the mass of voters in it, spent more time with the members of the campaign committee and with the key workers in the Labour organization.

We are not implying that one position was right and the other wrong, nor are we suggesting that one stance is typical of Conservatives and the other typical of Socialists. At this stage in the discussion, we are merely trying to identify the differences in candidate roles. In the last chapter we shall attempt to speculate on the question of whether these differences had any effect upon the outcome of the election.

Certain contrasts in the background and personal experiences of the two candidates are of some importance in understanding the conduct of the campaign. Mr. Carr was a solicitor and company director at the time of the 1964 campaign. While this appears to be a fairly typical occupational profile for a Conservative candidate, Carr did not come by it in a typical Tory fashion. He was born into a family of mean circumstances. His father had struggled up the economic and social ladder, but Carr never forgot his humble background. At a large outdoor rally one afternoon during the campaign, he was defending the Prime Minister's defense policy when he encountered severe heckling from a group of young unilateralists. As the exchanges grew more bitter, it became obvious that some in the hostile audience were attacking not only a defense policy, but the whole Conservative Party as an instrument of privilege, prestige, and power. A former peer was now the Prime Minister, and William Compton Carr, the Conservative candidate, symbolized the Tory peerage, Tory privilege, and Tory power. When this message got through to Mr. Carr, his face reddened, the veins in his throat expanded, and he shouted at his heckler, "I come from the same stable as you do, Mac!"

Not from exactly the same stable, we hasten to add, for Carr did have the advantage of education at good elementary schools and at the Leys in Cambridge. From 1936 to 1938, he was an airman in the R.A.F., and he rejoined the service as an air gunner in 1941. He still proudly wears a tie marked with the insignia of the Sergeants' Club. Between his tours of duty, he worked as a clerk and as a laborer. It was after the war, in 1947, that he took the three-year articles and qualified as a solicitor.

In talking with Mr. Carr, one could readily discern that many of his political values were directly related to his personal experiences. He was strongly committed to the basic programs of the "welfare state," supporting such policies as higher pensions, subsidized housing, and improved educational opportunities. He felt that the state should assume an active role in guaranteeing a minimum standard of living for every citizen. The pension plan he supported was identical in every essential regard to that outlined by Mr. Michael Stewart, the renowned Labour leader who represents the neighboring constituency of Fulham.

Carr was also willing to support limited state intervention in other sectors of the economy. He recognized, for example, that some nationalization was both necessary and desirable. He would level attacks, not upon the principle of public ownership, but only upon certain Labour schemes for nationalization, such as the proposed takeover of the steel industry.

Mr. Carr, however, was strongly opposed to any theme in Labour's philosophy that could be tied to the Marxian notion of class war. Indeed, it was his perception of this in Labour's appeals that sent him scurrying into the Conservative Party after his initial political interests had brought him into contact with the Socialist movement. Carr's richest invective was reserved for those who would emphasize the unity of the proletariat in its struggle against the bourgeoisie. He gave his strongest support to policies that were designed to provide the individual with security and to enhance his chances of improving himself socially and economically. A logical corollary of this position prompted him to strike out against party colleagues who explicitly or implicitly sought to advance the Tory cause by arguing that particular classes could claim the right to rule the country by virtue of their birth and training. One can hardly deny the existence of an air of snobbishness and condescension among certain elements of the Conservative Party. But under no circumstances would Bill Carr associate himself with the political outlook of these groups. It should come as no surprise that he was an early and strong supporter of Edward Heath in the leadership struggle, and it is one of the sad ironies of his political career that he was not in the House of Commons when Heath became the leader of the Conservative forces.

The Labour candidate, Ivor Richard, was born into the family of a mining engineer in a mining village in South Wales. He attended elementary school there and then won scholarships to Cheltenham College and later to Oxford. After completing his education at the university, he studied law at the Inner Temple in London. At the time that he was sharpening his political spurs in the South Kensington Labour Party, he was also winning a reputation as a talented young barrister in the law courts. In the middle of the 1964 campaign, he had to climb down from the political stump and journey to Westminster, where he donned his wig and gown and handled a case on leave to appeal to the House of Lords.

If we can associate Bill Carr with the "leftist" wing of the Conservative Party, we can identify Ivor Richard as being "center right" on the political spectrum of the Socialist movement. It may be that Richard's training in the law made him sensitive to the complexity of an issue and inclined him to weigh the difficult alternatives on the scales of pragmatism. Although he understood the emotional commitment of the "left" and shared with them a deep concern about social problems, he tended to be somewhat impatient with their oversimplification of issues and with their doctrinal rigidity. It must be emphasized, however, that, despite his pragmatic approach, he exhibited little tolerance for party colleagues who take refuge in expediency on basic policy matters about which he felt deeply.

Richard had a keen interest in foreign and defense policy. Like his opponent, he strongly supported Britain's entry into the Common Market. On defense matters, he was fervently opposed to unilateral disarmament, and had been associated with Hugh Gaitskell's organization in the long intraparty feud on this issue. While he did not argue that Britain should scrap her nuclear weapons, he was opposed to the Tory policy of purchasing Polaris missiles, contending that Britain could not afford the cost and could make a more substantial contribution to Western defense through the buildup of conventional forces.

In the purely domestic field, the Labour candidate was not sympathetic with a dogmatic approach to the nationalization of industry, although he was willing to go along with Labour's official policy on steel. He was much more interested in the expansion of educational opportunity, including the extension of comprehensive schools. Especially disturbing to Mr. Richard was the housing problem. When he visited some of the hovels in the Barons Court district, his blood pressure rose very rapidly, and on several occasions the sights he saw made him physically ill. These experiences reinforced his belief that housing accommodations should not be subject to the vicissitudes of the market and that much more action by the government was needed to relieve the shortage.

Although Ivor Richard was a devoted supporter of Hugh Gaitskell and was grieved by his death, he had not yet developed such a close attachment to the other leaders in the party. In rare moments of relaxation, when he might be discussing the historical trends in British politics, he would occasionally refer to the personality and influence of Lloyd George, the Liberal leader from his native Wales who had left such an impressive mark upon the British political scene.

This brief treatment of the political views of the two candidates naturally raises a question about whether their outlooks were congenial with the dominant opinion in their constituency parties. Mr. Carr tended to be to the left of the officers and many activists in his organization, while Mr. Richard was on several important issues to the right of most of the activists in his local party. The differences, however, were dramatic in only two instances.

In early 1963, when the Conservative Executive Committee was discussing resolutions to be sent forward for consideration by the Conservative Annual Conference, one of the members moved that the constituency party lend its support to a continuation of capital punishment. In the middle of the discussion, Mr. Carr took the floor and flatly announced that if the resolution were sent forward from the Barons Court Association and was debated at the Conference, he would be forced to rise and speak against it. Nevertheless the Executive voted unanimously to support capital punishment. The next motion on the floor was an expression of confidence in Mr. Carr as the sitting member of parliament and the prospective candidate from Barons Court. This resolution was also passed without dissenting vote. At no time during the 1964 campaign was there any indication that Carr's stand against the Executive Committee on an important issue of policy affected in any way the support he received from his organization.

When Mr. Richard's name was put forward as one of several to be considered for Labour candidacy in Barons Court, the local party was in the hands of the unilateralists who opposed Hugh Gaitskell. In his address at the selection conference, Richard stated clearly his views on defense which conflicted with those of the majority. But the unilaterist party adopted as its prospective candidate an avowed multilaterist. While his position on the defense question did not hurt his campaign in 1964, his stance on foreign policy, especially with respect to the Vietnam issue, prompted a few activists to work less frequently and with dampened enthusiasm in the contest held seventeen months later.

Although the two candidates held views that differed in detail on such matters as nuclear strategy and the comprehensive schools, and more fundamentally on housing, there were wide areas of agreement in their basic approaches to political problems. Even on the issues where the two men clashed sharply—housing is a good example—their differences were largely over the most effective means for reaching a goal to which both men were committed. But neither the candidates nor their party workers were really aware of any congruence of views. Carr was known among some Labour supporters as a "good constituency man" who was "progressive" in his outlook upon the welfare state; a typical comment of some trade union activists was, "He is a decent bloke—it's a pity that he is a Tory!" Little personal criticism was leveled at the Conservative candidate by Labour's campaign workers; they saved their ammunition for the party he represented. Those who felt the sting of social class distinctions the most could not take a charitable view toward any Tory, and Bill Carr happened at that moment to be the one who must be defeated.

The common Tory perception of Mr. Richard was far off the mark. Since he was new in the constituency and unknown in Conservative circles, he was not appraised as an individual. In the eye of most Tory activists, he was the candidate of a unilateralist, left-wing party, which was particularly stamped by "militants" from the Fulham wing of the organization. They did not realize that the party had settled down after 1962, and that, in any event, the candidate disagreed with a segment of the Labour workers on several important issues.

During the campaign, however, neither party cared very much about the personal policy preferences of the opposing candidates. The issues at stake were those defined by the differences in the manifestos of the two national parties. Since each candidate was in effect pledged to support the platform of his party, personal views that might be at variance were not really relevant and were not emphasized on the public platform. In order to understand the issue context of the campaign in Barons Court, therefore, it is necessary to examine the trends of national politics from 1959 to 1964, and to look at the policy stands taken by the two national organizations in their manifestos.

The National Setting: Parties and Issues

In the election of 1964, the Conservative Party brought to the British people a record which had been compiled during thirteen years in office. In several important respects it was an enviable record, symbolizing Britain's entrance upon a new course of development. When the Tories occupied No. 10 Downing Street in the autumn of 1951, the British people were still living under an austerity program necessitated by the reconstruction from World War II and by the burdens of conflict in East and Southeast Asia.

Ration cards which regulated the consumption of many basic commodities were still being used six years after the end of the war. The scars of 1940 were still visible on the face of London.

Aided greatly by the cumulative impact of Marshall Plan aid and by the shift to more favourable terms of trade for manufactured products following the Korean armistice, the economy began to blossom during the 1950s, while the Conservatives were in power. Most salaried people and the men on the shop floor began to receive bigger pay envelopes which, supplemented in many instances by the earnings of working wives, made possible the purchase of television sets, electric washers, "fridges," and even private cars—all symbols of a new affluence.

In 1959, Prime Minister Macmillan led his party into the general election with variations on the theme; "You've never had it so good!" To many voters this was an undeniable fact, and the British people went to the polls to deliver to the Conservatives an even bigger majority in the House of Commons than they had enjoyed previously.

However, all was not as well in the economy as the Government and vast numbers of the people believed. The Labour Party was quick to point out that those living on fixed incomes and pensions were not sharing in the nation's new prosperity. For some citizens, prices were rising faster than their incomes, and they knew from personal experience the subtle cruelty of a creeping inflation. But these economic problems ran far deeper than the difficulties which outraged the Socialists' sense of distributive justice. These were the problems that had been festering for almost half a century. The basic industrial plant in Britain was obsolete and contributed to the difficulty Britain was experiencing in competing with products from the continent and Japan. British products were gradually being driven off world markets by these foreign producers, who could usually make them cheaper and sometimes better.

And while its industrial plant was growing older, Britain's raw material base was becoming exhausted. In the mid-nineteenth century "Carrying coals to Newcastle" epitomized foolish waste and redundancy; in the mid-twentieth century it sometimes became necessary to carry coals to Newcastle. But even if the reserves of coal and other raw materials had not been disappearing, Britain would still have run into trouble. The industrial economy in the nineteenth century was built upon a foundation of iron, steel, and coal. An industrial economy in the mid-twentieth required additional ingredients—petroleum, petrochemical products, and non-ferrous metals. None of these basic raw materials is present in significant quantity in the British Isles.

The only way for Britain to meet the raw material deficiencies was by importing; the only way for her to pay for the imports was by exporting. But with an outdated industrial plant, with entrepreneurs who seemed reluctant to engage in aggressive competition on the world market and who were not used to operating on small margins, and with a labor force that appeared to be oriented more toward welfare than toward production, it was becoming increasingly difficult for the British to unload their exports without fundamental changes throughout the economy. Economic growth rates in Britain were lagging seriously behind those of her chief competitors.

The problem of lagging growth rates, of course, may be remedied on a short-run basis by reducing interest rates and by adopting other fiscal policies, including an increase in government spending to stimulate investment. But Britain was not entirely free to adopt such a solution because she was the holder of one of the two great international reserve currencies. A reduction in the bank rate is likely to send international investors scurrying. The rise in income that accompanies economic growth creates new demands for imports, and because of the income elasticity of imports in Britain, these new demands in the aggregate are always proportionately greater than the rise in income that spawned them. The simple fact is that the pound sterling cannot stand the battering it would take if dynamic, expansionist monetary and fiscal policies were to be pursued. Indeed, the traditional monetary and fiscal devices tend to be used in Britain more in response to the international position of sterling than to the situation in the domestic economy.

It was not long after the 1959 election that these long-term economic problems began to manifest themselves in current difficulties. In the early 1960s the crisis in sterling grew more severe, and the Macmillan Government responded by making adjustments in the tax structure so as to dampen consumer demand and by raising the bank rate to attract foreign capital. These deflationary measures could do little more than alleviate the pressure temporarily, and even this was achieved at the cost of increasing unemployment. In the long run something had to be done to increase productivity and to increase the ratio of exports to imports.

Constrained by the weakness of the pound from using expansionary monetary and fiscal policies, the Conservative Government turned to more direct intervention in the economy. The Tories instituted a temporary "pay pause" designed to hold down incomes until increases in productivity could justify wage increments. A National Economic Development Council (NEDC)—an agency made up of cabinet officials and representatives of management and labor—was established to formulate plans for the growth of the economy at respectable rates and to encourage labor and management to work together in meeting the targets. This was followed by the establishment of a National Incomes Commission, which was authorized to make public reports on the advisability of granting specific wage claims, taking into account the need to gear pay increases with rising levels of productivity.

While these measures represented attempts to strike at Britain's short-term and long-term economic problems, they did not achieve marked success. The pay pause was resisted by teachers, nurses, postmen, and workers in the London tube system. The trade unions tended to be suspicious of an incomes policy, especially one administered by Conservatives. Their fears were reinforced in July 1963 when the National Incomes Commission reported that one of its wage inquiries had been hampered by the unwillingness of employers in some industries to make available sufficient information concerning their profits.[5]

The Conservative Government also took another approach to the solution of Britain's economic problems. Since the 1950s the Liberal Party had been advocating that the country seek admission to the Common Market. In 1961, after much of the groundwork had been laid by the Bow Group and pressures were building up from the more liberal elements in the party, Tory leaders announced their intention to commence negotiations for entry. This policy met with opposition from some Conservative backbenchers, as well as some business interests which ordinarily supported the Government. The Labour Party was split on the issue, and the leading exponents of entry and nonentry could sanctify their arguments with university degrees in economics. Despite the political uncertainty at home, the Government dispatched Edward Heath to Brussels in 1962. After three months of tough negotiation, Heath returned to London in January 1963 without succeeding in his mission. At this point in time, the Treaty of Rome could not embrace both the Cross of Lorraine and the Cross of St. George.

It was difficult for many voters to see exactly how sterling crises and the Common Market directly affected them. But there was one issue which was basically related to the health of the economy and which was of direct concern to many citizens, especially those who lived in London and other parts of Southeast England. That issue was housing. On few questions did the philosophy of the Conservative and Labour parties differ so fundamentally. The Tory approach to the housing problem was to stimulate the construction of more housing units, and they conceived of this largely in terms of private building on a free market. In their view, construction had to be made an attractive capital investment. In line with its position on welfare—that Britain's limited resources should be

5. Francis Boyd, *British Politics in Transition, 1945–1963: A Short Political Guide* (London: Pall Mall Press, 1964), pp. 156–157.

used to provide a minimum level of living for all citizens and extra assistance should be reserved for those most in need—the Government felt that subsidized rentals should be used for the low-income groups, while the more affluent should be required to pay an "economic rent." The Labour Party, on the other hand, found it difficult to impose an economic rent in the public housing units, and in any event its adherents were opposed to a housing policy in which the capital required for residential housing would have to compete with capital in the most profitable sectors of British industry and commerce. To them, housing ought not to be subject to the law of the market, and public housing should be given priority over the construction of private dwellings.

In 1957–1958, the Macmillan Government took steps to alleviate the housing problem by introducing the Rent Act. The aim of this legislation was to exempt certain types of property from rent controls so as to encourage private landlords to improve their properties and to put more homes and flats on the rental markets. While the act did help to make more housing units available, it had other consequences that made the Government vulnerable to attack. With a limited free market returned to specified categories of rental property, some landlords took advantage of the critical housing shortage to exploit their tenants—a situation that was dramatically illustrated by the machinations of one Perec Rachman in West London.

Moreover, the price of land for home development skyrocketed, and the cost of private homes advanced accordingly. It was not unusual to find houses that had been bought for £700 before the war now being turned over for as high as £5,000. In the early 1960s, regardless of the cause and despite the advances that had been made, the housing problem remained crucial in Britain's industrial centers. The number of people living in slum properties was still high, and thousands of families were continued on the housing lists with little hope of securing the accommodations they needed. The situation in London was dramatically portrayed by the Milner-Holland

Committee, which pointed out in 1964 that 1,500 families (7,000 people) were homeless, being thrown on the mercy of the hostels and reception centers provided by local authorities on an emergency basis.[6]

The housing shortage helped to call attention to another problem—that of colored immigration in the large cities—which had been festering beneath the surface since the early 1950s and which had exhibited itself in a nasty form in the Notting Hill riots (not far from Barons Court) in the autumn of 1958. These people—West Indians, Indians, Pakistanis, and Africans—had migrated to England and Wales from the Commonwealth countries in search of jobs. Although the colored immigrants constituted only about 1.5 per cent of the total population, they were concentrated in urban centers like London and Birmingham where work was available, and in many places they were living in ghettos. The fact that these immigrants were indispensable to the economy in an era of full employment was frequently overlooked by the native residents, many of whom regarded the newcomers as aliens reaping the benefits of the welfare state and taking up housing space which should be reserved for their own people.

Local pressures for some form of control of immigration soon began to mount. Some backbenchers in each party grew a bit restive, and in October 1961 the issue appeared on the agenda for debate at the Conservative Party Conference. A month later the Government introduced the Commonwealth Immigrants Bill, which became law in April 1962. This legislation restricted admission to those Commonwealth immigrants who had obtained vouchers from the Ministry of Labour and could satisfy the authorities that they should not be barred for reasons of health, criminal records, or national security. Under the leadership of Hugh Gaitskell, the Parliamentary Labour Party vigorously fought the measure, although the Labour members of parliament conceded the need for

6. *Report of the Committee on Housing in Greater London*, Comnd. 2605 (London: H.M.S. Office, March 1965), p. 101.

medical checks. At the time the Socialists opposed the legislation in the House, more than three-fourths of the British people expressed their approval of the steps the Government was taking.[7]

When the legislation came up for renewal in November 1963, the Labour Party leaders reviewed their objections to the original bill, but recognized that some form of control was desirable. They proposed that quotas be worked out through negotiations with the Commonwealth countries, and that a determined effort be made to integrate the colored people into the community. By 1964 the immigration question had blossomed into an open issue in a number of constituencies, and was encountered on the doorsteps in many more where the candidates did not make public reference to it.

Another issue that could generate strong emotions from certain segments of the population involved an appropriate defense policy for the country. Despite its precarious financial position, Britain continued to make an important contribution to Western defense, spending 8.3 per cent of its national income directly on the defense budget, more than any other Western power except the United States.[8] These expenditures, however, constituted a serious drain on the economy, especially in light of the rapid technological changes that were taking place in the defense field during the late 1950s and early 1960s. Following through on a policy instituted by the Attlee Government, the Conservative leaders opted for a buildup of Britain's nuclear power, even at the expense of improving conventional forces. In 1958 they undertook the development of the Blue Streak missile system, but they were forced to cancel the project two years later, largely because it had become outmoded before it was made operational. The shift was then to the Skybolt missile, which was to be acquired at some future date from the United States after it had been developed by that country. This plan,

7. *Gallup Political Index*, Report No. 23, p. 37.

8. See Walter Goldstein, *The Dilemma of British Defense: The Imbalance between Commitments and Resources* (Columbus: Ohio State University Press, 1966), p. 23.

however, never came to fruition, for in December 1962 the Americans informed the British Government that they were scrapping the Skybolt. As a partial substitute, the United States agreed to provide Polaris missiles without warheads for British submarines, as well as the necessary support facilities. Thus the Macmillan Government was determined to stick to its policy of making Britain an independent nuclear power. But the cost was becoming increasingly high, and dependence upon the United States for the essentials made the policy subject to the vicissitudes of American defense strategy and vulnerable to attack by the chronic "Yankee-phobes."

Even before the abandoning of the Skybolt plan, the political sea had become a bit rough for the Conservative Government. Its deflationary economic measures, higher rents precipitated by the Rent Act, restrictions upon the building of council houses, the failure of the Common Market negotiations, and increases in the cost of living made the Tories open to criticism. The growing unpopularity of the Government was reflected in by-elections and public opinion polls. One of the bitterest pills the Tories were forced to swallow was at the Orpington by-election in March 1962, when a Conservative majority of nearly 15,000 was converted into a Liberal majority of 7,855. This adverse turn of events led the Prime Minister to reshuffle his Cabinet in July 1962, and one of the casualties was the Chancellor of the Exchequer—a removal that provoked bitter criticism.

The worst, however, was yet to come. In October 1962, William J. C. Vassall, a clerk in the Admiralty, was convicted of giving secret documents to the Soviet Union.[9] The Government was embarrassed by the publication of several letters linking Vassall with a Conservative junior minister. A special tribunal set up to investigate the matter cleared the minister of any blame, but pointed to weaknesses in the safeguarding of secret information.

The Vassall case was only a preliminary bout among unknowns

9. See *The Times*, October 23, 1962; November 15, 1962.

which prepared the audience for the main event. Early in 1963 a series of rumors and newspaper reports alleged that John D. Profumo, Secretary of State for War, had had improper relations with a young "model," Miss Christine Keeler.[10] Some veiled references to the matter were made on the floor of the House of Commons on March 21. Presumably in order to squash these rumours, the Conservative leaders prevailed upon Profumo to make a personal statement to the members of the House, and he did so the next day, denying any impropriety.

But the rumors continued to persist, and they soon took a more serious form. Miss Keeler lived with a Communist sympathizer, Stephen Ward, who was on friendly terms with Captain Eugene Ivanov, a diplomat at the Russian Embassy and a Russian intelligence officer. According to the rumors, Miss Keeler was having affairs with Ivanov and Profumo at the same time. This naturally brought the security issue to the fore again. When the Lord Chancellor was directed by the Prime Minister to undertake an inquiry, Profumo admitted his relationship with Miss Keeler, and on June 4 he submitted his resignation.

Members of parliament have little taste for investigating the personal life of another member or in passing judgment upon purely personal conduct. But, in their view, Profumo had committed an unforgivable offense: he had made a false statement in the chamber, and thus was guilty of "grave contempt" of the House of Commons. Profumo's action was a severe blow to the Government. A judicial inquiry was held, and although the investigation disclosed that there had been no breach of security, the report charged that the Prime Minister and his colleagues had not dealt with the situation effectively. At the time of Profumo's

10. For the official account of the Profumo affair, see *Lord Denning's Report*, Comnd. 2152 (London: H.M.S. Office, 1963). An interesting study of the incident is Jorgen S. Rasmussen, *The Relations of the Profumo Rebels with Their Local Parties* (Tucson: University of Arizona Press, 1966). See also *The Times*, March 15, 23, 1963.

resignation, a Gallup Poll showed that, in the opinion of nearly half of the respondents, Macmillan had not succeeded in defending his handling of the case, and 52 per cent of them expressed dissatisfaction with him as Prime Minister.[11] This was the nadir of the Conservatives' popularity with the electorate in the period from 1959 to 1964.

Dissatisfied voters and Labour M.P.s on the opposition benches were not the only groups that expressed displeasure with the Prime Minister. When the Profumo matter came up for debate in the House of Commons, several Tory members criticized the Prime Minister and his colleagues for not having investigated the case properly, and twenty-seven of them chose not to support the Government in the division lobbies.

On October 10, 1963, while the Conservative Conference was meeting in Blackpool, the man who had come to power after the Suez episode and had rallied his party to victory in 1959, announced his decision to resign. The front-running candidates for the succession appeared to be Richard A. Butler, Viscount Hailsham (Quintin Hogg), and Reginald Maudling. But in the intense and divisive struggle for leadership that followed, none of these three contenders won the prize. On October 18, the Earl of Home emerged as the Conservative choice, and he proceeded to form a new government, subsequently relinquishing his peerage under the 1963 Peerage Act and taking the name of Sir Alexander Douglas-Home.

The new Prime Minister did not receive warm applause from all the people in his party; in fact, two of its leaders refused to serve in his Government. As was to be expected, the adjustment in the lineup of Conservative forces created pressures for delaying the approaching election as long as possible. If it was to be successful at the polls, the Conservative Party would have to be united again, it would have to hammer out a set of appealing policies, and it would have to give the Prime Minister time to make himself known to the electorate.

11. *Gallup Political Index*, Report No. 41, pp. 106–107.

One of the few things that gave the Tories comfort during the period from 1960 until the election in 1964 was the trouble that brewed in the Labour camp. The election of 1959 had brought the party its third successive defeat, each by a larger majority. The prospect of another term on the opposition benches lowered morale in the organization, and conflicting viewpoints within the party over the reasons for the defeat made it harder to hold the potentially fissiparous movement together.

The first rupture in the Labour ranks occurred shortly after the 1959 election, as the party prepared to hold a postmortem on its performance at the polls. Hugh Gaitskell, the leader, was concerned with modernizing the party so that by streamlining its organization and remodeling the program it would be more capable of dealing with Britain's current problems. He and some of his colleagues felt that the party needed to improve its public image, and they were convinced that the traditional Labour policy on nationalization was both an electoral liability and an economic anachronism. They proposed, therefore, to amend the public ownership clause of the party constitution (Clause IV), which had stood as a basic goal of the party since 1918. To many of the faithful, these "revisionist" ideas represented a watering-down of fundamental Socialist doctrine, and the party's left wing joined forces with some trade union groups to defend this traditional symbol of the Labour movement. When the polemical smoke had cleared away, Clause IV was left standing as a "valuable expression" of the party's aims for the rest of the century. Many of those who eventually supported Clause IV were lukewarm about nationalization, but were willing to leave the commitment on the books so long as no real effort was made to implement it broadly.

Since the strong advocates of nationalization could not always agree on what additional industries should be taken over by the state, it was unlikely that the party would be torn by serious conflict over whether a specific industry should be nationalized. But there was one exception—the steel industry. Steel had been the object of controversy in the closing years of the Attlee Government, which eventually nationalized the industry. When the Tories came to power in 1951, they immediately took steps to "denationalize" it. Although in 1964, many Labour M.P.s were willing to accept the status quo, pressures within the party for steel "renationalization" were so strong that a plank for the takeover of the industry was included in the platform.

The debate on Clause IV was a good "dry run" for the intra-party battle over nuclear defense policy, which rocked the organization to its foundations. The Campaign for Nuclear Disarmament (CND), which was committed to the proposition that Britain should unilaterally rid herself of nuclear weapons, made inroads into the ranks of the Labour Party and some of the trade unions. The success of its efforts became painfully obvious at the Party Conference in Scarborough in 1960, when the delegates overturned the statement on defense policy recommended by party leaders, voting by a narrow margin over Gaitskell's vigorous opposition to support unilateralism. Shortly after this stinging defeat, Gaitskell was challenged by Harold Wilson for the leadership of the party, but he managed to retain his post by a vote of 166 to 81. During 1961 Gaitskell and his lieutenants set about to mobilize their forces and to launch a counter-offensive. With the aid of a new organization called the Campaign for Democratic Socialism, they took their case against the unilateral disarmers to the grass roots. In one constituency after another their supporters came back into majority control of their local organizations, and in October 1961 the conference overturned its decision of the previous year. Thereafter the CND fought a rear-guard action and gradually spent itself.

No sooner had the struggle over unilateralism died down when another foreign policy issue appeared on the horizon. Gaitskell, many of the party's top leaders, and a sizable number of Labour activists in the local constituencies opposed the attempt of the Conservative Government to take Britain into the Common Market unless certain guarantees were made in advance. An influential minority of Labour M.P.s, however, were convinced that there was no reasonable alternative to Britain's entry. But, after having just gone through the unilateralist struggle, the leaders of each faction were not disposed to draw political swords over the question. The issue was settled, at least for the time being, when General de Gaulle cast his veto and when the delegates at the 1962 conference in effect endorsed Gaitskell in his qualified opposition to Britain's entry.

When the conference adjourned, Gaitskell and the party he led stood in a stronger position than at any time since the 1959 campaign. The defeat of the unilateralists had infused new vigor into the organization at the grass roots, and it was more united in support of its leadership. But at this moment of triumph, Hugh Gaitskell died, and the party was suddenly thrown into a potentially schismatic struggle to elect someone to replace him. Three candidates were nominated: Harold Wilson, George Brown, and James Callaghan. The latter dropped out after the first ballot, and in the run-off Wilson defeated Brown by a vote of 144 to 103. Some of the loyal Gaitskell people felt forced to cast their ballots for Wilson, although it was difficult for them to forget that he had challenged Gaitskell's leadership at a time when his support was most needed.

Thus, just a year before the statutory life of the 1959 parliament was due to expire, both parties had selected new, untried leaders, each of whom was faced with the problem of having to win the allegiance of those party people who were only lukewarm over the choice that had been made. Early in 1964, both Sir Alec and Harold Wilson traveled widely throughout the country and made frequent appearances on television in an effort to present their views and to project their images before the electorate. Wilson sought to portray his party as a united organization which was capable of tackling the problems of modernizing the country and of introducing new technology and new life into the economy. The Prime Minister had a more difficult task. He had to demonstrate that a man of his lineage could meet the challenge of the times, and that he was competent to deal with more than just foreign affairs, which had been his speciality in the Macmillan Government. Although he treated foreign affairs in some of his speeches, wishing to make his party's stand on the defense question a campaign issue, he devoted considerable attention to Britain's economic problems, stressing, like Wilson, the modernization theme.

When the new leaders began to spar with each other in early 1964, Wilson and his party appeared to have a good advantage over their opponents in electoral support. In March, the Gallup Poll reported that 67 per cent of its respondents felt that Wilson was a good leader for the Labour Party. while only 40 per cent were satisfied with Sir Alec as Prime Minister.[12] In May, the poll revealed that 45.5 per cent of the voters intended to vote Labour in the forthcoming election, while the comparable figure for the Conservatives was only 30.5 per cent.[13] But the Tories held on in the Commons, and the gap gradually began to narrow. By the time of the dissolution, only two or three percentage points—within the range of sampling error—separated the two parties. All evidence pointed to a close election.

At the beginning of the formal campaign, each party issued its election manifesto. The policy stands taken in the manifesto represented a commitment by the party that if the voters awarded it control of the House of Commons, it would pass the necessary legislation to put its policies into effect. Every candidate in the party was under strong compulsion to support the manifesto of the national organization. In a concrete sense, then, the manifesto represented the national-issue setting within which the campaign in Barons Court was fought. For this reason it is useful to examine the stands taken by the manifestos of the two national parties on major issues, as well as the public opinion polls which reflected the distribution of voter opinion on each issue.[14]

12. *Gallup Political Index*, Report No. 50, p. 42.
13. *Gallup Political Index*, Report No. 51, p. 55.
14. The Gallup Poll reference for the particular issues are as follows:

The Independent Nuclear Deterrent

CONSERVATIVE: Britain must in the ultimate resort have independently controlled nuclear power to deter an aggressor.

LABOUR: The Nassau agreement to buy Polaris know-how and Polaris missiles from the U.S.A. will add nothing to the deterrent strength of the western alliance, and it will mean utter dependence on the U.S. for their supply. Nor is it true that all this costly defence expenditure will produce an "independent British deterrent." It will not be independent and it will not be British and it will not deter. . . . Our stress will be on the strengthening of our conventional regular forces so that we contribute our share to Nato defence and also fulfil our peace-keeping commitments to the Commonwealth and the United Nations.

PUBLIC OPINION: Mr. Wilson says that we should switch our defence spending from nuclear weapons to building up the navy. Do you agree or disagree with this suggestion? Agree: 24 per cent; Disagree: 46 per cent; Don't know: 30 per cent. (October 6, 1964.)

Sir Alec Douglas-Home says that having the H-bomb rules out any likelihood of a world war. Do you agree or disagree? Agree: 42 per cent; Disagree: 35 per cent; Don't know: 23 per cent. (February 13–18, 1964.)

Independent Nuclear Deterrent, *Gallup Political Index*, Report No. 54, p. 142; Report No. 50, p. 49. Control of Immigration, Report No. 44, p. 164; Report No. 51, p. 63. Nationalization, Report No. 54, p. 134; Report No. 47, p. 219. Rent Control, Report No. 45, p. 185. Control of Land for Housing Development, Report No. 54, p. 141; Report No. 45, p. 182.

Control of Immigration

CONSERVATIVE: A Conservative Government will continue to control immigration from overseas according to the numbers which our crowded country and its industrial regions can absorb. We shall ensure that the working of the Commonwealth Immigrants Act, which we passed in 1962 against bitter Labour Party opposition, is fair and effective.

LABOUR: We believe that the Commonwealth has a major part to play in grappling with the terrible inequalities that separate the developed and under-developed nations and the white and coloured races. That is why a Labour Government will legislate against racial discrimination and incitement in public places and give special help to local authorities in areas where immigrants have settled. Labour accepts that the number of immigrants entering the United Kingdom must be limited. Until a satisfactory agreement covering this can be negotiated with the Commonwealth a Labour Government will retain immigration control.

PUBLIC OPINION: Two years ago an Act of Parliament was passed which restricted the rights of coloured people coming into Britain from the Commonwealth. Do you approve or disapprove of this Act? Approve: 70 per cent; Disapprove: 19 per cent; Don't know: 11 per cent. (September 5-10, 1963.)

On coloured immigrants, is there any difference between the policy of the Conservative and the Labour Party's policy? There is a difference: 26 per cent; No difference: 34 per cent; Don't know: 40 per cent.

Which party has the best policy for dealing with the problem of coloured immigrants? Conservative: 22 per cent; Labour:

19 per cent; Liberal: 1 per cent; Don't know: 57 per cent. (March 19-24, 1964.)

Nationalization

CONSERVATIVE: The Conservative Party is utterly opposed to any extension of nationalization, whether outright or piecemeal. We propose to complete the denationalization of steel. Industries in public ownership will continue to be developed as modern businesses.

LABOUR: Major expansion programmes will be needed in the existing nationalised industries, and they will be encouraged, with the removal of the present restrictions placed upon them, to diversify and move into new fields. . . . Private monopoly in steel will be replaced by public ownership and control. The water supply industry, most of which is already owned by the community, will be reorganised under full public ownership.

PUBLIC OPINION: Do you think that there should be more nationalization, more de-nationalization, or should things be left as they are? More nationalization: 22 per cent; More de-nationalization: 24 per cent; Left as they are: 43 per cent; Don't know: 11 per cent. (August 27-September 1, 1964.)

Do you approve or disapprove of the re-nationalization of the steel industry? Approve: 30 per cent; Disapprove: 46 per cent; Don't know: 24 per cent.

Do you approve or disapprove of the nationalization of water supplies throughout the country? Approve: 34 per cent; Disapprove: 43 per cent; Don't know: 23 per cent. (November 21-26, 1963.)

Rent Control

CONSERVATIVE: In the next Parliament we shall take no further steps to remove rent control. Additional safeguards for tenants will be provided if shown to be necessary by the inquiry into rented housing in London.

LABOUR: Labour will repeal the notorious Rent Act, end further decontrol and restore security of tenure to those in already decontrolled rented flats and houses. We shall provide machinery for settling rents on a fair basis.

PUBLIC OPINION: Do you think that the Rent Act should or should not be repealed? Should: 52 per cent; Should not: 16 per cent; Don't know: 32 per cent. (September 12-17, 1963.)

Control of Land for Housing Development

CONSERVATIVE: Our regional studies, showing land needs for twenty years ahead, will enable planning authorities to release ample land in the right places and without damage to the green belts. This substantial increase in the supply of land will do more to stabilise land prices than anything else. Where major developments are in prospect—such as the many new towns and town expansions which are being started or proposed—land will be acquired well in advance and made available to private and public enterprise as necessary. The Finance Act 1962 brought short-term land transactions within the sphere of ordinary taxation. In considering any further measure to tax land transactions, the test must be that it should not adversely affect the price or supply of land. We reject the Labour Party's "Land Commission" as an unworkable and bureaucratic device, which would dry up the voluntary supply of land and slow down all our housing and building programmes.

LABOUR: Labour will . . . set up a Land Commission to buy, for the community, land on which building or rebuilding is to take place. Instead of paying the inflated market prices that have now reached exorbitant levels, the Crown Land Commission will buy the land at a price based on its existing use value plus an amount sufficient to cover any contingent losses by the owner, and to encourage the willing sale of land. . . . As a result of public acquisition, building land can be made available at cheaper prices; although the land will remain in public ownership, new owner-occupied houses built upon it will remain, under the new "Crown-hold" system, the absolute property of their owners as long as the house stands.

PUBLIC OPINION: Would you approve or disapprove of nationalizing land that is intended for building, leaving the remainder in private hands? Approve: 33 per cent; Disapprove: 40 per cent; Don't know: 27 per cent. (September 23-30, 1964.)

If you saw or heard anything about the Labour Party Conference at Scarborough (1963), were you favourably impressed or not by Labour's plans to set up a Land Commission to buy property and land required for building at what they decide are reasonable prices? Impressed: 27 per cent; Not Impressed: 25 per cent; Don't know: 26 per cent. (October 3-8, 1963.)

Summary

There were, of course, a number of issues on which the two parties were broadly agreed, except possibly for certain differences in emphasis or approach, and on some of these Labour did well in the polls. But from a glance at the popular support for party positions on issues of sharp disagreement, Labour appears to have been at a disadvantage except in the case of rent control. On the question of controlling the inflow of immigrants, the Labour Party had shifted position since 1961-1962, but the polls indicated that Labour was to a large extent still identified in the public mind as the organization reluctant to impose restrictions. That more than half of the poll respondents were not sure which party had the best policy on colored immigration was indicative of considerable confusion among the voters on the issue.

As is usually the case, the British voting public was more interested in domestic issues than in questions bearing upon foreign policy. During the first week in September, the Gallup Poll reported that 63 per cent of its sample had listed domestic affairs as the most important problems facing the country.[15] Economic affairs housing, and pensions captured the most attention from voters, but some interest was also centered on labor relations, education, roads, and health. The question of defense and armaments was ranked in the middle of the listing of issues.

The voters in Barons Court followed the national pattern in being preoccupied with domestic (or even local) concerns. Occasionally, as we shall see, a partisan at a public meeting might ask one of the candidates a question about defense policy, and at one of the "all-candidates meetings" the Conservative and Labour standard-bearers had a lively go-around on the independent nuclear deterrent. Questions about defense and foreign policy were raised, especially at Tory gatherings, by a small, though vociferous, minority. But, from the questions the voters raised at the indoor and street-corner meetings and the conversations they held with party canvassers on the doorsteps, the people in Barons Court appeared to be much more concerned about housing problems, pensions, and the question of colored immigration. It was largely around these issues that the 1964 campaign in Barons Court evolved. This campaign, which was long in preparation, is the focus for the remainder of this study.

15. *Gallup Political Index*, Report No. 54, p. 124.

Housing in Barons Court—block of new council flats in foreground and old Victorian housing in background.

Street scene in polling district with a predominant Conservative voting pattern.

Chairman of the GMC addressing the Labour adoption meeting.

Mrs. Bowman and Mr. Carr discussing strategy in the Agent's office.

Labour agent and candidate at Robert Owen House.

Labour activist addressing street-corner crowd.

Conservative candidate responding to questions.

Mr. Richard canvassing on the doorstep.

Mr. Carr with the Conservative "circus" discussing education with a constituent.

Prime Minister Douglas-Home supporting Mr. Carr's candidacy at street rally at Hammersmith Broadway.

Clerk in charge of Tory committee room talking to supporter on polling day.

Tellers (number-takers) at a polling station. (Tory on left, Labour on right; rosettes identify the parties.)

Labour committee room clerks checking off the registration numbers of Labour supporters who have voted.

The Count. (The mayor—at right center—wears the symbol of his office.)

CHAPTER 2 Preparing for the Encounter:
Precampaign Planning and
Organizing

The strategy of the Labour and
Conservative parties in Barons Court was basically the same in both
1964 and 1966, and probably resembles the plan of action followed
by any major party in a marginal constituency in any election. This
strategy consists of two simple steps: (1) to identify individually
all of the party's supporters, and (2) to make sure that each supporter goes to the polls on election day and marks his ballot for the
party's candidate.

A party, to be sure, may find it necessary to develop contingent
strategies. In 1964, for example, the leaders of the Labour Party
were prepared to make a systematic effort to persuade the "doubtfuls" and wavering Tories to vote for their candidate if in the last
week of the campaign it appeared that their pledges would not reach
target figures. The Conservatives, on the basis of a less explicit
rationale, did devote some resources—especially the valuable time
of the candidate and his wife—to the attempted conversion of un-
decided voters, and in 1966 they sent canvassers out after doubtful
voters in the strong Tory polling districts when the number of
Conservative promises remained below the targets. But in neither

party was the proselytizing of electors who had indicated a commitment to the other side a significant campaign objective. The party strategists believed that traditional loyalties strongly influence voting behavior, and that an individual's personal experiences, including the impact of government action upon him since the last election, as well as his reaction to the current national campaign, largely determine his action in the polling booth. If the prospective voter has made a commitment on the basis of these factors, he is not likely to be won over by canvassers on the doorstep. What did concern the leaders of each party, however, was the possibility that they might lose the election by a narrow margin because a significant number of their own supporters would not bother to vote. As will be noted later, even Labour's contingent plan in 1964 to invade the ranks of the doubtfuls was based upon the fear that an abnormally large proportion of their firm pledges would stay at home. The specter of losing the battle as a result of political apathy haunted both of the constituency organizations until the clock chimed 9:00 P.M. on polling day.

While the strategy of the two parties was simple in concept, the adroit and successful execution of the strategy presented more difficult problems. The complexities involved in strategy implementation grow more apparent and the reasons for precampaign activity become more obvious when we consider some of the hurdles that the agent in any marginal constituency has to overcome.

1. The number of voters in a parliamentary constitutency in Britain ranges from about 25,000 in a few of the Scottish districts to nearly 97,000 in Billericay, an area not far from London. For Britain as a whole, the average size of the electorate is about 55,000. In the London constituencies the number of registered voters varies from 35,000 to 71,000, with the average being about 51,000. It is important for each of the two parties to ascertain the voting intention of as many of these people

as possible as close as possible to election day. This was more essential than usual in 1964 because the public opinion polls, from the spring until the last survey published shortly before polling day, revealed that shifts in voter attitudes were continually taking place. In other words, each party in 1964 had to be especially industrious and cautious in compiling its list of voters who had given pledges to its candidate.

2. Each organization has to know throughout polling day which of its potential supporters have not yet cast their ballots, so that its workers can launch a drive for these votes before the polls close. To provide this information when it is needed, the party has to keep elaborate records of the voters as they come out of the polling stations so that the identifying mark of each supporter can be stricken from the overall list of pledges.

3. In addition to compiling information about voter intent so as to identify its supporters, each party has to gather and store specific information about the needs and requirements of its sympathizers. Some voters need proxy ballots, others require postal ballots in advance of polling day, and still others need transportation to the polling stations. Information of this type has to be stored in the organizational memory in such a way that it can easily be recalled in both aggregated and disaggregated forms. For example, it is important for the party to know definitely that it has to provide transportation for 800 potential supporters on election day; such information is obviously essential if the required number of automobiles and drivers is to be lined up in advance. But these aggregate figures serve no purpose unless the party also knows that Mrs. Bertha Smythe, who lives in the upstairs flat at No. 13 Primrose Lane, needs a car at 4:30 P.M. to carry her to the polling station at the

Normand Park Primary School on Bramber Road.

4. It is also imperative for each of the parties to impress upon the consciousness of the voters the name of the candidate it is sponsoring. Although British electors—more than their counterparts in other democratic countries—customarily vote for the party rather than the personality of the candidate, the election is technically nonpartisan, and the candidate's party affiliation is not listed on the ballot. For this reason the party has to make sure that its supporters know who the candidate is.

5. The parties have to recruit and organize a corps of workers who will carry the burden of campaign and election-day activities. The bulk of the manpower resources consists of volunteers who are theoretically in a position to do only what they choose to do when they want to do it, and can drop out of the organization when they grow unhappy. There are, as we have already indicated, few negative sanctions which a party can apply against "slackers" and "malcontents." For this reason the workers in a party have to be positively motivated to devote their time and energy on its behalf and to cooperate with other people to form a well-disciplined team.

6. It is also necessary for each party to prepare its budget carefully and to adjust its expenditures so that the statutory maximum will not be exceeded. In contrast with the regulations in American campaigns, relatively few loopholes exist in the law and its provisions are rigorously enforced. The limitations are rendered more difficult as a result of the outdated allowances which take no account of inflated costs.

Obstacles of this type are to be found in virtually every marginal constituency, and they have to be surmounted by any party which entertains the hope of winning a marginal seat. But Barons Court is a marginal constituency with two special characteristics that complicate even more the problems of executing the basic strategy.

First, Barons Court, as we have noted, is located in a section of London where the population is relatively mobile; put in British terminology, it has a high "removal rate." The register upon which the 1964 election was based was about a year old and hence was badly out of date. The two agents estimated that between 10 and 12 per cent of the people whose names were on the election list no longer resided at the addresses given in the register, but they were nevertheless eligible to vote in Barons Court if they could be located. The spring election in 1966 was fought on the basis of a newer register, but even so the problem of removals complicated the planning and execution of the campaign.

Second, as the census data show, a rather high proportion of the Barons Court voters live in rooming houses or in buildings with "bed-sitter" accommodations. These people tend to be highly mobile, living at a given residence for a short period of time and then moving to new quarters elsewhere in the constituency or in an entirely different district. But even when individuals of this type are residing at the addresses listed on the register, it is often difficult for party workers to contact them directly. Many of these people are single and nearly all of them have jobs, and they are less likely to be at home than is the case with members of an ordinary family. Moreover, when the canvassers call, they often experience difficulty in getting information as to the whereabouts of the voter they are looking for. Even though a building may be divided into a number of separate units, usually there is only one entrance (always locked), and there is the problem of getting someone to answer the door. If the party workers are lucky enough to get a response, the person who answers the doorbell often knows nothing about the individual living down the hall.

These, then, are the problems that have to be faced in Barons Court. Barring some dramatic shift in the voting behavior of the electorate (such as occurred in 1966), the party organization that can cope most effectively with these problems will win the parliamentary seat.

Grass Roots Planning from 1962 until the Eve of the Campaign

In 1964 the probable time for holding the election was anticipated far in advance of the formal dissolution of parliament. Each party thus had the chance to plan its approach diligently and to prepare the organization and the constituency for the election campaign. In fact, however, the Socialists were much more active than the Tories in the precampaign period. This difference in level of activity may be accounted for by two factors, one of which was advantageous to the Conservatives and the other to Labour.

A point in favor of the Conservative Party arose from the fact that the sitting M.P. was a Conservative. The Tories were not confronted with the potentially schismatic problem of having to select a candidate, nor did they have to project a new and unfamiliar face before the voting public. The Labour Party, on the other hand, was forced to address itself to both of these tasks.

But the Conservatives in Barons Court did have the problem of finding a suitable agent to direct the activities of their organization. The agent who had served the association ever since the formation of the constituency had moved to a different arena in 1963. His organizational record made him difficult to replace, and in the months following his departure, the party employed two agents in succession, both of whom resigned after short periods of service. The vacancy was then filled by a temporary agent recruited from the Central Office to direct the campaign in the 1964 election for the Greater London Council. It was not until the eve of the borough council election in May 1964—a scant six months before the general election—that Mrs. Bowman was appointed as agent for the Conservative Association at Barons Court. In contrast, the Labour Party, which had been troubled by a turnover of agents a few years earlier, had settled upon Mr. Clarke in the autumn of 1961, and he had plenty of time to study the constituency and to build up the political organization.

During a brief moment of relaxation over a "spot" of tea toward the end of polling day, when nothing more could be done but release more "knockers-up" and appeal to the deity, Mrs. Bowman was asked what she would do differently if she could start the campaign over again. With only slight pause for a sigh, she responded: "I would take eighteen months to learn about the constituency and another eighteen months to plan and organize the entire campaign!" Unfortunately for the Conservatives, she did not have thirty-six months at her disposal. As we review the long-range planning in the Labour camp under the direction of an agent who had three years to lay the groundwork, we can more fully appreciate Mrs. Bowman's regrets. The early formulation of Labour's plans and the building of its organization were an important ingredient in its victory in 1964. But before the party could go very far in formulating its plans for capturing the Tory-held seat, it had to choose a prospective candidate.

Choosing the Challenger

According to the rules of the national Labour Party, any parliamentary candidate who has just been defeated in an election automatically has his candidacy terminated, although the constituency party may decide to readopt him. In the autumn of 1961, when the selection of a candidate was placed on the agenda of the Barons Court Labour Party, Mr. W. T. Williams, who had won the seat in 1955 and lost it in 1959, was already representing another constituency in the House of Commons. Thus the Socialists had to consider a fresh contingent of prospects.

There was strong sentiment in the party for selecting a candidate as quickly as possible in order to give him ample time to "nurse" the constitutency and to make himself known to the party's workers and the voters before an election was called. The identification of the candidate and the fostering of his image were considered to be especially important in a marginal constitutency like Barons Court, where Labour might benefit from a physically active leader who would not only rally the party's traditional forces but would also appeal to uncommited voters and disgruntled Tories.

When the party began to collect the names of potential nominees, the acting agent (Mr. Clarke had not yet arrived on the scene) hoped that as many as thirty people would be nominated by the wards and the affiliated organizations. One might have anticipated that his target was not unrealistic. Barons Court was in many respects a desirable constituency for an ambitious, would-be M.P. It was "winnable," it was located in London (where life is enjoyable), and, being close to Westminster, it would be easy to attend to. As it turned out, however, the party leaders experienced some difficulty in securing people who were interested in being considered. The paucity of nominees was perhaps due in part to the self-flagellation which the party was subjecting itself to at the time over the question of unilateral disarmament. The acting agent contacted several trade unions to see whether they might be interested in making nominations, but the response was feeble. In seeking to determine which people they might sponsor, several wards invited prospects to speak at meetings of their members, and they urged activists from other wards to attend.

After a search for nominees which lasted for several weeks, a total of eight people were officially nominated by the wards or by other groups affiliated with the constituency organization. In addition to Mr. Richard, who was nominated by Grove Ward, the list included a married lady who had long been active in Labour politics in the London area, nominated by the South Hammersmith Cooperative Guild; a tutor-organizer of the National Council of Labour Colleges, nominated by the building workers' trade union (the AUBTW); the general secretary of the International Volunteers Service, nominated by the Clerical and Administrative Workers Union; a young journalist, who was chairman of the Labour Party in an adjacent constituency, nominated by the Executive Committee of the Barons Court party; and the assistant general secretary of the Fabian Society, nominated by the Union of Shop, Distributive, and Allied Workers. Also on the list of nominees were two leaders of the local party in Barons Court, both from the Fulham section of the organization. One was an insurance representative who had served as president of the local party, had fought eighteen local elections, and was currently a member of the London County Council. He was nominated by Margravine Ward, the Women's Section of the local party, and the Amalgamated Engineering Union. The other local nominee was an administrative secretary who currently served on the Fulham Borough Council. He was nominated by the old Barons Court and Lillie wards and by the Fulham Cooperative Party. Since the number of nominees was small, the party decided to regard the group as a "short list" and to get on with the business of selecting a candidate.

As is the usual practice in choosing parliamentary candidates, the General Management Committee met as a selection conference, on November 26, 1961. Even though the ordinary attendance at GMC meetings was about twenty-five, a total of forty members appeared at the conference. By this time, the assistant general secretary of the Fabian Society had withdrawn his name from consideration, leaving only seven competitors in the field. In accordance with the rules, each nominee delivered a fifteen-minute speech to the assembled delegates, outlining his views on the issues of the day, after which he was subjected to a period of questioning. When this phase of the conference had been concluded, the delegates proceeded to vote without discussion until one of the contestants had secured an absolute majority. After four ballots Mr. Richard emerged the winner.[1]

One would ordinarily expect that, with two local competitors in the field, the selection of Ivor Richard as the prospective candidate would have had a schismatic and debilitating effect upon the constituency organization. Although the votes and the alignment of political forces in a selection conference remain the closely guarded secret of the delegates, it appears likely that the two local prospects divided between them the votes of those who had strong parochial loyalties and in effect knocked each other out of the race. Since they were local leaders with notable influence, whose disaffection might seriously weaken the organization, it is worth recording that neither of the two men stopped to nurse his wounds or carried any grudge during the following months. One of them assumed important responsibilities in the campaigns which led to Richard's election in 1964 and to his reelection in 1966, while the other was selected as candidate in a nearby constituency a few months later and won a seat in parliament. It is also interesting to note that the Labour Party in Barons Court, which was strongly unilateralist in 1962, selected as its candidate a multilateralist who made no effort to conceal his views. Far from suffering conflict and dissension after the selection conference, the party grew more unified and began to exhibit new vigor. This development, however, was not simply a fortunate accident. While students of political life cannot discount completely the role of the goddess of luck, the unifying influence of the new agent, the prospective candidate, and some of the younger party officers was a great help in bringing stability to the organization.

---

1. Three of Mr. Richard's competitors at the selection conference found their way to parliament in either the 1964 or 1966 elections.

Organization and Planning in the Precampaign Period

The conference which selected Ivor Richard as the standard-bearer had scarcely adjourned when the Labour agent turned the attention of his party activists to preparing for the next general election. As a first step, he persuaded the GMC in January 1962 to establish a small campaign committee which was initially composed of five people, including the agent, the candidate, and the chairman of the constituency organization. It was impossible at that time, of course, to determine exactly when the election would be fought, and it was agreed that the members of the committee would continue to serve until their duties were discharged, even though the party itself would be electing new officers at its annual meetings. Later on, after the leading campaign officials had been appointed to their posts, they were requested to sit in on some of the meetings of the campaign committee.

The General Management Committee authorized the campaign planning committee to analyze the organization's needs in a general election struggle and to report periodically to the party's Executive Committee.[2] Meeting thirteen times between March 1962 and June 1964, the committee members interpreted their mandate broadly: they were to organize and plan all phases of the campaign, and they were to recommend to the party the practical steps that would have to be taken in order to carry out the general plan.

Early in its meetings, the campaign committee centered its attention upon the matter of party organization. The members appraised the level of organizational efficiency in the various wards, and where weaknesses were uncovered, they suggested that the delegates on the party's Executive should find time to visit with Labour members whose interest was lagging. When the wards were restructured in 1963 under the new arrangement for the

2. Information on the deliberations of the campaign committee is largely drawn from the *Minutes of Meetings of the Campaign Committee,* typed record of the Barons Court Labour Party, March 1962–June 1964.

London region, the campaign committee took note of the implications of the reform and requested reports of reorganizational progress from time to time.

The committee also experimented with a level of organization below the polling district in the hope that smaller units would facilitate the voter canvass and the distribution of literature, especially by outside help. Before long, however, it was discovered that units below the polling-district echelon were not practical, and the party decided to revert to the older pattern of organization. The party's concern with the detailed organization of its basic units is illustrated by the fact that the committee rooms for the campaign period and for polling day were arranged for in the summer of 1963—nearly a year and a half in advance, as events turned out.

The members of the campaign committee also analyzed the types of campaign tasks that would have to be performed, and they established a group of key offices, each of which was to be in charge of one aspect of the party's campaign. After having designated the functional tasks, the campaign planners then proceeded to examine the personnel resources available in the party and to appoint people to occupy the posts. The positions created were as follows:

OFFICE	DUTIES
Finance Officer	To take charge of the campaign fund and to handle expenditures
Meetings Officer	To arrange for public meetings during the campaign
Canvassing Officer	To direct all canvassing activities and to supervise ward secretaries in this work
Removals and Postal Vote Officer	To supervise the processing of postal and proxy votes
Press Officer	To write reports of the candidate's activities and his stand on issues and to get them printed in the local weekly press

Envelope Addressing Officer	To supervise the addressing of envelopes for the candidate's election address and appeals to special groups of voters
Transport Officer	To arrange for automobiles to carry voters to the polls

After having examined the party's organizational structure and assigning qualified personnel to the key spots in the campaign apparatus, the planning committee began to concern itself with certain specific tasks, many of which involved the functional offices which it had recently created. These additional activities of Labour's committee will be examined shortly. But before we discuss them, we should look at what the Conservatives at 84A North End Road were doing in the way of planning and organizing their campaign.

Had Mrs. Bowman known that her rivals had begun extensive preparations as early as the autumn of 1961, she would probably have realized how badly she needed thirty-six months of lead time to plan her campaign. Nearly everything that had been done by Labour over a two-year period had to be done by the Conservatives in about six months. Indeed, it could be argued that they had less than six months at their disposal, because the new agent had to familiarize herself with the party organization and its resources before she could be in a position to make crucial decisions, especially those involving the assignment of personnel.

Throughout the spring and summer of 1964, the Executive Committee and the Finance and General Purposes Committee met to consider questions of campaign planning and strategy, though not in the systematic and detailed way in which these matters were being handled at Robert Owen House. In early June the party organized a "strike force" to commence a systematic program of canvassing. Attention was focused alternately on specific polling districts, starting with the heavy Tory areas. The work of the volunteers, who met at the central headquarters for their instructions before moving into the target districts, was supported by two paid canvassers, called "missioners." The purpose of this effort was to "clean up" the register and get a start on the identification of removals. This activity also helped the agent familiarize herself with the constituency and to become acquainted with her most dedicated and reliable workers.

By the end of the summer the plans and organization of the campaign effort began to take more definite form. The agent established a campaign committee made up of the officers of the association, the ward chairmen, and other individuals who had been assigned responsibility for specific tasks before and after the onset of the formal campaign period. The committee met in late August to review, in informal consultation with a few key people, the strategy which the agent had developed. It may be an exaggeration, however, to refer to the plans that were discussed at this meeting as strategy. Perhaps the only real strategy that emerged was the decision to wage a short, dynamic campaign and to delay deliberately its public opening, while devoting particular attention to building up the organizational strength and kindling the enthusiasm of the party's activists. The Conservative agent believed that Hugh Gaitskell in 1959 had run his horses too soon and too fast, with the result that the campaign had not been peaked properly, reaching a climax a week or more before polling day. She felt that a party which was trailing in the opinion polls might have a tendency to panic and to start things off too quickly. Rather then run the risk of alienating the voters by too much public activity before the dissolution of parliament, the agent preferred to focus her attention upon completing at an early date the routine clerical work, such as addressing envelopes, processing the postal vote, and performing similar tasks which could be carried on behind the scenes. After ratifying these views, the campaign committee discussed the tactics that were needed to identify Conservative voters, to win over the doubtfuls, to energize the apathetic, and to get their supporters to the polls.

Designated members of the campaign committee were

responsible for applying certain of the campaign tactics, and their assignments, similar to those of the Labour side, can best be understood by listing the offices and describing them briefly.

OFFICE	*DUTIES*
Meetings Officer	To arrange all public meetings
Publicity Officer	To design posters and leaflets
Circuses Officer	To direct the circuses, the major campaign activity of the candidate
Canvassing and Mutual Aid Officer	To supervise all canvassing and to coordinate all mutual aid efforts
Central Committee Room Director	To be in charge of the clerical operations at 84A North End Road
Transport Officer	To arrange for automobiles and drivers to carry voters to the polling stations

Although the composition and role of the campaign committee resembled in some respects those of its Labour counterpart, there were nevertheless significant differences. As we shall soon observe, the Conservative campaign committee included a number of people who had had no previous association with the Tory Party in Barons Court. Moreover, the group was not a planning and deliberative body to the extent that the Labour committee was.

Mobilizing Resources in the Precampaign Period

The mobilization of a party's resources involves two distinct types of activity. First, the party must mobilize its *financial* resources by building up a "fighting fund" to cover the expenditures of the campaign. Second, it has to muster its *manpower* resources by recruiting and training its campaign leaders and its rank-and-file workers. Both of the parties in Barons Court spent a considerable amount of energy in mobilizing their resources during the precampaign period.

Finance. Perhaps the most spectacular contrast between British and American political encounters lies in the financing of the campaigns. In a marginal constituency in the United States, a candidate can easily find ways to spend all the money he is able to gather in, and for this reason a great deal of time and effort goes into fund-raising. In Britain, the laws on election specify a maximum expenditure which is largely calculated according to the number of voters in a district, but which also includes certain flat allowances for such items as the agent's salary. In 1964, each party in Barons Court was legally entitled to spend about £740, or approximately $2,072.00. In the United States, of course, there may be a big difference in the expenditures made by the two parties in a marginal area, depending upon the financial resources available to them. But in Britain it would be unusual if the two parties in a marginal constituency were unable to lay their hands on enough money to come up to the maximum disbursements permitted under the law.

As early as mid-1962, when the local elections were out of the way, the Labour Party took preliminary steps to build up its campaign fund. At that time the campaign committee compiled a list of potential contributors, and the treasurer of the constituency organization drafted a letter of appeal which was sent to some of the trade unions and to all party members and known supporters. By polling day Labour's various appeals for funds to meet campaign expenses had resulted in contributions from the following sources:

Transport House	£200
Individual Members and Sympathizers	186
Local Trade Union Branches	93
Ward Party Organizations	51
London Labour Party	20
Voluntary Contributions at Public Meetings	150*
Total	**£700**

* The most lucrative collection was taken up at a large public meeting in the Hammersmith Town Hall, which featured Harold Wilson as the principal speaker.

In the summer of 1964, the Conservatives began seriously to tackle the problem of building up their financial reserves. The finance officer of the campaign, who was also the treasurer of the constituency organization and the chairman of the old Margravine Ward, dispatched a letter to 1,578 members of the association asking for contributions and volunteer workers. By the final week of the campaign, 150 people had responded to the financial appeal which yielded about £600. Some of this money, however, was to be used to cover the regular expenses of the organization throughout the year. Besides the contributions from party members, the Conservatives received the following donations:

Junior Carlton Club	£200
Conservative Central Office	125
South Kensington Conservative Association	250
Richmond Conservative Association	50
Total	**£625**

These figures indicate that neither party suffered from a lack of financial sustenance. In comparing the mobilization of these resources by the two parties, however, several points should be considered. First, the relative ease with which each party managed to develop its financial reserves indicates that the winning of this marginal seat was important to the partisans both inside and outside the constituency. Second, Transport House invested significantly more in the Labour cause in Barons Court than the Tory Central Office poured into the Conservative campaign. Third, Conservative parties in neighboring constituencies which customarily pile up huge majorities were exceedingly generous with their friends in Barons Court, while Labour received no official funds from its comrades in nearby organizations. Fourth, the contributions from individual members were much more substantial on the Conservative side than they were in the case of Labour, reflecting the difference in the socio-economic bases of support. The donations to the cause by individual Socialists came in relatively small amounts.[3] Moreover, the Labour Party still had to struggle during the campaign to meet its ordinary housekeeping expenses, and on the night before the election some workers had to take time out to handle the weekly tote, which is an important source of revenue. The Tories, too, continued the sale of their tote coupons throughout the campaign, and the treasurer had to concern himself with the normal problems of association finance. However, it is fair to say that neither of the two parties had to consume much valuable time in raising funds at the expense of other, more crucial, tasks in the campaign.

Manpower. The mobilization of manpower resources—a much more critical task than the accumulation of funds—proved to be somewhat more difficult for the two parties. On the Labour side, the campaign committee, working with the agent, began to mobilize its key campaign leaders early in 1962. As we have already indicated, the committee established a number of administrative posts and then recruited suitable personnel to fill them. Shortly after this "general staff" was appointed, its members were briefed on the campaign plan and on their respective roles in it. With this core group fully assembled, the party leaders then proceeded to line up other key workers to assist in carrying out the various campaign tasks. The agent sent out a questionnaire to all Labour members indicating what the manpower needs were, and the people who responded constituted a reservoir from which workers were drawn during the campaign and on polling day.

3. The sense of dedication of some of the old-time Labour members was illustrated at the candidate's adoption meeting. An elderly gentleman walked to the rostrum and handed the agent £1, which he had frugally saved from his sixpence stamps for this purpose. Although similar cases of sacrifice by needy people are undoubtedly less frequent on the Conservative side, they do exist. One day during the early stages of the campaign, an elderly pensioner trudged up three flights of stairs and proudly deposited a half-crown piece on the agent's desk.

One of the important features in the Labour program for the training of key personnel was the sponsorship of a weekend "election school" at Gomshall, Surrey, on April 6–7, 1963, in collaboration with North Hammersmith. The residence school, which was arranged by the agent with the assistance of the regional organizer, was scheduled after the 1962 local elections had been held and the results analyzed. It was attended by twenty-five workers from Barons Court, including nearly all the ward secretaries. The curriculum of the training school—which was thoroughly covered, with time out for the requisite number of "tea breaks"— consisted of the following topics:

1. General Outline of the Aims and Plans of the Parliamentary Campaign, by the agent and the candidate.
2. The Purpose and Techniques of Canvassing and the Recording of Canvas Results, by the regional organizer, the canvassing officer, and two members of the campaign committee.
3. The Organization of the Postal Vote, by the agent at North Hammersmith.
4. The Campaign in the Wards up to polling day, including a discussion of staffing, recruitment of helpers, the assimilation of outside help, preparation of records, literature distribution, canvassing, and transport of voters.
5. Polling-day Organization, including a discussion of work in the committee rooms, number-taking at the polls, and the system of knocking on doors to insure that the Labour promises get to the polls.

In the closing session, the party's leaders set up a model committee room and demonstrated the procedures for running it.

The adequate training of campaign workers after their recruitment was especially important for the Labour Party. The organization had to rely primarily upon voluntary, part-time help, and many workers lacked experience in the sort of campaign effort which the party was planning. Moreover, the types of people that Labour was able to recruit differed markedly from those recruited by the Conservatives. The Labour women, for example, tended to be much younger, with less formal education, with less experience in clerical work, and with full-time jobs or home responsibilities. This meant that there was a great shortage of full-time workers who could afford to take time off from their jobs or who could forget about their work at home. Such a shortage naturally created problems of continuity in the performance of campaign tasks, since there were fewer full-time people to whom the agent could delegate specific responsibilities. Under these circumstances, it was important for as many volunteer workers as possible to be acquainted with the overall plan and the strategies to be employed, and for them to be given intensive training in the campaign jobs that they would be called upon to do.

As another feature of its recruitment program, the Labour Party in mid–1962 began to sponsor a series of women's coffee parties or "cottage meetings," especially in the more affluent sections of the constituency. These gatherings were usually held in private homes to which women were invited by printed invitation. The aim was to get some of these people interested in Labour politics and party activities and whenever possible to sign them up as members. Although not many cottage meetings were scheduled, the few that were arranged proved to be reasonably successful. With about thirty women in attendance, these gatherings gave them an opportunity to meet other people from the neighborhood and to listen to the prospective candidate discuss aspects of Labour policy. At one of the meetings, the sponsor managed to recruit ten new members for the party. This type of activity was reasonably successful in recruiting people who might otherwise not have been drawn into politics, and many of the recruits were useful in carrying out routine clerical tasks, especially the addressing and stuffing of envelopes.

Virtually all of the Labour people who were to play an executive role in the campaign were local party stalwarts who were well acquainted with their constituency. The canvassing officer, Mr. Carlyle Thomas, was a native of the Fulham portion of the constituency and an alderman on the local council; he was employed in the local power station and had to sandwich his political activities in with his regular job. The leader who arranged the public meetings was Mr. Wallace Franklin, a local councillor of long standing who had lived in the district for about forty years. Mr. Randall Stoney, who was selected as finance officer, was the regular party treasurer and a member of the borough council. In charge of the postal vote process was Mr. Christopher Blake, who had moved into the constituency from the East End of London three years earlier and had won a seat on the local council. The press officer, Mr. Lester Baldridge, had resided in the constituency for two years and was already serving on the local council. The individual chosen to be the candidate's aide to drive Mr. Richard about the constituency and to serve as his general utility man was Mr. Sydney Ainsworth, a graduate of Cambridge and former Conservative candidate at Rhondda East. Unilateralist views had brought him into the Labour party in 1960, and in his first campaign as a Labour Party member he secured release from his regular work so that he could devote all his time to campaigning. Besides visiting with many voters on the doorstep and accompanying her husband at public meetings and on social calls to special groups, Mrs. Richard was placed in charge of envelope addressing, most of which was done before the campaign formally got under way. She also prepared the list of voters to whom special appeals were to be sent. The only "outsider" who was given major responsibility was Mr. Russell Lowe, former agent at Putney and an administrative officer of the Electrical Trades Union, who was released from his regular duties with his union for full-time work in Barons Court. He processed lists of internal removals (voters who had merely shifted residence within the constituency and could not qualify for a postal vote) and performed other administrative assignments at Robert Owen House.

According to the general campaign plan, the ward organizations that were sufficiently strong were to be left on their own, to be guided by central directives but without too much interference from the headquarters on Shepherds Bush Road. The districts that had little or no organization, largely as a result of the recent realignment of the wards, were to be operated from the center. By the same token, any wards showing signs of weakness would be given supplementary help from the central headquarters.

This plan placed a great deal of reliance upon the ward officers (usually the secretaries), and these people were all local party leaders who for the most part had had long acquaintance with their areas. In full charge of Broadway Ward and polling districts Fc and Fd (the new Starch Green Ward) was Mr. Winston George, who operated the main committee room located in the home of Miss Vanessa Redgrave. A sign painter by trade, George had lived in his district for about twenty years, and was secretary of the ward and a member of the borough council. Grove Ward was under the leadership of Mr. Dana Ronald, a librarian at the British Museum who had joined the party in 1960, and his assistant, Mr. Adrian Adams, who was employed in a real estate office. Using their flat as a main headquarters, they regarded the proper organization of their ward as a challenge, and by 1964 it was in fighting trim. The area comprising polling districts La, Lb, and Oa (the old Margravine Ward) had recently lost its secretary through a change in residence. The ward, however, had enough experienced veterans to step in, including Wallace Franklin and Mr. Norton Howard, a long time resident of the area and a local councillor. Gibbs Green Ward fell under the direction of Mrs. June Avery, the secretary, and Mr. Barnett Edwards, chairman of the constituency organization and a member of the borough council. Similarly, Halford Ward was under the charge of Mr. Clark Barford, who was ward secretary, a local councillor, and a former mayor of the Borough of Fulham. The permanent organization of these five areas was considered to be strong enough to carry on their campaign activities by themselves, within the framework of the directives issued from Robert Owen House and in some instances with supplementary aid to be sent to them from the center.

The other two districts—Addison Ward and polling districts Hb and Ic—were to be run from the central headquarters at Robert Owen House. In Addison Ward, however, the committee room was in the home of Mr. and Mrs. Halperin, who had lived in the district for more than two decades, and they assumed responsibility for supervising the workers who were sent to them. In the case of polling districts Hb and Ic, the administrative responsibility was eventually undertaken by Mr. Kenneth Arnold, a young Canadian graduate student at the London School of Economics.

It must be noted that, with a few exceptions, these leaders had full-time jobs, which meant that they usually did not begin their weekday political activities until after they had their suppers in the evening. Moreover, apart from the agent and the candidate, no fewer than half of the people who were scheduled for key roles in the campaign were members of the local council, and they were frequently called upon to handle their local government responsibilities as well as their added campaign burdens.

The auxiliary organizations of the Labour Party played a less influential part in the campaign than did their counterparts in the opposing camp. Although the Young Socialists were extremely active in 1966, they were a smaller group in 1964 and consequently had fewer resources to draw upon. However, they did undertake some of the work on the doorstep, and in the precampaign period they were made responsible for canvassing the young voters in Broadway Ward and in the old Barons Court Ward. The Women's Section was also small, comprising twenty-three members. Some of the women in this group helped out with canvassing and the distribution of literature, but most of them spent their time addressing envelopes and performing other clerical tasks. In both the 1964 and 1966 campaigns, the envelope work proceeded ahead of schedule, but the agent purposely held up some of the material so that a few of the elderly ladies would have something to do when they reported for duty at the central headquarters.

Unlike the Conservatives, the Labour Party in Barons Court did not have the patronage of another constituency party which undertook work in the area as an organized project. Although many people from outside the district called in to offer their help, no constituency party was directed to come, and the agent made no appeals to Transport House for outside help. He regarded his organization as strong enough to stand on its own feet. There was, however, a sentimental link between the Labour Party in South Kensington and Barons Court, since the candidate had until recently been an active member of that organization and had been its standard-bearer in the previous general election. For this reason, a number of workers from South Kensington came into the constituency from time to time to lend a hand with the canvassing and other jobs. In addition, some outside workers who volunteered their services at Transport House were referred to Barons Court, because it was a marginal seat. But since there was no direct tie-up between the Barons Court Labour Party and a neighboring constituency party in this election, little precampaign planning was required to handle an influx of workers from the outside.

The mobilization of manpower resources at 84A North End Road took a very different form from that which was directed from Robert Owen House. Mrs. Bowman had not been in the constituency long enough to acquire as much knowledge about the skills and motivations of potential workers in her organization as Mr. Clarke had concerning his people. In order to cope with this difficulty, she established a centralized pattern of organization, directing all phases of the campaign from the main headquarters in North End Road, and she proceeded to recruit key workers from outside the constituency. The pattern of organization will be treated later in the discussion, but the use of key workers from outside Barons Court is of relevance here.

In selecting qualified people to supervise the functional tasks in the campaign, the Conservative agent relied heavily upon individuals with whom she had worked in previous election contests elsewhere. Of the seven administrative officers set up to handle the principal campaign assignments, four were filled by outsiders who had no previous association with the Conservative Party in Barons Court. The head of the central committee room was assigned to the organization by the Tory Central Office; in addition, the publicity officer, the head of the circus, and the absent-voters officer had all worked with Mrs. Bowman in other constituencies and were recruited by her specifically for this campaign. These four people from the outside supervised most of the functional tasks in the campaign, and in carrying out their assignments they devoted a vast amount of time to the cause. For example, the absent-voters officer, who was given almost complete authority over the processing of the postal vote, was employed full time by the association toward the end of the precampaign period until polling day. The head of the circus took three weeks from his regular employment so that he could spend all of his time in Barons Court. The head of the central committee room—a housewife who resided in a safe Conservative district—worked in the headquarters regularly for a month before the start of the campaign and then during the campaign itself. Although they were not assigned to any specific campaign tasks, the chairman and one of the vice-chairmen of the association invested a considerable amount of their time in the campaign effort, as did the treasurer, who served as finance officer.

In mid-August 1964, the Conservatives requested the ward organizations to draw up lists of their most active members. On the basis of these lists the party leaders sent out a questionnaire to 350 or 400 people urging them to volunteer for work as canvassers, envelope addressers, and literature distributors. About 80 per cent of these people responded, and 90 per cent of the respondents volunteered for one or more jobs. The volunteers were then requested to report for duty either at the main headquarters or at one of the ward committee rooms. As we shall see, however, some of these workers were not employed as efficiently as they might have been because of occasional mix-ups in the assignments, due primarily to an information overload in the party headquarters.

The Conservatives also relied heavily upon their auxiliary organizations for the mobilization of manpower resources. The women's organization, for example, assumed responsibility for many of the routine clerical tasks. Under the direction of Mrs. Green, a lady who had worked with the Conservatives for forty years, the women took over one of the rooms in the headquarters and addressed and stuffed thousands of envelopes, prepared most of the 12,000 or so pledge cards, and made out about 1,000 new canvass cards. Another ancillary organization—the West Kensington Young Conservatives—was given primary responsibility for the campaign in one polling district, and its members manned the committee room in that area after it was opened.

With only one researcher in each party and with campaign activities taking place simultaneously at the main headquarters and at committee rooms scattered throughout the constituency, it was virtually impossible to get an accurate count of all the volunteers who were working at any given moment. From all appearances, however, the Conservatives were able to mobilize more manpower but, as will be evident later, their workers were less efficiently deployed.

In contrast with the Labour Party, the Conservatives had formal connections with neighboring Tory organizations, and through a program of mutual aid they were in a position to employ a veritable army of rank-and-file workers from the outside. Throughout the campaign, the committee rooms that controlled activities in four of the twenty-four polling districts were staffed by outsiders. Working as self-contained groups which were independent of the ward organizations and responsible only to the agent, these Conservatives from other constituency parties did all of the canvassing, distributed the literature, and carried out all of the related activities in the polling districts assigned to them. While the handling of the campaign itself in these polling districts will be discussed in Chapter 3, it is worthwhile noting at this point that the division of labor necessitated by this arrangement required a good measure of pre-campaign planning and close liaison with the Conservative associations in nearby constituencies.

The most formal tie-up between the Barons Court party and sister organizations was with the large Conservative Association in South Kensington, one of the most distinctive constituency parties in England. According to some students of British politics, the strongest and most vigorous constituency parties are to be found in the marginal districts where both parties have a chance to win and where good organization is most likely to tip the balance. By the same token, the two parties in rock-solid constituencies, where one party cannot hope to win the seat and the other cannot lose it, are likely to be very weak, if not moribund. This analysis may be generally correct, but if so, the Conservative Association in South Kensington represents a startling exception. If the Conservative Party nationally were to lose every seat in the House of Commons but one, the lone survivor would very likely be the member from South Kensington. Regardless of how strongly the tide may run against the Tories nationally, there is virtually no action which the party can take that would defeat the Conservative candidate in this district. The only challenge left for the South Kensington Conservatives is to run up such an overwhelming majority that all competing candidates would lose their deposits.

Given the Conservative nature of the political map in South Kensington, one would expect to find the local party a weak organization—inactive because there are no enemies to conquer. But this is not the case; indeed, the opposite is true. The association has a large group of active members whose mission is not to campaign in South Kensington (where they do not even bother to canvass), but to help Conservative candidates in adjacent marginal constituencies. In 1964, by the time the formal campaign opened up, the South Kensington people had already prepared all of the envelopes needed for the election-address mailing in their own constituency and had thus freed resources to help the campaigns in other districts. At a general meeting of the association held in early September, the agent explained to the large assembly of members the plans that had been worked out to assist in the marginal contests, including the one in Barons Court. We have already noted that the South Kensington party made a sizable financial contribution to the fighting fund of the Tories in Barons Court. The two agents also worked out an agreement whereby a group from South Kensington would staff the committee room and run the campaign in one polling district (Je in Broadway Ward).

The campaign in three other polling districts—Fc and Fd in Starch Green Ward and Gb in Grove Ward—was run by a group of outside Conservatives under the leadership of Mrs. d' Anton, herself a resident in a safe Tory district on the outskirts of London. Mrs. d' Anton was something of an entrepreneur who rounded up a flock of her personal friends from several constituencies and brought them to Barons Court for the duration of the campaign. Mrs. d' Anton was the type of volunteer leader that is much more plentiful in the Conservative Party than in the ranks of competing groups. Her name suggests that the family can trace its ancestry back to the Norman Conquest; she carries herself with the grace and quiet self-confidence appropriate to such a lineage. An intelligent, well-educated, and attractive lady, Mrs. d' Anton has a great deal to offer a political party. When these qualities are combined with her obvious leadership skills and her financial position, which makes possible regular care for her children so that she can devote all of her time to a campaign, a political party has a prize recruit for a position of responsibility. The British, of course, have a long tradition of voluntary service to the community—a tradition that permeates the ranks of Conservatives, Liberals, and Labour alike.

But the environment that produces people like Mrs. d' Anton not only places high value upon voluntary contributions to the general welfare, but also tends to equate untiring assistance to the Conservative Party with devoted service to the community.

The Conservatives were also the beneficiaries of volunteer labor which was sent to Barons Court by the Tory Central Office. When these people appeared at North End Road, they were treated as individual volunteers and given specific job assignments. As in the case of the Labour Party, little precampaign planning was involved in handling these people.

Scouting the Terrain

One of the most important activities in the precampaign period is the canvassing of voters on the doorstep. Ideally, the aim is to contact every elector whose name appears on the voting register. The results provide the party leaders with an early assessment of how strong their support is and what issues might be important to the voters in the locality. The information gleaned from this activity also enables the party to identify the people who have moved to another part of the constituency or to some other district —intelligence that is essential if the organization is to get its absent supporters lined up in plenty of time.

The Labour Party began its canvassing activities in preparation for the general election as early as the autumn of 1962. At that time special attention was given to the young electors who had just reached voting age. After this group had been identified from the register, the prospective candidate prepared a letter which was sent to each of these new voters, and the Young Socialists went into two of the wards to canvass them. Early in the spring of 1963, the ward organizations were urged to canvass all of the entries on the "B List"—people who had moved into the district during the previous year—and during the summer months the party workers, rather than spending time on the recruitment of new members, busied themselves with the marking of the B register. In the fall of 1963, the party, under grants made available by Transport House and the London Labour Party, employed three paid canvassers for a six-week period to go into sections of the constituency that had never been adequately canvassed. The objective of this canvass was not only to uncover supporters for Labour, but also to give the party leaders a measure of the intensity of Conservative strength in selected upper-class areas.

When a new election register was issued in February 1964, both parties realized that this would be the final list of eligible voters for the parliamentary election. This list also served as the basis for canvassing for two local elections in the spring of 1964, and both parties obviously derived some benefit from the markings made on the register at that time. But neither party could afford to lean too heavily upon this early information. The canvassing during local elections is usually not as thorough as that conducted during a general election. In any event, six more months were to elapse before the parliamentary election was scheduled, and a good portion of the information was obsolete by then owing to the high rate of removals and shifts in public opinion.

Cognizant of these problems, the Labour Party in the summer of 1964 put into effect a special plan for its canvassing activities. The plan called for a two-stage approach. During the first stage—in effect, throughout the summer—party workers would contact as many people as possible who were *not* known Labour supporters —people whose political allegiance was unknown, doubtful, or even Tory. It was assumed that, since the public opinion polls at this point showed the fortunes of the Conservative Party to be at a low ebb, voters who indicated a preference for the Tories were beyond redemption. During the second stage, attention was to be concentrated upon the known Labour sympathizers and the doubt-fuls in order to secure as many promises as possible. During this phase of the canvass, voters who were known to have Conservative sympathies would be completely ignored, since contacts by Labour workers might serve to activate the opposition. This canvassing scheme would undoubtedly delay the processing of Labour's absentee voters because the workers were leaving their most lucrative areas until later in the political season.

From the beginning, the Labour canvass was geared to a specific set of targets. During the early months of 1963, the campaign committee began a discussion of how many Labour promises would be needed in order to win the seat. In seeking an answer to this question, the agent, the candidate, and the party chairman conferred with the regional organizer, and together they made some calculations based upon the local election held in May 1962. After allowing for a maximum Liberal vote of 5,000, they concluded that Labour would need 16,600 votes to win. However, since about 25 per cent of the Labour vote ordinarily failed to turn out, they needed to set their target of Labour pledges at 22,213. With these figures in mind, the committee authorized one of its members to relate this target to each of the wards on the basis of the 1962 election returns. A month later, the committee examined and approved the targets, which were listed for the old wards (before they were reorganized) as follows:

Barons Court	3,388
Lillie	5,175
Margravine	4,560
Ravenscourt	1,720
Grove	3,765
Brook Green	1,630
Broadway	1,975
Total	22,213

The reorganization of the wards, of course, necessitated a readjustment of the targets, which was done shortly before the commencement of the formal campaign. In considering the 1964 campaign in Barons Court, it is important to recognize that specific canvassing targets broken down by wards were a significant element in Labour's strategy. Their success at this time prompted them to pinpoint the quotas even more specifically in 1966, when they set targets for each polling district.

By August 1964, Labour's canvassing efforts had resulted in a marked register which had notations for slightly more than 50 per cent of the voters. At that time the canvassing officer called a meeting of all ward secretaries and key workers to inform them of where the party stood and of what its canvassing needs were. He indicated that further canvassing of certain areas of Conservative strength would be unwise, and that henceforth a concerted effort should be made to contact unknown and doubtful voters in districts likely to be more sympathetic to the Labour cause.

This directive marked the transition from stage one to stage two of the precampaign canvassing plan. At this transition point, even before parliament had been dissolved, the canvassing reports revealed the following results:

For Labour	Against	Removed/Dead	Doubtful	Unknown
16,715	4,450	1,188	1,811	21,884

In Chapter 5 we shall attempt to make an assessment of the accuracy and usefulness of the canvass. Suffice it to say at this juncture that after a period of sustained canvassing in areas of known Conservative strength and among voters whose allegiance was unknown, Labour workers had uncovered slightly more than 4,000 voters against them (Conservatives, Liberals, and others)—only about one-fourth of the number they found supporting their cause.

An early scouting of the terrain also provides necessary information about a party's supporters who have moved from the residence listed for them in the register and who must be handled in a special way if the party is to claim their votes. Anyone who had moved after the preparation of the election register was entitled to vote in Barons Court, but only in Barons Court. Voters who had moved elsewhere in the constituency (internal removals) had to be traced. Since many of these voters might erroneously assume that they had been disfranchised by their change of residence, it was important that literature and information about the location of their polling station be sent to them, and that the party be notified of their transportation needs. Voters who had moved outside the boundaries of the constituency were entitled to an absentee ballot, or, in British terms, a postal vote. Also eligible to cast ballots by mail were the sick and disabled and people whose employment took them away from home periodically.

Needless to say, the processing of postal votes is a time-consuming and a resource-devouring task. For potential supporters who have moved out of the constituency, the party has to find their new addresses and to send them the necessary claim forms, at the same time requesting them to return the completed forms to the party headquarters or to post them directly to the registration officer at the Town Hall. Claim forms for the ill and infirm require a doctor's signature, and very often the postal vote officer or a canvasser has to take care of this personally. Similarly, those who are eligible for a postal vote because of their employment generally require personal wals by party workers. All postal votes have to reach the Town Hall clithin a fortnight of polling day. It is to the advantage of a party to get as many postal votes as possible processed during the pre-campaign period so that it can free its manpower resources for other work during the regular campaign. Servicemen, merchant seamen, and others whose obligations take them to sea or to foreign countries are eligible for proxy votes. A party has an interest in assisting its supporters to arrange for proxies, though the procedures are somewhat less complicated than the processing of postal ballots.

The leaders of the two parties in Barons Court realized that the postal vote could be a critical factor in the outcome of the election for this marginal seat. The feeling was widespread in both camps that the 1,585 postal votes cast in 1959 had been a strategic factor in the Conservative victory. In light of the continuing high rate of removals in the constituency in 1964 and a voting register that was a year old, party leaders recognized that a significant proportion of the electorate would be eligible for a postal vote. The Labour people were particularly concerned about the postal vote in this election for several reasons. First, they felt that many of the removals were working-class voters who were likely to be Labour supporters if they could be located. Second, they recognized that in previous elections the Conservatives had managed to process the postal votes more systematically than they had been able to do, and that, since an outdated register would result in a higher rate of removals to process, they would be at a disadvantage with the Tories on this score unless they devoted more resources to it. Third, they believed that a Labour removal was much more difficult to trace than a Conservative removal. In the opinion of some Labour activists, middle-class Tory voters were more likely to leave forwarding addresses and were more inclined to exercise their voting privileges than were voters of working-class status. Moreover, many landlords were reluctant to give the new addresses of their former tenants to Labour canvassers but readily provided the Conservatives with this information. While this may be a reasonable evaluation, it may also be a reasonable rationalization for a party that invariably comes off second best with the postal vote.

In conducting their canvassing throughout the summer of 1964, the Labour Party took steps to handle internal removals and postal votes. The basic information concerning removals was obtained from housing lists or, more usually, was unearthed by the canvassers, who filled out a removal card when they encountered such a case, attempting whenever possible to secure the voter's new address. These cards were then turned over to the ward secretaries, who were expected to make from them the appropriate notations on their own records and to relay the cards to the removals and postal vote officer. An analysis was then made of the removal cards to determine whether the voters who had moved were Labour supporters. Since the processing of removals involves considerable manpower cost, no attempt was made to trace voters or to send out the necessary forms unless the party leaders were reasonably sure that their expended energy would result in added Labour votes. For this reason they were concerned only with known Labour supporters. In the earlier stages of the work on removals, the processing was done largely by the removals and postal vote officer and his staff of six or seven volunteer helpers. But as time went on, some of the ward organizers took over part of this work on their own. To the extent that this happened, the handling of removals became less synchronized, and it was difficult to determine just how many removals and postal votes the party had actually processed.

When a voter had moved elsewhere in the constituency, the usual procedure was to have him traced to his current address and to have a canvasser contact him. He was also sent a form letter from Robert Owen House telling him what polling station he needed to go to and offering him transportation. An election address was enclosed in each envelope. When an action card indicated that an elector was ill or otherwise incapacitated, a party worker called upon him to get his signature on a claim form for a postal vote, and the party took the initiative in securing a doctor's signature. In the case of a voter who had moved outside the constituency, someone on the volunteer staff sent him a set of instructions and some campaign literature, along with the application for a postal vote, which he was requested to mail to the town clerk before October 1. Thus, the Labour organization was content to leave a great deal to the initiative of the potential postal voter himself.

In their precampaign efforts to scout the terrain, the Barons Court Conservatives pursued a different strategy, partly by choice and partly by necessity. Because of the turnover in agents, whatever thought was given to the planning of the canvass prior to the spring of 1964 had little effect. Furthermore, with different agents serving during the two local elections of that year—and each of them new to the constituency—it was difficult to plan the canvassing for these elections so as to derive maximum benefit for the approaching general election.

Immediately after the campaign for the borough council in May, when Mrs. Bowman received her baptism of fire in Barons Court, she was in a position to pour her energy into preparations for the parliamentary election. Her first concern was to "clean up the election register and to get a leg up on the postal vote." As we have already pointed out, a canvassing squad, including two "missioners" who were supported financially by volunteer donations from the association, went into operation in June.

In contrast with the Labour approach, the Conservatives directed their early canvassing efforts toward the areas of Tory strength. The main reason for this decision was their concern to get an early start on the removals and the postal vote. Their assumption that the removal rate would be higher in the strong Tory districts than in the heavily Labour areas finds support in the census data recorded in Chapter 1.

Although the leaders of the Labour Party entertained the notion that a higher proportion of the absentee vote was potentially Labour rather than Conservative (probably a realistic view, except for Tory sympathizers who claimed postal votes on grounds of occupation), the processing of postal ballots was a much more important aspect of the Tory strategy, and more resources were allocated to it. The Conservatives were convinced that their slim margin of victory in the 1959 election—913 votes—had been due largely, if not entirely, to their greater efficiency in handling the postal vote. In 1964 many of the party leaders nurtured little hope of retaining the seat unless they could duplicate or even improve their proficiency in rounding up these votes.

When a Conservative canvasser discovered a residence that was no longer occupied by the voter listed on the election register, he made a notation on the canvass card and sought to obtain the voter's present address from the new resident or from a neighbor in the same block of flats. The information that Mr. John Doe had moved away, together with his new address (if this had been ascertained), was reported immediately to the constituency headquarters at North End Road. When the report reached the headquarters, the party's records were checked for any available information concerning Doe's voting preference. If the canvasser had been unable to discover the new address, one of the workers was assigned the job of tracing it. When the new address became known, the Barons Court party contacted the Conservative agent in John Doe's new constituency (where Doe was not eligible to vote in this election), requesting him to dispatch a canvasser to Doe's present residence so that the voter's political loyalty could be determined or reaffirmed. If this canvassing report indicated that John Doe was a likely Tory supporter, the voter was requested to fill out the claim form for a postal vote. The agent in the new constituency then returned the form to the Barons Court agent, who saw to it that the postal vote application was properly lodged in the Town Hall. In this way, nothing was left to chance or to the voter's personal initiative. The external removal was not entrusted to request the postal vote form or to send it in; all of this was handled by the party organization.

From late August until the deadline for filing postal vote applications, the Conservatives changed their procedures for processing the absentee ballots somewhat. Although a discussion of this modification takes us into the formal campaign period, its treatment at this point will enable us to complete the picture. On August 24, the Conservative Central Office put into effect a "priority removal scheme" so that the weight of the entire national organization could be thrown behind the handling of the postal vote for the marginal seats. The new system for exchanging information between constituencies on the movements of voters was based upon the use of yellow, pink, and brown cards which were marked with a diagonal stripe and had the word PRIORITY written across the top in red letters. These priority cards were supplied only to the party's agents in marginal territories. When Conservative workers encountered the name of a removed elector whose voting intention was unknown, a yellow card was filled out and sent to the agent in the constituency to which he had shifted residence. The agent was then expected to give priority to the canvassing of this voter, and if it was determined that he had Conservative leanings, he was to be given assistance in completing the postal vote form, which was sent immediately to the agent in the marginal constituency and then forwarded to the Town Hall. A pink card was used in the case of a known Conservative voter whose application for an absentee ballot had already been properly registered. This was sent, usually with campaign literature, to the agent in the new constituency who was supposed to have a party worker canvass the voter, give him the literature, and remind him to send in his postal vote at the proper time. After the elector had been contacted in this way, the pink card was returned to the agent in the marginal constituency to indicate that the visit had been completed. The brown card was used for the known Conservative voter who had moved away and could not obtain a postal ballot. When this was sent to the agent in the new constituency, he dispatched a canvasser to check on the elector's voting intention, to encourage him to return to his old constituency on polling day, and if necessary and possible to offer him transportation facilities. (Conservative voters who had moved out of Barons Court were brought to their old polling stations on election day from as far away as Cambridge.)

While the Conservatives in Barons Court benefited from this priority system, they went even further to ensure a high return from the absent voters. When the registration officer in the Town Hall published a list of all voters who were eligible for postal and proxy votes, the Conservative organization sent a copy of the candidate's election address to every elector, regardless of the appraisal of his voting intention. In addition, on the day after the ballots were mailed by the returning officer, the Barons Court Tories dispatched swarms of canvassers throughout the London area to call on those who were listed as supporters. Their assignment was to make sure that these voters had received their ballots and to urge them to mark their ballots promptly and put them in the mail.

Voters who had moved to a new residence but who continued to live in the constituency—"walking removals," in Tory parlance —were not eligible for an absentee ballot and were required to return to the polling district where they were registered if they desired to vote. Any walking removal of Conservative inclination was offered transportation to his old polling station. A week before polling day, the headquarters sent a form letter to the Tory removals without postal votes reminding them of the polling stations where they were entitled to cast their ballots. Enclosed in the letter was a form—together with an addressed envelope and a stamp—requesting transportation at a time convenient to the voter, and he was invited to fill it out and return it to the main committee room.

It should be obvious by now that if a political party wishes to capture a sizable proportion of the absentee votes, it must be prepared to invest a good slice of its manpower resources in the necessary leg work and the compilation of careful records. From the end of the summer through polling day, the Barons Court Conservatives employed Gladys Holcomb as the full-time absent voters officer. She had a great deal of campaign experience and had worked with Mrs. Bowman in previous elections. Her job was to supervise all of the activities involving absent voters. She kept elaborate records and handled the necessary correspondence. The register of absent voters who were declared eligible to vote by the returning officer, together with the records compiled by the Tory headquarters at North End Road, provide us with materials for a gross analysis of absentee voting and the payoff resulting from the careful search for these voters. According to the records, a total of 2,183 voters applied for and received postal votes, of which 1,638 were actually cast. Of the total number of applications (2,183), 1,677 were lodged directly by the Conservative organization. It is likely that some of the remaining 506 were actually lodged by Tories without the knowledge of the organization. Of the 213 votes that were authorized to be cast by proxy, the Conservatives at North End Road were able to account for 200. In light of these figures, it is highly probable that the Tories gained a considerable edge over Labour in the processing of absentee votes, although the latter had undoubtedly improved in performance over previous elections. They also made offers of transportation to about 200 external removals who had no postal vote, although no final check was made to determine how many of these voters were actually brought to the polls by the Barons Court party or by Conservatives in other constituencies. In addition, the party organization offered transportation to 500 walking removals, but here again it is impossible to know how many took advantage of the offers. Considering only the postal and proxy votes, it appears likely that the Conservatives' effort brought them returns that accounted for about 10 per cent of their total vote. If the removals who probably accepted transportation to the polls are added, the proportion rises to nearly 15 per cent.

Publicizing the Candidate and Appealing to the Electorate

There can be little doubt that the incumbent has an initial advantage in virtually every election, especially when it comes to publicity. His previous campaigns have made him known to the voters, and his position as a public official provides him with plenty of opportunities to keep his name before the public.

In 1961, when Ivor Richard was chosen as the prospective Labour candidate in Barons Court, the party's leaders realized that he was not well known among many Labour members and that he was virtually unknown in the constituency at large. Early in its deliberations, the campaign committee laid plans to project the image of the candidate and to involve him in the public affairs of Barons Court. It was agreed that Mr. Richard should meet as many party members as possible, and the committee prepared a roster of inactive Labour people to whom he might pay a personal visit. It was also agreed that he should engage in the canvassing activities so as to become better acquanted with the party activists and at the same time meet some of the Barons Court voters on the doorstep. In addition, the campaign committee drew up a list of civic groups in the constituency with which he might become associated. At one point, it was planned that he should attend a meeting on cuts in the education budget, which was being sponsored by Labour representatives on the London County Council, and that he should get on the protest committee. In any public meetings to be held during local election campaigns, the committee felt, the prospective candidate should be given the opportunity to speak from the rostrum. The committee also decided that a series of open-air meetings be held at the marketplaces in the Hammersmith and Fulham ends of the constituency so that Richard would have a platform from which to convey his views to interested passersby. These street-corner meetings were started in the summer of 1963, and when they were taken up again during the following summer, they were continued throughout the campaign. In an effort to reach an important element of Labour's constituency, the agent and his colleagues in early 1964 sent a letter to forty-three trade union branches inquiring whether they would like to have the candidate speak on particular policy questions. About fifteen of them extended the invitation.

From the beginning the party made a deliberate effort to get the local weekly press to publicize the views of the opposition candidate for the Barons Court seat. At its first meeting in March 1962, for example, the campaign committee agreed that Mr. Richard should challege Mr. Carr on the housing issue at the annual meeting of the GMC, and that reports of the challenge be fed to the press. Since GMC meetings are not open to the public, Richard's speech would have little impact upon the electorate unless it were picked up by the press. Formal responsibility for keeping the candidate's name in the newspapers fell to the press officer.

The attempt to promote Labour's cause through the commercial press was supplemented by the publication of a party propaganda organ called *The Citizen*. For two issues of the paper which were to have wide distribution Mr. Richard prepared statements on housing and education. In a similar publicity venture, the party in January 1963 distributed 10,000 copies of *Let's Go for a Better Britain*. The purpose of this selective distribution was to make an appeal to segments of the electorate without having to list the cost as a campaign expense, in the case of a sudden election.

Although in Britain many local parties doubt that the holding of small public meetings is a very effective campaign technique, both the Labour and Conservative organizations in Barons Court felt that they should expose their candidates to the electorate in open forums. The view was that some voters like to have an opportunity to see the aspirants in action, that public meetings have at least some utility in inspiring the party faithful, and that a political organization becomes vulnerable to criticism by the opposition if it schedules no meetings at all.

Early in its deliberations, the Labour campaign committee decided that there should be a very limited number of small public meetings, and plans were eventually made, long in advance of the campaign, for three of them to be scheduled and the halls booked. The committee also expressed a wish for one large public meeting featuring Mr. Harold Wilson, the party's leader. The members of the committee believed it advisable to schedule this meeting no later than the Monday before the election rather than on the eve of the poll so that it could be covered by the local press. (The weekly newspapers always appear on the stands on Wednesday or Thursday.) Wilson was lined up as the main speaker long before the start of the campaign, but the Labour planners made an effort not to publicize the fact until the appropriate time.

In addition to these efforts at building up their candidate in Barons Court, the Labour leaders made an attempt to polish the image of their party, to make it appear as a modern, up-to-date organization. As part of the new symbolism, the party workers painted and spruced up the headquarters at Robert Owen House, and their industry was appropriately rewarded in 1962 when the organization won first prize in the "Brighter Premises Competition," which was sponsored as a feature of the Festival of Labour. To help project the new image, the agent, after some initial resistance from a few Labour stalwarts, managed to get the traditional colors and layout for posters and displays changed in favor of a somewhat gayer design, more in tune with the new age.

Since their candidate was the sitting M.P. who had been active in constituency affairs for more than a decade, the Conservatives in Barons Court were not under as much pressure as their opponents to deliberately project Mr. Carr into the limelight during the pre-campaign period. Through his membership in numerous civic groups and his involvement in various local service activities, as well as through his wife's participation in local affairs, Carr enjoyed frequent contact with the opinion leaders and other influential people in Barons Court.

Although the Conservative candidate obviously derived benefit from incumbency status, his party leaders were not content to ignore publicity activities during the precampaign period. They were not especially pleased with the coverage they had been receiving in the local press, which, in the view of some, was somewhat slanted against them. Partly in an attempt to get independent publicity, the Conservatives began to rely heavily upon their own newspaper, the *Barons Court News*. In the spring and summer issues in 1964, lead articles by Mr. Carr put forward his views on such issues as housing, education, national defense, and social welfare. The issue in September 1964, however, in addition to publishing the candidate's stand on the major issues, devoted much more space to "Bill Carr" as a personality and to an exposition of his record since his election to parliament.

The publicity office established by Mrs. Bowman was quite different from that set up by Mr. Clarke on the Labour side. Mrs. Bowman was interested in having on her staff an individual who was skilled in the art of poster design and layout and in the writing of effective appeals. During the precampaign period, she recruited for this post a friend who had been associated with her in previous political encounters. Although the man selected as publicity officer was not a professional, he possessed the skills of a good commercial artist and had considerable expertise in public relations. In his role, however, he bore no responsibility for dealing with the press or for directly publicizing the candidate in the constituency.

In its discussion toward the end of the summer, the Tory campaign committee approved a schedule of public meetings which were to be held during the campaign and were to be arranged by the meetings officer. It was agreed that nine public gatherings should be scheduled between October 2 and October 12 at various locations throughout the constituency. The candidate, of course, was to appear on the platform at all of these meetings, but in three of them he was to be supported by other Conservative members of parliament. Besides these small gatherings, which were to give interested citizens an opportunity to meet Mr. Carr, the party leaders made plans to hold two major rallies in the constituency. The first one, scheduled for October 8, was to feature a major address in the Hammersmith Town Hall by the Rt. Hon. Quintin Hogg speaking in behalf of Mr. Carr. At the second rally, which was planned much later, the Prime Minister was to appear at an open-air meeting at Hammersmith Broadway just five days before the election.

While both of the parties made plans to employ the traditional publicity techniques—public meetings, posters, and campaign literature—the Conservatives also decided to expend significant resources, especially large amounts of the candidate's time, on the "circus." This activity is organized around the candidate, who travels in a jeep equipped with a loudspeaker. Completing the entourage and an important part of it is a squad of canvassers. After the circus is formed, the group moves into a neighborhood and then drives through the streets announcing that the Conservative candidate has arrived to visit with any citizen who wishes to see him. The canvassers descend upon the doorstep to perform their usual task, simultaneously informing the residents that the candidate is available to meet with them. The Conservative plan called for a circus every morning and every afternoon (Saturdays and Sundays excepted) during the campaign proper. It was the hope of the party leaders that the entire constituency would be covered once, and that the strong Conservative areas would get the treatment twice. A peripheral part of the circus plan was to have the bulk of the crew eat lunch at a different pub each noon.

When in April the Prime Minister announced that an election was not likely to be held before autumn, party workers could feel reasonably assured, though not completely certain, that they would be free from electoral worries for three or four months. The months of June, July, and August, when people go away on holiday, are usually not considered to be a "ripe time" to entice voters to the polls. Throughout the summer the Labour people in Barons Court could adjust and refine the operation of their party machine, keeping it active enough to prevent rusting but not pushing it so hard as to wear it out before the campaign got underway. The Tories had to use the summer to build their organization and to try to put together parts that had not been properly meshed into a workable machine for about eighteen months.

But the leaders and workers in each organization knew that there had to be an election by November. And when the traditional vacation period began, the two parties grew restive and clearly increased the tempo of their activities, though these were not always visible to the public eye. As the last of the British voters began to return from their holidays, the key workers in the Labour and Conservative camps realized that the curtain would soon rise on the battle of Barons Court, 1964.

CHAPTER 3

Waging the Battle:
The Campaign

On September 15, 1964, the London press reported to the British reading public that the Prime Minister, Sir Alexander Douglas-Home, had ended a whistle-stop tour in Dover the night before and had flown to Balmoral Castle to hold an audience with the Queen. No official announcement of the trip or its purpose was issued from No. 10 Downing Street; none was necessary. Even the politically unsophisticated knew that the legal life of the present parliament would expire within a few weeks, and that a general election was in the offing. According to British custom, the Prime Minister was expected to advise the monarch in person on the proposed dates for the dissolution of the parliament and the scheduling of the election.

Shortly after his consultation with the Queen on the morning of the fifteenth, Sir Alex returned to his official London residence and announced to the country that the election had been set for Thursday, October 15. Meeting with the Privy Council on September 25, Her Majesty signed the proclamation of dissolution which was then rushed to the House of Lords for the Great Seal to be affixed. These bows to tradition and the fine print of the election law were a signal to political leaders throughout the country that the dress rehearsal was over, and that the campaign proper was now underway.

Adopting the Candidates

The Conservative and Labour parties in Barons Court were each ready for the opening scene—the formal meeting to invest its prospective candidate with formal candidate status. Following a prearranged schedule, the Labour people went into action immediately. Since their man was the M.P. and was limited by certain legal proprieties, the Conservatives held back for a few days.

The Labour Party scheduled its adoption meeting for the evening of September 24 at Robert Owen House. This gathering, which was restricted to party activists (of whom forty-two attended), opened quietly. An air of solemnity and determination cast itself over the small room in the basement of party headquarters as the motion was made and unanimously accepted that Ivor Richard be adopted as the Labour candidate for parliament in Barons Court. Restrained murmurs of excitement broke into the somber atmosphere as Mr. Richard rose to accept the candidacy and its challenge, and to thank his colleagues for the honor they had conferred upon him. It soon became apparent that this was not the Mr. Richard of the "stump," seeking to dazzle the street-corner crowd with verbal pyrotechnics. Nor was this the Mr. Richard of the bar, scoring points with judge and jury by his erudition and logic. This was Ivor Richard the candidate, who now had a chance for the first time to win a seat in the House of Commons, speaking to his key workers. Whether he would win the seat depended in good part upon how well these people would carry out their assignments during the next three weeks. The new candidate discussed briefly the state of the Barons Court party; then he outlined the issues of the campaign, and concluded with a rallying plea for united action for victory.

After the enthusiastic applause had died down, the meeting was turned over to the agent. When a party's activists gather at the opening of a campaign, they are concerned about strategy and tactics as well as issues, and on these matters the agent—not the candidate—was the spokesman. It was a feature of Labour campaign organization that the key workers were brought together from time to time so that they could be briefed on the overall plan, and how their work fitted into it. The adoption meeting served as one of these occasions.

Mr. Clarke started on a professional and businesslike note. He briefly reviewed the campaign objectives and then presented a detailed analysis of what needed to be done and when. He issued a report on the party's financial resources, marked out a schedule for literature distribution, gave an account of the open-air and public meetings which had been planned, indicated what was being done in the way of press and television publicity, and, finally, outlined the plans for canvassing. After answering questions concerning strategy and tactics, the agent changed the substance and tone of his remarks, concluding with a comment which, to an Anglophile, would suggest that the values of a cricket match dominate political contests in Britain: "If we win, we can afford to be generous; and even if we lose, we must always behave properly!"

This appeal struck a responsive note, and the cadre of the party affirmed that Labour was asking to be entrusted with the grave responsibility of governing the country, and that party workers who come into contact with the public must present the image of an organization which has the capacity to discharge its responsibility with distinction.[1]

1. The Labour adoption meeting in 1966 was somewhat different from the one held in 1964, and the difference stemmed largely from the fact that the party was trying to retain the seat rather than having to win it back from a Conservative incumbent. The challenge is slightly less exciting when the candidate occupies the seat than when party workers are confronted with the prospect of getting a new M.P. of their own political faith. Moreover, as the

Five days later, on September 29, the Conservatives held their adoption meeting in Constitution Hall off Hammersmith Broadway. But this was no meeting of cadre. All members of the Conservative Association were invited, and by 8:00 P.M. the hall was comfortably filled with almost 200 people. The meeting was planned so that it would have some of the touches of an American presidential nominating convention. The association president, Sir Samuel David, gaveled the meeting to order and immediately launched into a nominating address. He listed the notable qualities and achievements of the man who had served Barons Court in the House of Commons. When he presented Bill Carr to the throng as the Conservative candidate for reelection to this post, pandemonium broke loose. The Young Conservatives surged from the back of the hall into the aisles, waving their banners high and chanting, "Bill Carr! Bill Carr!" All that was missing to make the demonstration worthy of the Cow Palace was a brass band and some hot-dog hawkers. Mr. Carr was nominated by acclamation, and when the demonstration had subsided, the newly proclaimed candidate rose to deliver his acceptance speech.

While speaking to the assembled Tories. Mr. Carr was really addressing the voters in Barons Court. The meeting had been

---

incumbent, the member would have had to take certain policy stands which would not have pleased all of the activists within his local party. In 1966, this was true of Mr. Richard. Some of the workers in the Barons Court party differed with him on his attitude toward the homosexual bill and on his support of Labour's official policy on Commonwealth immigration and the war in Vietnam. As a result of these policy disagreements, the vote on his readoption was not unanimous. The Vietnam issue prompted two GMC members to abstain, and Richard's support of the homosexual bill precipitated one negative vote. On the latter issue, the Burkean influence on British politics was especially noticeable. When the dissenter asked Mr. Richard by what *mandate* had he supported the homosexual legislation, he quickly responded: "When you sent me to parliament, you sent as your *representative* and not as your *delegate*. On a given issue before the House, it is my responsibility to make up my mind after I have listened to the debate!"

scheduled so that it could be covered in the next issue of the local newspaper. Reporters were invited to attend and were handed advance copies of Carr's remarks. In outlining the campaign issues, the candidate made a strong appeal to his constituents to support the Conservatives. He condemned Labour for its declared intention of having Britain give up her nuclear weapons and thus rely upon the United States for the country's defense. He castigated the opposition for its "cynical change of front" on the immigration question, charging that in 1962 the Socialists had opposed restrictions and were now supporting controls until agreements could be worked out with the Commonwealth countries. He then praised the record of the Conservative Government in economic and social affairs, emphasizing the prosperity theme and the gains in housing construction. His concluding remarks predicting another victory for the party stimulated cheering and loud applause. The meeting was closed with the singing of the national anthem.

The Labour and Conservative adoption meetings not only accomplished the legal purpose of adopting the candidates, but also enabled the two parties to officially disband their organizations. Thus, in the eyes of the law each party organization was transformed into an "informal" group of supporters for the candidate, working for his election under the leadership of the agent. The main reason for this action was to avoid having to include the costs of normal party activities in the list of campaign disbursements.

But here the similarity between the two adoption meetings ceases. If the differences were merely simple distinctions in tactics at a given point, they would be of little consequence. A single meeting is likely to have no measurable impact on the outcome of an election, even in a marginal constituency. The differences between the two adoption meetings, however, are symptomatic of much greater differences between the two local organizations. The Conservative candidate was oriented more to the constituency as a whole than to his local party organization. He saw himself as the representative of all the people in Barons Court, and he saw no reason why the party organization should not operate well without his special attention. The new agent, while preferring to have the candidate linked more closely with the party organization, was not in a position to change the stance of a sitting M.P. who had been active in local party and constituency affairs for several years.

While not ignoring the const'tuency, the Labour candidate and his agent were much more concerned with their party organization and its active cadre. They devoted more time to maintaining the support of the key workers and increasing their effectiveness. This difference in approach between the two campaign teams was not only reflected in the adoption meetings, one of which was exclusive and organizationally oriented and the other inclusive and constituency oriented, but in other actions of the two candidates and two agents as well. This may have been one of the factors responsible for the differences in performance which were manifested during the campaign. We shall have occasion to examine this problem later in the study, where it will be discussed in the context of other campaign developments.

Patterns of Campaign Organization

At the nucleus of the Labour Party organization in Barons Court was the agent, Alan Clarke, who directed the campaign from his office in the central headquarters in Robert Owen House. From this vantage point he saw the campaign in its total perspective, and in his quiet way was in full command of its operation. A special mimeographed *Election Guide*, which he had carefully drawn up, specified in detail the assignments of the leading campaign officials, and it contained an elaborate flow chart indicating the chains of authority in the organization. The *Guide* made it clear that the "agent directs our campaign, because in a battle there can be only one line of command. His aim, like that of all of us, is a Labour victory, so it is up to every worker to cooperate." It was explicitly understood that only the agent and the candidate were to communicate directly with Transport House, the trade unions, the Cooperative Party, newspaper reporters, printers, and poster firms. Only the agent was entitled to disburse funds during the campaign; only he could place orders and obtain supplies of any sort.

Being responsible for this campaign, the agent was, of course, in constant touch with the candidate, who also had an office in Robert Owen House. Their relations were always cordial. They had come to the constituency at about the same time and had worked closely together in trying to unite the party and get it properly organized for an election contest. The fact that they had grown to respect each other's views permitted them to carry on their relationships in an informal atmosphere. There was no sharp jurisdictional separation between the two men based upon an organization-policy dichotomy. They frequently consulted with each other on questions of organization, strategy, and campaign issues, and consensus was easily arrived at. As a rule, however, the agent directed the candidate's daily activities. He kept a schedule of meetings and interviews which had been lined up for the candidate and his wife, he usually suggested the areas to be covered by the loudspeaker van and the proper timing for these excursions, and he helped to make arrangements for the Saturday meetings on the street corner. On more than one occasion he made a few suggestions to Mrs. Richard when she was requested without much notice to fill in at public meetings.

The atmosphere of congenial informality which pervaded the central headquarters made for a type of collegial policy-making during the campaign. Although the agent was responsible for directing its course and could in theory have asserted his prerogative, Mr. Clarke always made it a practice to consult with his colleagues when crisis developed and problems of strategy and tactics arose. We shall have occasion later to note what some of these crises and problems were. But it will suffice now to indicate that the crucial campaign decisions were made by the agent in collaboration with the candidate, the party chairman, the canvassing officer, and sometimes a ward leader, if he was the person who happened to encounter the difficulty.

In directing the campaign effort, the agent for the most part ran a decentralized operation. Although this was his inclination in any event, he really had very little choice in the matter. Robert Owen House did not have enough large rooms to accommodate sizable groups of volunteer workers, and there was no regular paid staff except for a part-time typist. The only large-scale activities which were carried out entirely at the center were literature folding, envelope stuffing, and window-bill pasting. All the other work had to be done at ward level, in the smaller committee rooms, and in private homes.

Mr. Clarke deliberately delegated responsibility at two echelons of his organization—to certain campaign officials at the center, and to designated organizers at ward level. We have already observed that the campaign committee, long before the dissolution of parliament, had established special administrative offices and had filled them with reliable party veterans. Although all of these people carried out their assignments under the agent's direction and reported directly to him, he permitted them to have relatively slack rein in performing their executive tasks. He expected them to do their jobs, and so long as he felt that they were getting results, he made no effort to intervene. The autonomy of administrative officials was revealed in handling the question of whether the candidate should be permitted to examine the canvassing returns. In 1964 the canvassing officer refused to disclose them, while in 1966 the candidate was made privy to this information. On both occasions the agent left the matter to the discretion of the official in charge. For him to offer subtle suggestions was characteristic of the agent's style, and, since his lieutenants were familiar with his modes of behavior, they invariably interpreted these hints as directives.

Two of these administrative officials—the canvassing officer and the removals and postal vote officer—had especially close contact with the leaders in each of the wards. The canvassing officer had several meetings with the ward organizers, and from time to time he issued directives to them on canvassing targets and priorities. Moreover, the officials in charge of the wards were required to send him progress reports which grew more frequent as the campaign advanced. In the case of the removals and postal vote officer, the flow of communication was much more one-way; since the ward organizers had complete instructions on how to handle voters who had left their places of residence, they needed only to fill out the appropriate cards and forward them to Robert Owen House, where they were picked up by the official responsible.

As we have already seen, some wards were in healthy condition, and the agent decided to give the leaders in charge of these areas a relatively free hand in discharging their obligations under the campaign plan. This meant that, within the general framework of his instructions from the central committee room, the ward organizer was in full charge of running the campaign in his baili- wick, and he was expected to recruit enough manpower resources to get the job done. He appointed a subleader for each polling district and delegated to him the task of literature distribution. The ward organizer lined up his canvassers and designated the particular areas to be covered. In addition, he prepared a roster of workers and a time schedule for the purpose of getting work assignments taken care of during the campaign and on polling day—committee room clerks, number-takers and messengers for polling stations, car donors and drivers, and knockers-up. When he ran short of workers for any of these tasks, he immediately notified the people in the central committee room, who tried to send him supplementary assistance.

This pattern of organization required a two-way flow of information. Officials at Robert Owen House—the agent or one of his administrative lieutenants—issued instructions to the ward leaders, and they in turn sent messages to the center in the form of reports or calls for assistance when they encountered problems. As suggested earlier, the fact that the agent could confidently allow some wards to move ahead on their own enabled him and his aides to manage campaign operations in the weaker districts from the central committee room. In the 1966 campaign, the organization in all of the wards was sufficiently strong to permit an entirely decentralized operation.

With such division of labor and heavy reliance upon ward organization, the Labour agent had to make sure that all of the gears were meshed and the machine was running smoothly. Long before the campaign was begun, he had taken pains to set the machinery up properly by arranging for the training school for key workers and by publishing the *Election Guide*. His office served as a collector of information, both from Transport House and from inside the constituency, and this information was the basis of instructions which were fanned out to the ward organizers. Mr. Clarke's communications to administrative personnel were concise and to the point, leaving no room to doubt as to what the assign- ments were. He had instruction sheets for every type of worker— the key campaign officials, the ward organizers, and rank-and-file members and ordinary workers who volunteered for routine jobs. Moreover, on two different occasions during the campaign he arranged for a meeting of the key workers and other activists to bring them into the picture by briefing them on the progress of the overall effort and the work still to be accomplished. These gather- ings also provided short interludes of social relaxation, which were important for morale purposes. As the integrating force within the campaign organization, the agent made it a point to chat with the members of his central staff and the ward organizers at least once a day, and he visited each committee room from time to time to see how things were going and to offer words of encouragement and commendation to the workers.

In the Conservative camp, the tempo of activity was noticeably increasing at 84A North End Road even before the formal adoption of Mr. Carr. By ten o'clock each morning, the work rooms on the second, third, and fourth floors were bustling with industry as new canvass cards were being readied, envelopes were being stuffed, and literature was being prepared for distribution. In the main secretarial office, half a flight above the street level, the phone rang incessantly, and Gladys worked more intently on the postal vote cards as the deadline for filing them approached.

At the center, both organizationally and architecturally, of this political beehive was the agent and her office. The office was located one full flight of stairs above street level, between the secretarial office and the work rooms. Everyone who had reason to go beyond the secretarial office had to pass by the agent's door. Judging by the crowd that was usually gathered in the office, one might conclude that most of the people who walked down the hall stopped in for a little chat.

For a number of reasons—ward organizations that had not been completely revamped after the reorganization of London government in 1963, the newness of the agent, the heavy reliance upon outside help, and, perhaps most importantly, the absence of a long period of planning and preparation—Mrs. Bowman decided to run a campaign that was highly centralized in operation. Virtually all of the clerical work, most of the canvassing, and most of the tasks concerned with the postal vote, the public meetings, publicity, and the circus were handled directly from 84A North End Road, In addition, all of the outlying committee rooms were controlled directly from central headquarters.

Not only was the campaign operation centralized at the main headquarters, but, through no choice of her own, within the headquarters establishment almost every detail of the campaign was directed from the agent's office by Mrs. Bowman herself. If a canvassing problem arose in one of the committee rooms, it would be taken directly to Mrs. Bowman, because the canvassing officer was either at his place of regular employment or was so busy distributing canvass cards that he was unable to deal with the matter. A question involving literature distribution came directly to the agent's office. Many of the groups that were preparing canvass and pledge cards at 84A took their problems directly to Mrs. Bowman, usually bypassing the clerk in charge. In only two operations—the handling of the postal vote and the direction of the circus—could the agent be assured that the people in executive positions would be available and able to handle their responsibilities with dispatch.

While the high degree of centralization in campaign administration formed the most obvious contrast between the Labour and Conservative camps, an even more crucial difference was the absence in the upper echelons of the Tory organization of local personnel to whom the agent could confidently delegate authority. Later in our analysis we shall indicate the reasons for this and its impact upon the efficiency of the Conservative campaign.

Mrs. Bowman's job was complicated by still another factor. Not only was she involved in many matters of petty detail which consumed her time and energy and kept her from focusing upon more important affairs, but she was also forced to undertake the work of building morale and smoothing over the minor disputes and irritations which invariably arise in a campaign organization. The fact that a relatively new organization had to be set up for this campaign and a number of workers had to be brought in from the outside was probably conducive to more personality conflicts and emotion-laden disagreements over small matters than might otherwise have developed. In a voluntary organization that has been in existence for a longer period of time, the normal processes of attrition, combined with the absence of effective negative sanctions to prevent withdrawals, tend to eliminate or to segregate into different groups those people who do not adjust well to each other. But the Conservative campaign organization had not been in existence long enough for this to happen, and the centralized pattern of organization made this natural adjustment more difficult.

Mrs. Bowman had just the right touch to deal with the minor irritations which were bound to arise in a central headquarters where thirty or forty people were thrown together in routine tasks to be performed under pressure of time. A word of encouragement here, a tap on the shoulder there, five minutes for a cup of tea with the right person—this was about all that was needed. Her boundless enthusiasm, her driving energy, and her own heavy work load set an example at the headquarters which helped to promote good relations among the campaign workers and to prevent minor aggravations from seriously hampering the output.

Problems that arose outside the headquarters tended to be a bit more serious, partly because minor irritations were unlikely to come to the agent's attention until they had begun to fester. When, for example, a personality clash might occur in one of the wards between a local party worker and an outside volunteer who had come to Barons Court to help with the work, the agent was faced with a delicate problem. As she pointed out, "I need the outsiders because the ward organization is just not strong enough to do the work alone. But after the election is over, the outsider will be gone, and then I shall need the ward workers to build up the organization." She was an expert in smoothing ruffled feathers, and she managed to keep both types of workers industriously employed in the campaign. The only cost was the time and energy of the agent, but these were precious commodities in the Tory camp.

The best visual representation of the organization and operation of the Conservative campaign could be obtained by spending an hour or so in the agent's office almost anytime during the campaign. At any given moment, from five to fifteen people were likely to be crowded in the little room, some waiting to see her about a campaign matter, a clerk searching through the files for a memo, another answering the telephone. More likely than not, at least one phone would be ringing, unless they were all being used.

What prevented chaos from developing was an agent who could answer the phone, draft a memorandum, and respond to someone's query all at the same time.

If the agent was the center of the campaign organization and operation, the candidate was the focal point of its purpose. All of the work and activity was aimed at getting him elected. Mr. Carr spent most of his time away from 84A North End Road—with the circus, on the doorstep, on the stump, or at a private reception or public meeting. He did have an office at the central headquarters (it was the most peaceful spot on the premises), where he spent some time writing letters, talking with constituents who had come to call, and preparing his speeches. While at 84A, he spent much time conferring with Mrs. Bowman. The formal line of demarcation between the duties of the candidate and the duties of the agent were well observed. The agent was responsible for organization and operations, the candidate for policy. Mrs. Bowman always yielded to the prerogatives of Mr. Carr on policy matters. If, for example, a newspaper reporter arrived at headquarters to inquire about the party's stand on a certain issue, she would refer him to the candidate. Even when the candidate was away from headquarters, she would not respond. Mr. Carr, however, became involved from time to time in operational problems. He had worked longer and harder and more thoroughly in the constituency than any other member of the association, and was extremely knowledgeable about the area and its inhabitants. For this reason the new agent found herself drawing upon his fund of information and experience when campaign decisions had to be based upon an exhaustive understanding of the constituency.

As was to be expected, the agent and the candidate did not see eye to eye on the handling of some policy issues, and they held differing views on effective campaign practices. It would be erroneous to conclude that their different approaches to some policy questions in any way affected the efficiency of the campaign organization. As indicated earlier, Mrs. Bowman respected the authority of the candidate on policy matters; she rarely discussed these issues with Mr. Carr (except in relationship to campaign literature) and she never challenged him on a campaign issue. This kind of relationship appears to be the norm in the party, and it was strictly and willingly obeyed in Barons Court.

The differences between candidates and agent over campaign activities—particularly the activities of the candidate and his wife—were of more consequence. The norm in the Conservative Party on this division of labor is also clear: campaign strategy and tactics are under the jurisdiction of the agent. But Mr. Carr's long experience as a party worker in Barons Court, even before he stood for parliament, gave his competence on campaign affairs in Barons Court a special weight because the agent was a newcomer to the constituency. Mr. Carr—and Mrs. Carr, too, for that matter— did their jobs as outlined explicitly in the campaign plan. But they did not feel that they were always being used most effectively, and this had at least some effect upon their outlook in the campaign effort.

The relationship between the candidate and his agent involves an even more important, if more subtle, point. The effective use of the candidate (and his family) in a campaign entails something more than the adherence to an explicit plan. In the course of a campaign, there arise contingencies which have not been planned but which nevertheless require action. In some cases, the responses to these contingencies have to be virtually spontaneous. Agents and candidates who have worked together for several years get to know and to appreciate each other's *modus operandi*, and they are able to reach an implicit understanding. This was the basis for much of the cooperation between Mr. Richard and Mr. Clarke in the Labour camp. But in the case of the Conservatives, the candidate and the agent had not been together long enough for this level of under- standing to develop.

Relations with External Organizations

Any local Labour Party in a general election must inevitably interact with officials in the echelons above it, especially the regional agent and some of the functionaries in the national organization at Transport House. It was to be expected that the administrative officials in the national party would keep their eyes on Barons Court because it was highly marginal and was regarded as a "bellweather" constituency. As an official in Transport House indicated to one of the authors, every issue that was important in the national campaign was in contention at Barons Court, with a few other factors thrown in for good measure.

To begin with, the officials in the regional office and Transport House helped the Labour Party in Barons Court with some of its organizational ventures and with its publicity. We have already noted that the regional organizer assisted in sponsoring the training school for campaign workers, and he aided in the setting of the canvassing targets. Almost daily during the campaign Mr. Clarke received formal memoranda from the national agent calling his attention to deadlines for lodging applications for postal votes, the regulations on the filing of nomination papers, the need for insuring the automobiles to be used in the campaign, and similar matters. Transport House sent to the candidate regularly a mimeographed publication entitled *Today*, which supplied statistics and quotations (from both Labour and Conservative leaders) to be used as ammunition in his public utterances and on the doorstep if he needed them. The regional officer also helped the party's leaders line up supporting speakers for the public meetings. We have already seen that Transport House made a substantial contribution to the party campaign fund, and in addition the agent secured large supplies of campaign literature from the national office, which he sent over to the ward organizers for delivery to voters.

The authorities in Robert Owen House periodically sent

canvassing reports to the regional office, along with accounts of how party workers were being received on the doorstep. These increased in frequency as polling day approached and the national leaders grew interested in using returns from marginal constituencies to offset the influence of the opinion polls, which indicated a deadlocked race. Moreover, a leading official from the regional office made two or three trips weekly to Robert Owen House to examine the canvass figures and to consult with the agent and the candidate about the problems and progress of the campaign. The ultimate decisions on strategy and tactics, however, were made by the local party leaders.

The most crucial interaction between the Labour Party in Barons Court and Transport House was generated by the issue of Commonwealth immigration. When this issue showed signs of becoming a serious problem for canvassers on the doorsteps in traditionally strong Labour areas, the agent consulted with Transport House on how to deal with it most effectively. Even more perturbed was the candidate, who held several telephone conversations with an official in the national headquarters about the issue, suggesting that Labour make its position clear to the voters by having a top party leader assure them that the statute would not be repealed. Transport House, of course, was keeping a watchful eye on the immigration issue, and since Barons Court was a key seat, it was included in a survey which was designed to assess the potential impact of the question on voting intention. Toward the end of the campaign, the canvassing officer was requested to make a spot check of selected areas to detect any significant shifts of loyalty among regular Labour supporters. That this great amount of contact with Transport House was atypical is suggested by the fact that in 1966, when the polls forecast a clear Labour victory and the national leaders were pursuing their interests in marginals with a sitting Conservative M.P., the regional organizer made fewer trips to Shepherds Bush Road, and the agent sent only four canvassing reports to Transport House.

Compared with its opponents, the Labour Party did not have a great deal of contact with sister organizations in adjacent constituencies. Although Labour benefited from the help of large numbers of outside volunteers, particularly from college students in the closing days of the campaign and from members of the South Kensington party throughout the campaign, none was assigned officially to work in Barons Court. The local party, however, did collaborate with several other constituency parties in West London in sponsoring the big public rally at which Harold Wilson was the main speaker. In addition, Mr. Richard was a supporting speaker at a number of smaller meetings held in nearby constituencies. This type of activity, through which he intended to give a helping hand to other Labour candidates, especially those fighting hopeless battles, probably worked to his advantage to some extent. His political views and his lively appearance as a candidate tended to attract some young partisans to his side, and a few voluntarily left their own barren districts and began to labor in the Barons Court vineyard, where their efforts were more likely to bear more fruit.

Probably Labour's closest association was with the party in North Hammersmith. This liaison, however, did not result in many workers coming across the line from North Hammersmith, for that organization appeared to be intent upon consolidating its advantage over the Tories there. Their relationships were more involved with finance. In order to save on campaign expenses, the two agents and their candidates decided to collaborate in the publication of their election addresses. The plan was to have the inside of the brochure the same for both constituencies, with a localized outside section featuring the photographs and personal messages of the respective candidates. This meant that both groups had to agree on the programmatic statement which was to be common to both documents. In the course of the deliberations, Mr. Richard expressed the view that the immigration question was likely to be an issue in the campaign, and that Labour's position should be made clear in their election addresses. This outlook was resisted by the Labour

M.P. from North Hammersmith, who felt that public feelings about immigration were exaggerated and that the issue would not be influential in the election; to mention it in the brochure, he felt, would merely draw attention to an unfortunate social question. It was impossible to have the discussion continue for very long, because the copy for the election addresses had to be in the hands of the printer that day if the parties were to receive a special rate on publishing costs. Given this pressure, a decision had to be made quickly, and it was expected that Mr. Richard would defer to a sitting M.P., especially one that had sat in the House for fourteen years. The result was that the brochure did not mention immigration. As it turned out, of course, the immigration question did generate an undercurrent of dissension within Labour ranks during the campaign, and, as we shall see, the Barons Court leaders were forced to do some soul-searching and to expend additional resources in trying to clarify the party's position.

On the Conservative side, the association in Barons Court had ties with the Central Office in Smith Square, but their relations were rather formal and stylized, and hence not very salient to the main themes of this study. We have already taken note of the fact that the national organization provided some funds for the campaign, and it dispatched some workers from other constituencies to Barons Court. The Central Office also arranged for the appearance of the Prime Minister and Mr. Hogg in the district. Supplies of various leaflets could be purchased through the national headquarters, but association leaders were not greatly attracted by this literature and did not secure much of it. More regular communications were provided by a series of memoranda sent nearly every day from the Central Office. But, under the pressure of happenings in her office, the agent was unable to keep up with them.

At regular intervals throughout the campaign, the agent reported to officials in the Central Office the results of the canvass, and she responded to questions about those issues that were found by the canvassers to be bothering the voters. Later in the campaign,

Lord Blakenham, chairman of the national Party, paid a visit to the central committee room, accompanied by the Central Office agent and several other high party officials. They discussed the progress of the campaign, but the call seems to have been largely for the purpose of boosting the morale of the Barons Court workers. Although the Central Office supported the effort in Barons Court in the ways mentioned, it played no role in actively directing the course of the local campaign. Questions of strategy, tactics, and their execution were decided at the constituency level.

Entering more into the picture in certain respects were the relationships between the Barons Court Conservatives and their counterparts in the adjoining constituencies. We have already referred to the excellent relationship which existed between the Tory organization in Barons Court and the Conservatives in South Kensington. The South Kensington people gave both financial support and manpower assistance on a systematic basis to their Barons Court friends—aid that was of considerable importance in the campaign.

Over the boundary at the top end of Barons Court was North Hammersmith, where Labour had piled up a majority of more than 6,700 in 1959. On the eastern and southern boundary lay the constituency of Fulham, which, though technically still marginal, had been held by Labour in the previous election by a margin of nearly 3,000 votes, and it was not to be expected that the Conservative candidate there would be able to defeat the popular and highly respected Michael Stewart. Nevertheless, the Conservatives in both of these constituencies waged vigorous campaigns, somewhat to the dismay of the people in Barons Court.

A slight problem with the North Hammersmith association arose from the fact that its workers had hung posters featuring their candidate on display sites which were just within the confines of the Barons Court constituency. As already indicated, party affiliation is not listed on the ballot, and it is important that each voter be able to identify the candidate which his party is sponsoring. The Conservatives in Barons Court thought that some of their supporters might become confused by these posters and might go to the polling stations with the name of the wrong Tory candidate in mind. Early in the campaign, Mrs. Bowman called the matter to the attention of the North Hammersmith association, but her injunction that the boundaries of the constituency be adhered to was not always easy to enforce. Her willingness to express her concern declined when she discovered that on one occasion a group of Barons Court workers had distributed literature in one of the streets of North Hammersmith, reminding the Tories to vote for Mr. Carr.

There were also faint rumbles of discord between the Barons Court party and the Conservatives in Fulham. A strategic location for the open-air meetings sponsored by the Fulham Tories was right on the boundary line of the two constituencies. The Conservatives in Barons Court had some objection to the Fulham people setting up their speakers' stand in this location, not only because the voters might become puzzled as to who their Conservative candidate really was, but also because the Fulham standard-bearer was enunciating a line on certain issues that was more conservative than Mr. Carr's. Even though the Barons Court agent and some of the association officers were themselves somewhat more conservative on these questions than Mr. Carr, they felt that many marginal voters would have to be won over to the Tory side if they were to win the seat, and that these people were more likely to be attracted by the "progressive Toryism" of Bill Carr than by the views of their neighbor in Fulham. The objections of the Barons Court Conservatives to these street-corner meetings on the constituency boundary grew more vocal when they discovered that on one occasion a Labour leader from Barons Court had managed to get the microphone from the Fulham Tories and had taken over their meeting.[2]

2. See below, p. 143.

Because the boundary lines of the constituency are sometimes hard to distinguish, especially for outside workers, incidents like these were difficult to avoid. But even when there was an overlap, it is unlikely that campaign appeals to the wrong people had much effect upon the voters in Barons Court. Insignificant in themselves, these events merit brief attention only because they made slight inroads upon the time of the agent, who has more important things to do.

Having examined the main patterns of organization within the Labour and Conservative camps, we are now in a position to investigate the campaign activities in which they engaged. These activities involved two basic objectives: to identify in the consciousness of the electors the respective candidates and the policies they stood for, and to single out their respective supporters so that they could each marshal their battalions of promises to the polls on election day.

Campaign Publicity: Identifying the Candidates and the Issues

After September 24, when Mr. Richard had become the formal candidate, the Labour campaign shifted into high gear. The Conservatives, however, had not yet opened up their campaign to the public, since Mr. Carr was not to be adopted until September 29. On the Saturday afternoon, Mr. Carr took his American researcher by the arm and said, "Let's go down to the marketplace and scout the opposition!" The two men left the headquarters and walked briskly down North End Road toward Fulham Broadway. The sidewalks were filled with weekend shoppers crowding into the stores or patronizing the outdoor vendors whose barrows line the streets every Saturday. Near Fulham Broadway the Tory candidate and his companion encountered a group of people clustered around a small platform which was appropriately bedecked with Labour insignia. They were listening to a short, slender, highly animated speaker who appeared at first to be more interested in prompting the members of the audience to heckle him than in scoring substantive points on the issues of the day. He excelled in repartee, and the themes he stressed were punctuated with tones that left no doubt about his political loyalties. Leaning over to his American colleague, Mr. Carr whispered, "That's Alderman Thomas there. Some say that he is a left-winger, but he is a powerful opponent on the street corner!" At this point Mr. Richard, who was standing near the platform, recognized that the Tory candidate was in the crowd. Dashing over to his American researcher, he exclaimed, "Look who is here! I've never heard of a parliamentary candidate coming to a meeting of his opponent!"

Soon Mr. Richard ascended the platform and, taking the microphone in hand, began to address the crowd. It would not have taken a stranger long to guess that he had practiced before the bar. The words flowed in well-turned phrases, and he developed his points clearly, sometimes pungently. He handled his hecklers with relative ease, sometimes with a thrust but more often with the parry, asking them to hold their questions until he reached that particular subject. After listening to his Labour opponent hold forth for a few minutes, Mr. Carr locked arms with his American visitor and walked away, commenting dryly: "We won't make any effort to heckle him. Hecklers will just put some life into him!"

This little vignette is interesting for several reasons. It was the only time in the entire campaign when either organization made a deliberate attempt to discover what the other side was doing. Moreover, this was the type of street-corner activity in which both parties spent a great deal of time on Saturdays. The candidates felt that speaking in the marketplace afforded them an opportunity to present themselves to the voting public.

Street-Corner Meetings

It may be that few voters can be won over by street-corner appeals, but some can probably be lost. Handling a street crowd in expert fashion is an art in its own right; inexperience and ineptness may be dangerous. Just a few hundred yards from the spot where Mr. Carr observed Ivor Richard on the stump, the Fulham Conservatives later that afternoon had parked their jeep equipped with a loudspeaker and were holding a meeting. Alderman Thomas wormed his way through the crowd to heckle the Tory. After a few verbal exchanges he bested the speakers, and he then climbed on the jeep and was virtually handed the microphone. While the Conservative speaker ineffectively protested that this was hardly cricket, Alderman Thomas preached the Socialist gospel over the Tory loudspeaker powered by Tory electricity, as he stood on the deck of a Tory jeep which was decorated with the Tory blue. Accounts of the incident spread rapidly through parts of Fulham and Barons Court. Some Conservative leaders in the latter constituency fumed when they heard the story, and their displeasure was focused not upon Thomas (for whom there was almost begrudging admiration, even though his behavior could not, they felt, be classed as proper for a gentleman) but upon the Fulham Tories for having demonstrated, right on the boundary of Barons Court, a bumbling lack of authority and control.

As pointed out earlier, the Labour people made considerable use of the Saturday meetings on the street corners. They had started them as early as the summer of 1963, and they continued them from the summer of 1964 throughout the campaign. The meetings, which usually began around midday and broke up shortly after sundown, took a certain amount of planning. The officers in charge managed to ensure a space in the street by having their party colleagues who had access to cars or scooters park them overnight and then remove the vehicles just as the speakers appeared with their van, posters, and sound equipment. The people responsible for these meetings were usually successful in attracting a crowd by planting a member of their own organization in front of the portable platform and having him heckle the speaker. After a crowd had formed, hecklers from the opposing camp often appeared on the scene and cleverly engaged in this activity on their own. The crowds usually numbered from fifteen to thirty at any one time, and the speakers were probably able to reach about 150 to 200 passersby for short periods of time in an afternoon. Although it is unlikely that the street-corner meetings resulted in large numbers of "conversions," some speakers felt that they occasionally struck a responsive chord among a few wavering voters, and that, in any event, the gatherings helped to publicize the candidate, assisted in raising the "temperature" of the campaign, and let the politically apathetic know that Labour's flag was flying. In addition to the Saturday meetings, Mr. Richard addressed six open-air meetings at factory gates and other convenient locations.

The Tory street-corner meetings were as frequent as Labour's once the campaign got under way, and attracted about the same number of people and a few more hecklers. But, in contrast with both Barons Court Labour and the Fulham Conservatives, Mr. Carr did not stand before the crowd to make a speech. His opening remarks were usually designed to bring out the hecklers, and no one could suggest any similarity to a speech to impress a judge and jury. He was on the street to duel in behalf of his party. He rarely used the microphone, and, since his voice rivaled fog horns on the Channel coast in decibel potential, no one missed the electronic amplification. As in the case of Labour, street meetings helped him, at least to some extent, to keep his name before the voters as they wandered by on their way to do the Saturday shopping.

Indoor Meetings

The indoor meetings of a British election campaign used to be a popular event, when competing forms of entertainment (like home television) were more rare and political excitement ran higher. Since the 1950s, however, party leaders have often experienced difficulty in filling the halls; and they tend now to hold the smaller public meetings, as distinct from the big rallies, down to a minimum. As one party agent put the matter in a slightly exaggerated way. "When we schedule a small public meeting and the number of speakers on the platform exceeds the number of people in the audience, it is better to call the whole thing off!"

The small meetings, however, are still used as a campaign device in most constituencies, though in deemphasized form. Party leaders believe that some voters like to have an opportunity to see their candidates in action so that they can assess their potentiality as members of parliament. Moreover, some of the candidates themselves, especially if they are good speakers, relish the chance to appear at indoor meetings. In point of fact, a good proportion of the people who go to the small rallies are the party activists, and the speakers often find themselves delivering the message to those who entered the fold long ago. For these people, of course, a public meeting usually serves to build up their morale, to spur them on to greater effort, and perhaps to provide them with arguments that they can use in their own campaigning. Some activists prefer to skip these meetings and spend their time canvassing, while some may stop in for one of the later speeches after they have done some work on the doorstep.

As early as March 1963, the Labour campaign committee had decided that the party should sponsor only a limited number of small public meetings in selected areas of the constituency. With these instructions in hand, the meetings officer, in consultation with the agent and the candidate, made arrangements far in advance for four indoor gatherings. The meetings were scheduled to permit local press coverage and were publicized through press notices and the distribution of hand leaflets. The first meeting, held on October 2 in a good Labour district in the Fulham wing of the constituency, featured Mr. Carol Johnson, M.P., and Miss Vanessa Redgrave, but only about thirty people attended, probably because it clashed with a large rally in the Fulham Town Hall. The next indoor meeting, which was held three days later in an area of large housing estates, had as outside speakers Mr. Robert Mellish, M.P., and Mr. Douglas Jay, M.P., who drew an audience of about fifty. The third meeting was held on October 9 in a strong Labour area on the Hammersmith side, and featured the Rt. Hon. George Strauss, M.P., and Mr. Ben Parkin, M.P., who spoke to a group of sixty. The last indoor gathering was scheduled on October 12 in the strong Labour territory of Margravine Ward at the Fulham end of the district, with Mr. Ray Gunter, M.P., as the supporting speaker, and this meeting attracted a somewhat larger crowd. At each of these four meetings, Mr. Richard was the concluding speaker and took time to answer questions at the end of his formal presentation. Apart from their publicity function, these meetings provided opportunities for an appeal for funds and the sale of Labour's election platform.

The large public meetings, which featured nationally known speakers, were a marked contrast with the smaller indoor gatherings. In association with several other constituency parties in the vicinity, the Labour organization in Barons Court sponsored a huge public rally at the Hammersmith Town Hall on September 28, with the national party leader as the drawing card. Two of the auditoriums were filled to capacity, as about 1,200 partisans scrambled to find seats within a short time after the doors had opened, and another 500 stood outside the building. The local press described it as the biggest rally held in London since the war.[3] Four Labour candidates from this area, including Mr. Richard, shared the platform with Mr. Wilson, taking their turns in addressing the main audience and in speaking to the people assembled outside. Mr. Richard, unfortunately, had the worst of the draw, for he had barely started his speech when Wilson appeared in the hall and was led to the platform amid tumultuous applause and the flashes of photographers'

3. *West London Observer*, October 1, 1964.

cameras. (The Labour people in Barons Court made certain that their candidate had a better speaking position at the Wilson meeting in 1966.) A financial appeal by a well-known television comedian brought forth a large collection for Labour's fighting fund.

The Conservatives placed more emphasis on the small, local meetings than the Labour Party did. Nine meetings were scheduled on five different days. On three days—October 5, 6, and 7—two evening meetings were planned to be held in different parts of the constituency, one to begin at 7:30 and the other at 8:00. Mr. Carr started off the first meeting, and after a short address and a short question period he went to the other meeting, which had been kicked off by one of the local stalwarts. At three other meetings, Mr. Carr shared the platform with members of the Conservative Ministry, the Rt. Hon. Robert Carr (no relative), the Rt. Hon. William Deeds, and the Rt. Hon. Sir John Hobson.

Attendance at these meetings was disappointing to the Tories. The most they ever managed to attract into the meeting place was a little over thirty, and at all of them a large proportion of the audience was made up of loyal party workers who came more to cheer than to be persuaded. Total attendance at all nine meetings was probably just a little more than total attendance at a fewer number of Labour conclaves. The low attendance could hardly be attributed to lack of publicity. For several days before a meeting, workers distributed announcement leaflets door-to-door in the neighborhoods closest to the meeting halls, and on the afternoon of the event, the sound truck went up and down the streets inviting people to come. It is more likely that the small, neighborhood political meeting is losing its appeal in England; only the national figures can bring the people out for a political rally.

The star attraction of the big indoor rally sponsored by the Conservatives was the Rt. Hon. Quintin Hogg, the Minister for Education and Science in Sir Alec's government. On the evening of October 8, just a week before polling day, the Town Hall in Hammersmith was filled to overflowing with spectators who had come to listen to (or to heckle) one of the most controversial figures in the Conservative Party. At this point in the campaign he was the special target of Labour partisans because of a retort he had made at a meeting in Plymouth two days earlier. While Hogg was discussing the "standards of public life," a heckler had shouted, "What about Profumo?" The Minister's response, made more dramatic by gestures of accusation, stirred a troubled political brew: "If you can tell me there are no adulterers on the front bench of the Labour Party, you can talk to me about Profumo!"[4]

Sex and politics are an explosive mixture at any time, and many people who gathered in the Town Hall on this occasion were expecting fireworks. They were not disappointed. A noisy group of hecklers began to disrupt the meeting shortly after it was opened by the chairman, but when Mr. Hogg arrived on the platform, their jeering was temporarily muffled by the enthusiastic applause of the Tory partisans. When the main speaker stepped to the rostrum, however, he was subjected to an almost continuous barrage of chanting, catcalls, and foot-stamping—a type of behavior that was far removed from the clever heckling of the British tradition. Completely unruffled and with a grim smile on his face throughout most of the disturbance, Mr. Hogg hung closely to the microphone and churned his way through the stormy passage. At one point, in listing the achievements of the Government in the field of education, he turned upon the young hecklers with the remark, "And I think I am right to say, looking at your poor, little faces, that we need a lot more education in the future!" After he had concluded his remarks, he clasped his hands over his head and struck the pose of a boxing champion, and as he left the hall the police cleared the way for his automobile. It is important to point out that the Labour Party in the constituency had nothing to do with the rowdyism at this meeting; indeed, the leaders were somewhat distressed when they learned about it. This type of

4. *Daily Telegraph*, October 7, 1964. Hogg tried to clarify his remarks the following evening (see *ibid.*, October 8, 1964).

behavior had increasingly become the pattern at many of the political rallies of all parties throughout the country, and it reached its peak a day or so after the Hammersmith meeting. At this juncture the rowdyism was condemned by the national leaders of the three parties, and an appeal was made for a return to the traditional British style of heckling.

In addition to the chairman, who made some preliminary remarks, only two speakers addressed the group before Mr. Hogg put in his appearance. One of these was Mrs. Maud Danforth, a recent convert from the Labour Party, who elicited hysterical screams and shouts from the hecklers. The other speaker was Mr. Carr himself, and although the hecklers were in full voice, he refused to be shouted down and managed to present his analysis of some of the local problems in Barons Court.

The staging of these large rallies by the respective parties was markedly different. Part of this was due to the fact that several constituencies joined together to sponsor the Wilson meeting. This meant that Labour candidates from several constituencies were entitled to share the microphone. The Tories shied away from cooperative ventures with their neighbors, and the Central Office was probably willing to let them have full sponsorship of the Hogg meeting because of the bleak Conservative prospects in North Hammersmith and Fulham.

A second difference in the staging of the two large rallies may have had even more significantce. Not only did several Labour candidates claim a share of the spotlight, but local constituency officials, ward officers, and key workers were given seats on the platform. In fact, the platform was crowded, just like the main part of the auditorium. At the Conservative gathering, on the other hand, the chairman of the association was the only constituency worker who was on the platform, and he chaired the meeting. Mrs. Danforth also sat on the platform, but she had no long record of service to the Tory cause in Barons Court. The fact that local workers were given recognition at one meeting and not at the other reflects an important difference in the orientation of the local leadership in the two parties toward the party organizations as such. These differences in outlook may be of some significance—a matter that will be considered further in Chapter 5.

Conservative Outdoor Rally

In addition to this large meeting in the Town Hall, the Conservatives scheduled a major rally near Hammersmith Broadway on the Saturday before the election. The Prime Minister was to be the featured attraction of this meeting, and the local Conservatives made elaborate preparations for his appearance. There was a great deal of worry that certain rowdy elements might try to break up the meeting—that the commotion at the Hogg meeting might have only been a dress rehearsal for the main event. While the Conservatives were worried about the safety of the Prime Minister, they were also concerned about the physical well-being of the interested citizens who would assemble to hear him. They were also aware of the possibility that a few rowdies displaying poor campaign manners might help to prevent a shift of some middle-class voters to Labour, especially if there was good television coverage of their bad behavior.

After entering into negotiations with the police, the Conservatives were granted permission to hold their meeting in a small street just off the Broadway, where thousands of people would be doing their weekend shopping. The street, however, could not be blocked off for the entire day; the police agreed to close the street to traffic if and when the assembled crowd filled the entire passageway.

On Saturday morning, a large flat-bed truck equipped with a strong loudspeaker and decorated with Tory posters and colors was parked on the side of the street. At ten o'clock several speakers, including Mr. Carr, began to attract a crowd. The speakers and sound equipment faced the sidewalk, and the crowd gathered in a space about twenty feet wide between the truck and a wall on the far side of the walk. The television men set up their cameras in the second- and third-floor windows on the opposite side of the street.

Those who were interested in disrupting the proceedings appeared shortly after the local Conservative speakers began to address the crowd. Some of them appeared to be in an aggressive mood. To them, Sir Alec was the exponent of a foreign policy they detested, and though he had surrendered his title, he was in their eyes the symbol of the aristocracy which they despised. But Mr. Carr proved to be the master of the situation. He was at home in an open-air meeting when a pugnacious challenge forced the adrenaline to flow through his veins. In his characteristic style, he laid the microphone aside and thundered out a justification of Tory defense policy.

A number of other Tory speakers from Barons Court took their turns on the platform, holding forth before largely hostile crowds during the morning and early afternoon. About half an hour before the Prime Minister was scheduled to arrive, the crowd began to grow larger. As people moved about to obtain a more favorable view, the largest number of them found places in the street behind the truck, while the early arrivals were in effect pinned between the vehicle and the wall. Then, just before the Prime Minister was to go on stage, the Conservatives shifted the microphone to the back of the truck so that it faced the largest part of the crowd. This meant that the hecklers who had come early to get favorable locations found themselves to the side and partly behind the speaker and in a very poor position to make their interjections effectively. At the same time the television cameras, which were focused upon the main speaker, were in a good position to pick up the rowdies in the background whose behavior became more frantic when they realized that they had been outmaneuvered.

At about 2:30 the Prime Minister mounted the makeshift platform and addressed a relatively quiet crowd of about 2,000 people who had taken time out from their shopping to listen to the country's leader.

Other Activities of the Candidates

The crowds at the small indoor meetings were not large, and even the huge audiences at the mass rallies represented only a tiny proportion of the electors in Barons Court. For this reason each of the two parties recognized the need to project the personal image of its candidate before those voters who would not take the initiative to attend a public meeting.

On the Labour side, Mr. Richard's desire to meet as many constituents as possible prompted him to accept several invitations to address private gatherings, including a workingmen's club, a convent, and a policemen's residence. He also held personal interviews with about fifteen delegations of citizens who came to solicit his views on issues of great concern to them. The candidate, of course, received a large number of communications from electors through the mail, and he usually spent some time in the morning answering them. While most of these letters requested him to make his position clear on a major campaign issue (such as housing or nuclear disarmament), some asked him for his opinion on such matters as Sunday observance, decimal coinage, kindness to animals, and parking meters, and occasionally a voter would describe in lurid detail a pet scheme which he felt sure would cure Britain's economic ills and for which he sought the candidate's support.

Labour did not organize a "circus" in the formal sense of the term. Mr. Richard made frequent trips around the constituency with a loudspeaker attached to his automobile, but no canvassers accompanied him and he did not stop to chat with voters. An extra set of sound equipment permitted the use of portable tape recordings, which included messages from the candidate on housing and pensions, from Vanessa Redgrave to women voters on the cost of living, and from an ex-Conservative lady on why she was voting Labour this time. Each of these recordings emphasized the name of Ivor Richard. Mr. Richard's consultation with people who wished to speak with him about particular issues was handled as a separate operation. When a canvasser encountered one of these "problem cases" on the doorstep, he filled out an "action card" giving the relevant information. The card was then sent through the ward organizer to Robert Owen House, where it was filed along with other cards from the same neighborhood. The candidate or his wife would then take the cards and make an effort to visit all of the people listed on them. Following through on these action cards, Mr. and Mrs. Richard made approximately 150 personal visits to the homes of voters who seemed perturbed about a particular issue. Although this personal attention resulted in the reaffirmation of loyalty by many potentially disaffected voters, it consumed a great amount of the candidate's time as he dashed about the constituency trying to catch people when they were at home. In the 1966 campaign, the Labour campaign leaders made a distinct effort to cut down on the number of action-card cases so that the candidate would have more time to devote to ordinary canvassing.

Like the Socialist candidate, Mr. Carr visited nursing homes and convents and accepted invitations to talk with small groups of voters. Most of his time, however, was spent with the circus, in which Mrs. Bowman placed great confidence—and for understandable reasons.

When she was the agent in Holborn and St. Pancras South during the 1959 campaign, she had worked with Mr. O'Brian in organizing the circus, and it was generally agreed that it had been an effective campaign device. In 1964 Mr. O'Brian was available for duty again, and Mrs. Bowman persuaded him to donate his services to Barons Court, where he was made responsible for the circus on a full-time basis. In addition to the director, the circus claimed the attention of a volunteer worker sent out by the Central Office who drove the jeep throughout most of the campaign, and a few canvassers who were available for work during the day. In other words, the Conservatives allocated considerable resources to this type of promotion activity.

The aim of the circus was to present to the voters in Barons Court the image of a party that was vital and, if possible, ubiquitous. "Make them think that we are everywhere at the same time!" was the way Mr. O'Brian put it. Each day, Monday through Friday, he would designate two neighborhoods in the constituency to be covered. If these areas were in polling districts that were not being canvassed from the main headquarters, notices were dispatched to the appropriate committee rooms requesting that canvassers be on hand in these neighborhoods by the time the jeep arrived. As indicated earlier, the plan was for the jeep to swing around the neighborhood several times while O'Brian announced over the loudspeaker that the candidate was in the vicinity and was available to greet anyone who wished to see him. At the proper time the canvassers were expected to swarm upon the doorsteps, and, before securing the ordinary canvassing information, they were to tell the occupants that the candidate was within reach for a brief doorstep chat if they were so inclined. The names and addresses of the people who wished to see the candidate were relayed to the jeep, where Mr. Carr could pick them up and make his calls.

In 1964, however, the circus rarely worked out according to plan. Often there were not enough canvassers for the operation to have the desired effect. More important, the candidate was not satisfied with the type of personal contact with voters which the circus provided. The friendly but brief and superficial greeting that was called for was a difficult ritual for Mr. Carr to perform; when a constituent wanted to discuss a problem with him, he wanted to devote a little time to dealing with it properly. It was not unusual for him to spend half an hour on a voter's doorstep earnestly discussing a problem with him. In the meantime the canvassers would have completed their work and other constituents would be growing impatient waiting for him to appear. On one occasion, for example, Mr. Carr became involved in a lengthy discussion with an elector on the BOAC specifications and procurement of the VC 10. At another time he spent about half an hour discussing the problem of school admissions with a perturbed mother. On both of these problems, as well as on others, he displayed an impressive knowledge of intricate and technical detail. Later investigation revealed that these two people who had consumed so much of the candidate's valuable time were dedicated Socialists who had never voted Conservative and were not likely to start doing so in 1964. But even if Mr. Carr had been aware of this fact at the time (he did not have this information), he would probably still have bent an understanding ear to their problems and their opinions. He conceived of himself as the member of parliament, not for Conservatives alone, but for all of the people in the constituency. While this type of behavior on the part of an M.P. toward his constituents reflected a commendable attitude, it nevertheless tended to slow the circus down and to generate frustration among the canvassers and other workers. Instead of presenting the picture of a vigorous organization, the circus sometimes conveyed the image of a sputtering machine which was capable of only halting movement.

On at least one occasion during the campaign, however, the circus achieved its avowed objective. Owing to a late morning start, the last stop before lunch came well after the lunch period. Just as the jeep pulled into a courtyard in front of a large block of flats, a dozen energetic canvassers appeared on the scene. The loudspeaker blared forth the news that the Conservative candidate was available to greet any resident. As the canvassers moved up from one floor to another, the Tory workers in the courtyard below could see the voters pasting the blue *Carry On, Carr* signs in their windows. Mr. Carr waved pleasantly to his supporters and took the microphone to thank them for putting up the window bills. He climbed up the stairs to see those residents who had expressed a wish to meet him, but since the hour was late and the hunger pangs were gnawing, he did not become engaged in any long discussions. This was a circus that exhibited a dynamic organization. While it may not have won over many voters, it did enhance the spirit and morale of the canvassers and other partisans who had participated in it.

Literature Distribution

Recognizing that street-corner and public meetings and the candidate's personal contacts would reach only a small percentage of the voters, the Labour Party launched a big effort to identify its candidate and its policies through a program of literature distribution, within the limits established by the statutory ceiling on expenditures. More than a year before the campaign was formally opened, the leaders had laid plans to seize the initiative in the political encounter. Within three days after the Prime Minister's announcement, the first piece of campaign literature—in the form of 20,000 brochures which featured Mr. Richard in congenial pose and a statement of his career and qualifications—was in the homes of Barons Court electors. According to a systematic program of distribution, 12,000 broadsheets with a standard Labour appeal on the inside and the back and a localized front page were sent out during the weekend of October 2–4 to voters in strong Labour areas; the deliverers were instructed to begin in their best streets and then to work out until there were no sheets left. The main item for mass distribution was the candidate's election address, which was delivered by free post to every voter on the register on October 9 and 12, just prior to polling day. The inside of the brochure, which, as we have seen, had been drawn up jointly with the North Hammersmith party in order to cut expenses, outlined Labour's program for housing, education, pensions, and the improvement of the health service, including the abolition of charges on prescriptions, the development of hospital services, and the raising of nurses' pay. In the realm of economic policy, this piece of literature promised the introduction of a national economic plan designed to stimulate enterprise, the development of an integrated transport system, the "restoration of the steel industry to the nation," and an incomes policy under which productivity and earnings would rise together. A short section on foreign policy stressed consultation and cooperation with Commonwealth nations, as well as increased trade and more aid in the furtherance of their development. The party promised to work toward "all-round disarmament," the strengthening of Britain's regular forces, and greater control by NATO partners over the alliance's nuclear weapons. In an effort to portray Labour as the party of progress, the standard portion of the brochure berated the Conservatives for the country's lagging rate of economic growth, asserting that economic expansion under new leadership would more than handle the cost of improved social services. As indicated earlier, no mention was made of Labour's stand on the question of Commonwealth immigration. The remainder of the election address, which was localized for Barons Court, included a photograph of the candidate, a separate picture of his wife and child, and a personal message from him stressing the need for better housing, education, pensions, and social services, and for fresh leadership to revitalize Britain.

In addition to these distributions, the party through its canvassers delivered selectively 1,000 standard leaflets appealing to old folk, 2,000 on the issue of high rents, 4,000 to women on the cost of living, 5,000 "candidate called" miniature leaflets, and 2,000 brochures entitled *Points from Labour's Plan*, which was an abbreviated version of the party's election platform. All of these items were distributed selectively in an effort to achieve the best possible impact. In addition, the Labour people distributed a limited supply of leaflets featuring quotations from Harold Wilson on the immigration question. This appeal emphasized that the Labour Party intended to retain control over the admission of immigrants until an agreed program had been worked out in consultation with the members of the Commonwealth. Labour, the leaflet pointed out, had opposed the Government's program of restriction because the Commonwealth nations had not been consulted and because it was based upon color prejudice. It promised that Labour would introduce legislation to ban racial incitement and discrimination, and it asserted that the real problem was the shortage of housing, which had existed long before immigration, and that bad landlords—colored as well as white—would be forced to mend their ways.

In the precampaign period, the candidate had sent out printed letters to the young voters and to people who had recently moved into the constituency. As the campaign advanced, certain groups of electors were drawn from the register, and a personal appeal from the candidate was enclosed in the envelope with the election address. These included 500 letters to nurses, another letter to 500 young voters, and 2,500 to the tenants of higher-priced flats which were vulnerable to rent decontrol but which would be subject to recontrol if Labour won the election. The candidate's aide supervised the dispatch of these special appeals to certain categories of voters from lists that had been prepared by Mrs. Richard.

While the task of preparing and distributing literature is an arduous one, and, in contrast with canvassing, the workers who engage in it see no quantifiable results for their labor, occasionally the reaction of an irate voter provides a brief interlude of comic relief. A day or two after a district had been saturated by his literature, the Labour candidate received the following letter from one of his constituents (whose vote he could hardly rely upon):

Dear Sir:

One of your canvassers put the enclosed leaflet through my letter-box.

Kindly note that the letter-box is not a thing to put rubbish through. It is for the mail and *Conservative literature.*

Yours very sincerely,

A Conservative

Mr. Carr's election address emphasized the theme that *The Tories Do Care* about such things as housing, education, and the social services, and that the average voter who is concerned with such matters would be better off voting Conservative than Labour. Attention was also drawn to the differences between Tory and Socialist defense policy and to the "thirteen years of prosperity" which the country had enjoyed under Conservative governments. The back of the address was reserved for a more "human interest" portrait of Bill and Mrs. Carr and of their long and impressive record of community service.

The Conservatives in Barons Court did not use as many different leaflets with separate appeals as the Labour people, and, with the exception of the "Rent Act" leaflet discussed below, they did not develop and distribute literature aimed at particular elements of the electorate.

Two leaflets purchased from the Central Office were given constituency-wide distribution. One focused exclusively on the defense issue and stressed the point that Britain must have nuclear weapons under her own control. The second listed on one side ten reasons for voting Tory and on the other side ten reasons for not voting Labour. Again, the big issue on both sides of the leaflet was defense.

Two major leaflets were prepared locally and were widely used. One reiterated the theme that *The Tories Do Care*, but emphasized the point that in a marginal constituency like Barons Court every vote counted, and that Bill Carr with a majority of just 913 votes could easily be defeated by the apathetic, stay-at-home Tory. The other leaflet listed all of the meetings sponsored by the Conservatives and was circulated in the neighborhoods near the meeting places a day or so before the meeting was to be held in that area. A special message advertising the Prime Minister's open-air meeting in the constituency was also distributed. The Tories gave their canvassers calling cards which were to be left at the doorstep when a voter was not at home along with a small card with Mr. Carr's picture and a short appeal to vote Conservative. But it is clear that Labour in Barons Court spent more time and money on more literature which was more selectively distributed. After the campaign, when Mrs. Bowman was asked about the campaign literature, she indicated that she would have preferred more selective appeals. But her own lack of planning time, her unfamiliarity with the constituency, and the use of a publicity officer from the outside made this impossible.

Confrontation between the Two Camps

An interesting feature of the campaign arose from the fact that the two parties had very little direct contact with each other. The leaders of each party had analyzed their problems and had mapped out plans to resolve them, and they exhibited virtually no interest in what the other side was doing. The prevailing attitude among the leaders in each camp could be expressed in this comment: "We have a job to do, and we have to get on with that job regardless of what the opposition does." On the Labour side, one could detect only casual comments that bordered on curiosity, and these invariably came from rank-and-file workers. Thus, for example, before the Conservatives had formally adopted their candidate, a worker who had come into the headquarters for canvass cards might remark, "I wonder when the Tories are going to get started." Or later in the campaign a canvasser who had just come in from a tour of the doorsteps might observe, "The Tories were out in full force in Grove Ward tonight."

In the 1964 effort, the two agents had virtually no direct communication with each other except for the formal exchange of election addresses for their respective files. The same pattern obtained in 1966, apart from two incidents which required telephone conversations between the two organizations. On one occasion a report reached the Labour agent that the Conservatives had hung banners from windows in some parts of the constituency. After investigating the matter, he got in touch with his opposite number in the Tory organization and informed her that banners were illegal under the election law. The communication was a courteous exchange, and the banners were immediately dismantled. A day or so later, a worker from North End Road telephoned the Labour agent to inform him that a car with a loudspeaker was going about the constituency with only a driver in it, and that it was illegal for an automobile driver to be broadcasting. When Mr. Clarke indicated that the driver was not using the loudspeaker but that the voice was coming from a tape recording, the explanation was satisfactory to the Conservatives.

By the same token, the two candidates had little contact with each other and there were few signs of confrontation between them. Although the level of campaign activity was high and both sides worked intensively for the parliamentary seat, they did not create the image of a personal contest between the two men. Mr. Carr had represented the constituency for five years, but the challenge of his record as an M.P. was not a significant part of the Labour campaign. Instead, the Labour people centered their criticism upon the record of the Tory Government. Similarly, the Conservatives did not attack Mr. Richard, but sighted their guns upon the Labour Party and its election manifesto. While the two men occasionally spoke in terms of verbal challenges, there was little actual dialogue between them in the sense that the public statements and challenges of one would be immediately answered by opposing statements and counterchallenges by the other.

Two factors help to explain the lack of personal confrontation between Mr. Richard and Mr. Carr. As is true in nearly all constituencies, there was no detailed coverage of the campaign each day by the communications media. References to Barons Court were to be found only occasionally in the London daily press, and the coverage by radio and television was even more sparse. The weekly editions of the local press in West London did carry frequent and extensive accounts of the campaign and occasionally they would report a challenge by one candidate to the other. But the fact that these newspapers appeared only three times after the announcement of the election stopped them from becoming the vehicle for a sustained exchange between the two candidates for the benefit of the public. Moreover, Barons Court is not an integrated community to the extent that some constituencies are, and there are no nonpartisan interest groups whose political concerns tend to coincide with the boundaries of the constituency itself. In constituencies where such groups exist (as, for example, a local rate-payers' association), it is natural for them to invite all of the candidates to appear at the same meeting. But there was little opportunity for these types of gatherings in Barons Court. The Fulham branch of the Campaign for Nuclear Disarmament did invite all of the candidates to appear before a meeting of "ban the bombers," but it failed to generate much discussion. Only the Liberal candidate, Mr. Knott, appeared in person, while Richard and Carr sent along the questionnaires they had filled out, and these were read to the group.

Two churches in the constituency came the closest to serving as catalysts for discussion between the candidates, although they could hardly set the stage for a major confrontation when the two audiences comprised a total of seventy-one people, including the candidates' wives and the two American researchers. The first was held early in the campaign at the Broadway Congregational Church, and the second encounter took place a week later at St. Mary's Church. The two major candidates, along with the Liberal standard-bearer, attended both meetings, and after each of them had made an introductory statement, they fielded questions from the audience. While there was a head-on clash between Mr. Richard and Mr. Carr on the question of the independent nuclear deterrent, and to a lesser extent on the role of the "public," i.e., private, schools in the educational system, these meetings did little to dramatize a struggle between two personalities. There could be only a minor confrontation because most of the questions from the audience evaded the major issues of the campaign, centering instead upon such moral questions as Sunday observance, the responsibility of government officials for moral standards, the censorship of obscene publications, and the curtailment of crime. Somewhat to the amazement of the Labour and Conservative candidates, they found themselves agreeing with each other on most of the religious and moral questions; as a rule they tended to join forces in an attack upon their Liberal opponent who revealed a position, not at a point between the major parties, but on the moralistic end of the spectrum and somewhat on the periphery of British political life. A similar meeting of these candidates was held before a group of old-age pensioners, but it too did little to generate a direct confrontation.

Apart from their association in this type of setting (in 1966 they had no joint meetings at all), the two candidates rarely saw each other. Their contacts were limited to an exchange of friendly hand-waves (usually followed by a private comment to their supporters) when their conveyances occasionally crossed paths on the hustings, and to an exchange of greetings at the count, when they both paced nervously up and down the aisles waiting for the final result.

Canvassing: Identifying the Party Supporters

The stumping, the public meetings, and the loudspeaker vans—all aimed at identifying the candidates and projecting the image of the parties—represented the most visible and the most spectacular features of the political campaign. But each party gave primary attention to and employed the bulk of its manpower resources in the canvass of voter intention and in the processing of information which the canvass made available. The canvass in Barons Court provides an interesting comparison between the two parties, because the planning and execution of canvassing activities at

Robert Owen House were different from what took place at 84A North End Road.

Labour Canvassing

When the campaign began, the Labour Party in Barons Court was conducting a mass canvass of unknown and likely Tory voters to determine their allegiance. Canvassers from all the wards would assemble at a given spot, using the agent's car as a "mobile committee room," and they would concentrate their efforts upon a designated area. On September 29, 1964, however, the pattern of canvassing activity was changed in accordance with the campaign plan, and in the well-organized wards the work on the doorstep was turned over to ward organizers. As noted earlier, in those wards where the organization was weak, central headquarters assumed responsibility for the canvassing or supplemented the existing organization.

At this stage in the campaign, the plan called for the canvassers to work everything except names on the register that had already been marked as "against," whether Conservative or Liberal. Special attention was paid to the "unknowns," who still numbered more than, 17,000, and ward organizers were urged to use their most experienced workers for this task. Similarly, the canvassers still paid some heed to voters who were listed as doubtful, and again the canvassing officer requested that experienced canvassers be used. But the main objective at this point was to recanvass all known Labour supporters whose sympathies had been detected by the recent canvass or from the canvass cards which had been used during the local elections earlier in the year. In contacting these Labour voters, the aim was to secure firm promises of support for Ivor Richard and to encourage them to put up a window bill. They were also requested to vote as early in the day as possible, since early voting made the tasks of election-day organization much easier, reducing the pressure during the after-supper rush hours.

The picture of the canvassing process will be placed in sharper focus if we examine briefly the operation of one of the ward committee rooms.[5]

The main committee room in Broadway Ward was located in the home of Miss Redgrave in St. Peter's Square, and was in charge of Mr. Winston George, the ward secretary and one of the local councillors from the district. In his role as organizer, George was in charge of six polling districts in Broadway (Ja through Jf) and two polling districts in Starch Green (Fc and Fd), which had been attached to his command for purposes of this election.

His long residence and active political life in the area had enabled George to develop thorough familiarity with his district; he knew many of his constituents by name, and was aware of their problems. As a ward representative on the borough council, he maintained contact with many of the residents between elections, and the organization, especially in the heavily Labour polling districts, was reinforced by close personal ties. Certain parts of the territory under his supervision, especially polling district Ja, were difficult to organize and to canvass properly because of the type of housing accommodation. A large rooming establishment, for example, housed between 750 and 800 ordinary workers, many of them Irish immigrants, but it was impossible for the party's activists to contact them directly because canvassers were not permitted on the premises. In another part of the district, more than 150 nuns lived in one home, and these people, together with a large number of nurses in a nearby hospital, were also difficult to canvass. All in all, there were about 2,000 voters in Broadway Ward who for the most part lay outside Labour's communication system. In certain establishments which canvassers were unable to enter,

5. Any of the several committee rooms could be selected for this purpose, since, as we have observed, they were organized in a highly efficient manner. The committee room described here has been chosen largely because of convenience and clarity and because the Liberal candidate was very active in this ward.

an effort was sometimes made to have the trade union representative or some other spokesman spread the word about the election among the residents and arrange to have some literature placed in the resting rooms.

Councillor George was fascinated by the challenge of efficient organization, and he worked hard to build an effective campaign machine. "A newcomer who shows up for work in a committee room will stick around," he said, "if there is an efficient organization." As ward organizer, Mr. George recruited a large proportion of his workers, and often sent them written notes to confirm their duty schedules. When these workers reported to the committee room in the evening, he quickly assigned tasks to them and suggested that they get on with their jobs. When some volunteers did not wish to canvass or were regarded as likely to be ineffective on the doorstep, they were sent out to deliver literature or were given other assignments. The people who were scheduled to go out canvassing were handed canvass cards by the ward organizer and told where to go. He had prepared in advance a set of small photomaps, and each doorstep worker was given a map of the streets he was to cover—a safeguard against his getting lost and a time-saver in terms of the instructions that had to be given. Thus, the work was well laid out for the canvassers, and there was a minimum waste of time.

When each canvasser returned to the committee room, the ward organizer went over the cards with him, asking questions about particular markings and making the final decision in cases of questionable responses. Mr. George made the permanent markings on the cards in ink. (The canvassers were always instructed to use pencils. The purpose of this was to enable the organizer, when the card was taken out again, to distinguish those voters on the card who had already been canvassed from those who had not been at home on earlier visits.) He then checked the information on the removal cards and action cards which had been filled out by the canvassers as they encountered changes in residence and problem cases. George's most important work, however, was to transfer the information from the canvass cards to his marked register. He was especially alert for any shifts in voting intention, whether to or from Labour, and he indicated these in colored ink. After the tally clerks had compiled the results of the evening's work on a street-by-street basis, George would carefully examine them and mumble to himself, "Tonight, according to our previous records, we had a 2 per cent shift away from Labour," or "We did all right on South Black Lion Street—we are well over our promises, compared with last time!"

In going over the information brought in by his canvassers, Mr. George made a report on removals and sent it to the removals and postal vote officer. As the campaign advanced, however, he began to process some of the removals himself. He also pulled the action cards together and sent them to the agent at Robert Owen House, but when he noted reports of certain disgruntled Labour voters, he sometimes went to have a chat with them on his own. Every two or three days, he totaled up the canvassing returns and sent a progress report to the canvassing officer. The ward organizer was usually in touch with the agent once a day to let him know how things were going, and when a problem arose and he needed extra help, he immediately contacted the people in Robert Owen House. He reported from time to time on the impact of the immigration issue and the complaints of council tenants, and occasionally he requested that the candidate pay visits to certain voters.

More than the party organizations in the other wards, the Labour people in Broadway Ward had to be concerned with the Liberal candidate. Until recently a resident in this district, Mr. Knott had stood for the borough council on several occasions from Broadway Ward and had developed a reputation in this area as the champion of the council tenants and a defender of hardship cases. As a third-party candidate for the seat in parliament, he sought to appeal to the Irish vote, which was heavily concentrated in Broadway Ward, by denouncing the partition of Ireland and casting himself as a "fighting Irish lawyer." He devoted most of his attention to local issues, and he frequently attacked the local council for the alleged neglect of its responsibilities. He demanded better housing, better schools, and better traffic controls, and he vigorously protested against inequitable rent increases for people living in council properties and against noisy diesel hammers and other disturbances to local residents. These appeals enabled him to make some inroads into Labour territory, especially in polling districts Jb and Jc. Councillor George and his workers were kept busy defending the local authority on the doorsteps of disaffected voters and writing letters to the newspaper in answer to Mr. Knott's charges. (On the eve of the 1966 campaign, they took pains to lay down several motions at the last meeting of the borough council in a bold attempt to "take off some of the shine" from the Liberal candidate by anticipating his attacks at an early stage in his campaign.)

During the campaign, Broadway Ward relied upon approximately twenty activists to carry on its campaign activities, although many more workers were tapped for duty on polling day. The number of canvassers who went out into the Ward on any given evening varied from three to fifteen, and generally averaged about ten. The pattern was similar for the other wards, which usually recruited from eight to ten canvassers in an evening. This meant that the bulk of the Labour canvassing in Barons Court was done by about sixty people, most of them residents of the wards in which they canvassed. Some wards, of course, were able to do their canvassing more efficiently (and probably more accurately) and more completely than others. Occasionally there were minor breakdowns in the machinery, as, for example, when a group of workers spent part of an evening canvassing on the Fulham side of the constituency instead of in Barons Court. But on the whole the laborious task of canvassing was carried out, with small waste of time and resources, by experienced people who were familiar with the neighborhoods.

From time to time, there were complaints that not enough

canvassers were available. Toward the end of the campaign, however, more volunteer workers from the other constituencies began to report for duty, and, according to the agent, about thirty people from the outside were used in canvassing activities. Mr. Clarke made an effort to distribute this supplementary help as equitably as possible among the several wards; otherwise, the ward organizers who had done well in organizing their canvasses would be likely to resent the fact that outside manpower was being sent to areas where the party workers had not been so industrious. Understandably, however, the pressures of the last few days of the campaign required that some groups of outside volunteers be dispatched to polling districts where the canvassing tended to lag. In the canvassing work on Sunday afternoons, Labour enjoyed the services of Miss Redgrave and a small group of television stars who added a bit of color to the doorstep activity and brought the party some publicity. On the last weekend of the campaign, some of the local councillors were recruited for added canvassing duty in the weaker districts, and some canvassing on a mass basis was organized out of Robert Owen House.

In its attempt to identify potential supporters, the Labour Party was able to establish some contact with Commonwealth immigrants, although it is impossible to determine the effect of this work. Late in September, a group of seventeen West Indians invited the candidate to appear at one of their apartments to discuss the issues of the campaign. His wife went with him. Richard explained Labour's stand on the immigration question, and then he discussed the future of the Commonwealth. As it turned out, the latter theme was inappropriate and was received with a dull silence of disinterest. In the hour-long discussion which followed, the immigrants—a very sophisticated group—raised questions about the parochialism of British education at the elementary level and recounted their experiences with discrimination in their daily lives. Toward the end of the meeting, some of them asked how they might assist the candidate in his campaign. The upshot of this event was that some of these people contacted certain ward secretaries who were thoroughly familiar with their territories, and they were put to work at their own request canvassing colored neighborhoods. In one ward particularly, the secretary was able to identify the colored voters for these special canvassers, who proceeded to contact immigrant electors in a "quality canvass," i.e., to establish rapport with influential people in the neighborhood and let the word filter through to larger groups of people who were accustomed to "personalzied politics." How many immigrant voters rallied to the support of Labour is a question that cannot be answered, but this activity certainly did the party no harm.

The party leaders took very seriously the information unearthed by canvassers about Labour voters who exhibited displeasure at one or another of Labour's policies and showed signs of abstaining or possibly even shifting allegiance. Where action cards indicated people suspected of moving away from the party's support, the candidate, his wife, or a local councillor made it a point to get in touch with them and try to win back their loyalty. Not all of these waverers, of course, had grown disenchanted with Labour over the immigration issue; more frequently their complaints had to do with housing or some local grievance for which they blamed the party, but for which it may not have been responsible. Sometimes the change in attitude was due to misinformation the voters had picked up. But whatever the source of disgruntlement, the candidate and his aides picked up the action cards periodically and dashed off to private homes to see what the trouble was. On one occasion, early in October, Mr. Richard visited six families who were reported to be shifting from Labour support into the doubtful category. He discovered that five of these cases were the result of faulty canvassing, and he was able to win back the loyalty of the household that had actually shifted. It must be realized, however, that the immigration issue generated considerable unrest among Labour voters, and since its impact could not be accurately gauged, it was a source of worry for party chieftains. As indicated earlier, the canvassing officer supervised a number of spot checks in Labour areas to make certain that the vast majority of the troops were holding firm.

Similar concern about the shifting sentiment of Labour voters was displayed by the Labour leaders in the 1966 campaign, largely over the question of increased rents for council tenants. Key party workers, including the candidate, made a strong effort to reinforce their support among the voters in council properties, and they tried to make a special appeal to these groups. Offsetting this slippage, however, was the discernible movement of some middle-class voters into the Labour camp, as revealed by the canvassing returns. On March 21, 1966, the canvassing officer reported to the agent that there was a slight swing toward Labour in most places and a much bigger swing in some districts. While he recognized that these shifts might be explained in part as the result of improved canvassing, especially in some Tory areas, he was convinced of a relatively big swing in some of the "educated" (but not high-income) districts and among middle-aged groups—people who had been reluctant to move into the Labour column in the previous election. Since these are the voters whom the Tories allegedly represented, he concluded, this appears to be a highly significant movement. On the eve of poll the organizer of Avonmore Ward—strong Conservative territory—counted a total of 62 shifts from Tory to Labour and 107 shifts from Tory to "doubtful" or "won't vote."

In the 1964 campaign, as the electioneering activities reached a climax, the canvassing officer began to fear that the party had not yet secured enough firm promises to claim the seat. On October 10 he dispatched a highly confidential letter to all ward organizers appraising them of this fact, and indicating that 1,800 additional promises were needed to win the election. He urged the ward secretaries to concentrate on areas that were likely to be the most profitable, but that in the last few days of the canvass it might be advisable to call upon voters who had been listed as Tory on the register, particularly in districts where shifts in allegiance might have taken place, probably as a result of rent increases under the old Rent Act. The canvassing officer then established quotas of additional Labour promises for each ward:

Ward	Quota
Avonmore	150
Gibbs Green	300
Halford	400
Margravine	400
Broadway	250
Grove	100
Brook Green	200

In the wards that were investigated after the communication had been issued, the organizers turned extra pressure on their canvassers in an effort to meet the new quotas.

No local party organization ever reaches the goals that have been set for it, because the targets are usually beyond what is realistically attainable, or is really expected. In 1964, the Labour Party was not able to collect all of the promises its leaders had hoped for, although the number recorded was respectable and represented many hours of hard work on doorsteps by a relatively small group of dedicated activists. What is noteworthy about their final canvassing results was the fact that the number of electors whose voting intention was unknown to them was still quite high, slightly more than 11,000. About 76 per cent of the electorate had been contacted. When the last canvassing reports reached the canvassing officer, he was able to compile the results as shown in Table 3.1.

According to the Labour appraisal, the unaccounted for electors in Avonmore Ward were largely Conservative votes, as was a sizable portion of those in Brook Green Ward. What the "unknown" electors in Gibbs Green Ward would do was anyone's guess. The large number of uncanvassed in Broadway Ward was due in part to the transient rooming houses, convents, and similar establishments which were difficult to penetrate; possibly 1,500 to

Table 3.1—Final Canvassing Returns : Labour

AREA	FOR LABOUR	AGAINST	DOUBTFUL	REMOVED/ DEAD	TOTAL CANVASSED	NOT CANVASSED	ELECTORATE
Avonmore	1,510	1,226	340	76	3,152	2,198	5,350
Broadway	2,636	1,246	263	578	4,723	1,738	6,461
Brook Green	1,600	849	185	471	3,105	1,255	4,360
Gibbs Green	2,429	2,079	450	751	5,709	1,890	7,599
Grove	3,626	981	982	1,066	6,655	551	7,206
Halford	3,214	1,053	651	580	5,498	846	6,344
Margravine	3,700	622	386	209	4,917	1,756	6,673
Starch Green	533	506	102	208	1,349	706	2,055
Total	19,248	8,562	3,359	3,939	35,108	10,940	46,048

2,000 of these unknowns, party leaders felt, were unused Labour votes. They laid claim, however, to a good share of the unknown votes in Grove, Halford, and Margravine wards. On the eve of polling, the canvassing officer was reasonably confident that Labour had enough promises to win, but he warned his colleagues that a favorable outcome depended upon how efficient the organization was in getting its supporters to the polls.

Tory Canvassing

As suggested above, the planning and execution of canvassing activities on the Conservative side followed a different pattern from that of Labour. At the end of August 1964, the Tories commenced a new canvass on fresh canvass cards. Although on the surface this does not appear to be a momentous decision, it does magnify greatly the manpower requirements to make the canvass effective. The manpower needs are amplified in two ways: (1) A complete set of new canvass cards must be prepared, and this means that an entire register must be marked so as to identify every party member, every removal, every deceased voter on the register, and every voter who has received a postal vote, and then the register has to be cut up and pasted on the canvass cards. (2) In view of the fact that it is virtually impossible to complete a fresh canvass in a month or six weeks, it becomes necessary for the information derived from previous canvasses to be integrated with the findings of the current canvass so that a maximum number of pledges can be realized. While the preparation of the canvass cards can be completed before the campaign proper, the collation of new information with information from the old cards must inevitably be done in the last hectic days of the campaign. Although the costs in terms of time and manpower are necessarily high, a fresh canvass brings worthwhile results to a political organization. Since the canvassers are not professional interviewers, their findings on the doorstep are likely to be influenced by their own predilections and by the information they have about a given voter before they ring the doorbell. An interviewer who has no knowledge concerning the previously stated attitudes of an elector is more likely to make an accurate appraisal of his voting intention than one who has access to an earlier canvass report. He has no cue on the fresh canvass card which might prompt him to interpret an ambiguous response one way or another.

Once they had decided upon a fresh canvass to be conducted quickly, the Conservatives laid plans for the management of the operation, and its pattern was much more centralized than Labour's. Over 50 per cent of the canvassing was directed from the central headquarters in North End Road. In considering the remainder, we have already seen that four polling districts were canvassed from two committee rooms which were manned entirely by workers from other constituencies, and that one polling district was the responsibility of the Young Conservatives; the balance of the constituency was canvassed from ward committee rooms which were under the supervision of workers in those wards.

The officer in charge of the Conservative canvass was Mr. John Markham, an example of the experienced personnel which the Tories were able to bring into their organization. For several years he had served as a Conservative agent, but he decided to change his occupation, not because of a diminished interest in politics or in the Tory cause, but because he disliked the pressures to which an agent is invariably subjected. Since his work as an agent had provided him with valuable experience in the management of political campaigns, he was entirely familiar with the strategic and practical problems involved in directing a canvass of voter intent.

Each day Mr. Markham came directly from his regular employment to 84A North End Road. At about six o'clock the volunteers who were to canvass out of the main headquarters began to arrive for their evening's assignments. Each canvasser met with Mr. Markham to receive the canvass cards, instructions on how the canvassing was to be done, and directions on how to get to the area he was to cover. This centralized system, however, tended to create some administrative problems. Between sixty and a hundred canvassers turned up for work five evenings each week throughout the campaign period. Over half of these volunteers came from outside Barons Court and most of the entire group of volunteers arrived in the half-hour period between 6:00 and 6:30. The canvassing officer handed out the assignments from a table on the second floor, and the volunteers formed a line on the stairway, waiting for their cards and instructions. Despite Mr. Markham's industrious efforts to get the canvassers on their way, many of them had to wait for fifteen or twenty minutes before they could get their materials, and, after having already put in a full day's work in their regular employment, some of them were not in the best of spirits by the time they were dispatched to their jobs. The line formed again between 9:00 and 10:00, when the canvassers returned from the doorsteps, for they had to report directly to the canvassing officer and explain some of their markings, indicating removals and voters who needed to see the candidate. An observer could hear occasional grumbling at what some canvassers perceived to be the inefficiency of the procedure.

The Conservative leaders had anticipated the problem and had assigned a Young Conservative to the canvassing officer to help direct the canvassers to the proper streets. Unfortunately, however, this arrangement did not work out successfully. As a result the congestion persisted throughout the campaign. This bottleneck naturally had certain consequences for the organizationsl effort. The most obvious was the waste in man-hours which could have been more effectively used in actual canvassing. Less obvious but of considerable importance was the decline in the morale of the volunteers. While no systematic survey could be made of the morale factor, some of the canvassers remarked as they left the building that they could ill afford to donate an evening of work only to be kept waiting in line. Since these feelings were not usually expressed

176

to a party official, it would be difficult for anyone to contact the dissatisfied canvassers again and try to get them back into the organization if they decided not to come back.

When the last of the canvassers had reported in, Mr. Markham's work for the evening was only half finished. He had to calculate the number of responses in each of the categories listed on the canvass cards in order to get the daily and cumulative totals. The removals had to be identified, and if the canvassers had not been able to ascertain the new addresses, special instructions had to be drawn up for the daytime crews which were charged with tracking them down. It was a rare evening when all of this work was done by midnight, and occasionally it was two o'clock in the morning before the final tasks were completed.

The canvassing that was directed from the ward and polling-district committee rooms was not inhibited by the bottlenecks which developed at the main headquarters and operated very much as in the Labour committee room described above. The number of canvassers who showed up on a given evening, rarely more than twenty-five and never over forty-five, was manageable. Except in those polling districts which were being canvassed entirely by outsiders, a much higher proportion of the volunteers were acquainted with the local area and did not require detailed instructions on how to reach the streets they had been assigned to.

It was noted earlier that the Conservatives also ran two committee rooms which were responsible for canvassing in four polling districts and which were manned entirely by outsiders. Except for problems that arose from lack of familiarity with the area and some minor irritations with members of the local association, these committee rooms were operated very much like any other outlying unit.

As we have already seen, the gathering of information on the political sympathies of voters through the canvass is only the first step in the development of an information base which is necessary for an efficient polling-day operation. The Conservatives prepared an individual pledge card for every voter who had indicated to the canvasser his intention to support the Conservative candidate. This pledge card contained the voter's name, his address, and his election registration number. The responsibility for preparing these pledge cards—a time-consuming operation, since there were more than 10,000 of them—fell to women volunteers who were available for work during the daytime hours. As a rule these were the same women who had prepared the canvass cards for the fresh canvass. One of the rooms in main headquarters was reserved for their activities, and day after day from mid-morning until late afternoon from seven to twelve ladies worked assiduously preparing canvass cards in the early phase of the campaign and copying names of Tory voters from canvass cards to pledge cards in the later stages of the campaign.

The leader of this group was Mrs. Green; she had given more than thirty years of service to the party's cause. She had been involved in this type of clerical operation in many previous campaigns, and knew exactly how to organize it. Most of the women who worked with her were members of the Women's Branch in Barons Court, and they represented a spectrum of the middle class and some elements of the aristocracy in British society. On many days during the campaign, one could observe a long, black Rolls-Royce parked on a side street next to 84A, with a chauffeur crouched behind the wheel, usually reading a popular magazine. This was a sign that Lady North was sitting at a table in the second-floor room of the headquarters copying in a firm and dignified hand the names of hundreds of Tory promises on pledge cards. In the same room one could find a matronly member of the lower-middle class whose accent revealed that she had not had much opportunity for advanced education and who probably had to watch her monetary resources rather closely.

The organization of this group of clerical workers was an important asset to the party in many respects, but it also placed some restraints upon campaign officials. On the positive side, the agent could be assured that the vital clerical operations would be carried out competently in the traditional manner. As a somewhat limiting factor, however, there was little chance that the agent or the person in charge of the central committee room would be able to modify traditional procedures even if they thought that they had a better way of doing things. The organization of Mrs. Green's group also introduced an element of inflexibility into the allocation of manpower resources for urgent tasks. The women who handled these clerical assignments were a tightly knit group which usually had set tasks to perform. If more help was needed for some rush job, another group could have been set up in another room and put to work under the supervision of the clerk in charge. The ladies working with Mrs. Green, however, wanted to stay together as an integrated unit, and even if this group had more help than could be used efficiently, it was difficult to persuade the women to form part of a new group with a different assignment.

Although the rigidity of this clerical operation was a source of potential conflict, difficulties were never allowed to blossom, because the agent quickly perceived the situation and tolerated the autonomy of the group instead of trying to make changes which might have generated hurt feelings. The clerk in charge continued to indicate her displeasure in subtle ways from time to time, but before long she too adjusted to the situation.

The battery of workers at central headquarters not only recorded information on voter intent but also processed additional information from the canvass cards. As we have already indicated, the Tory canvassers were instructed to be on the lookout for re-movals and to secure the new addresses if possible, and this information was channeled to central headquarters where the absent voters officer picked it up. The procedure was to provide eligible voters with absentee ballots, and, after the deadline for filing postal votes, to line up transportation for people who had to return to Barons Court in order to vote, as well as for people who had changed residences within the constituency. The appropriate information on transportation needs had to be put in the hands of the transportation officer.

The canvassers were instructed to request information only concerning the voting intention of the respondents, but alert interviewers were often able to pick up additional information volunteered by the people with whom they spoke. This was especially true of certain disaffected Tory voters. A small merchant approached by a Conservative canvasser might respond with a dissident flourish, "I have always voted Tory, but after the bl———y retail-price-maintenance fiasco, I'm sitting home on polling day!" In such a situation, the canvasser was not to argue with the disaffected individual but was to suggest that he might like to speak with the candidate or the candidate's wife. In many instances the canvasser would receive a favorable reply, and he would make a notation on the canvass card to the effect that Mr. Craig Jones of 32 Beryl Road was unhappy about "R.P.M." and would like to chat with Mr. Carr. This information was then relayed to the canvassing officer. This was similar to the action-card procedure which was employed by Labour.

With each trip of the circus Mr. Carr had the name of at least one voter who wished to see him, and the candidate would make it a point to visit him at his residence. Sometimes Carr would spend an entire evening trying to locate voters who had not been at home when he had called during the day. In actual fact, however, a good many of these action cases were handled by Mrs. Carr, just as Mrs. Richard helped to perform this task on the Labour side. At about ten o'clock each morning Mrs. Carr collected her list of disenchanted supporters who had been discovered in the previous evening's canvass, and went on her way to make personal visits in behalf of her husband. She would often be gone for hours at a time making her rounds of the constituency and trying to contact those who were not at home on her first visit. Indeed, as the candidate's "alter ego," the wife had such a difficult and time-consuming job that one wonders whether a bachelor could ever operate a truly effective campaign in a marginal constituency. Both of the researchers in this study marveled at how the candidates' wives were able to spend their daytime hours walking briskly up and down the stairs interviewing voters, or preparing name lists for special literature distributions, and then appear on the platform at their respective public meetings looking charming and alert.

On the Monday before polling day, the canvassing machinery began to grind to a halt. The following afternoon, the final canvassing returns were available for study. They were recorded as shown in Table 3.2. These results—from a 63 per cent canvass—were cause for some alarm. Mrs. Bowman knew that the election could not be won with just 11,529 pledges. Her only hope was that 5,000 Tory voters would emerge from the 22,000 registered voters who were either listed as doubtful or had not been canvassed by the Conservative organization.

Reaction of the Parties to Crisis

Every campaign generates crisis situations, some of which develop from unforeseen events and some from the policy issues that have crystallized during the encounter. The campaign in Barons Court was no exception, for crises evolved in both the Labour and Tory camps, and the leaders of the two parties were called upon to develop strategies and to plan tactical maneuvers in order to deal effectively with emerging problems. A brief glance at the nature of the crises which developed during the two campaigns and how each organization responded to them will help illuminate some of the differences between the parties and their campaign strategies, and will also serve to underscore some of the issues which were perceived as having salient influence upon Barons Court voters.

In the 1964 campaign, the Labour Party in this constituency

Table 3.2—Final Canvassing Returns: Conservative

| AREA | FOR TORY | AGAINST TORY | | | DOUBTFUL | REMOVED/ DEAD | TOTAL CANVASSED | NOT CANVASSED | ELECTORATE |
		Labour	Liberal	Other					
Avonmore	2,218	922	14	0	302	174	3,630	1,720	5,350
Broadway	1,353	921	99	0	812	399	3,584	2,877	6,461
Brook Green	892	452	27	0	398	614	2,383	1,977	4,360
Gibbs Green	2,193	1,520	55	0	823	963	5,554	2,045	7,599
Grove	1,603	1,773	50	2	1,161	831	5,420	1,786	7,206
Halford	1,153	955	33	0	831	411	3,383	2,961	6,344
Margravine	909	918	14	0	526	237	2,604	2,437	5,041
Starch Green	785	405	10	0	96	176	1,472	583	2,055
Poll Dist. Oa	423	378	33	0	257	86	1,177	455	1,632
Total	11,529	8,244	335	2	5,206	3,891	29,207	16,841	46,048

faced only two emergency situations, a minor one which grew out of an unforeseen event and a major one which developed from a festering social issue. The critical point in the minor problem was reached on the evening of September 30, when the postmen in Hammersmith indicated that they would not work overtime if part-time employees were hired in post offices anywhere in London. If carried out, this threat would have posed a serious problem for both parties in Barons Court, for extra postal help was needed to get the election addresses delivered in time. The agent, the candidate, and several other party officials discussed the matter and began to make plans to handle the situation. It was agreed that if the threat grew more serious, Mr. Richard would make a public statement about it and, if necessary, talk to the postmen at a meeting. In the meantime the agent was to sort out the organizational problems which would be raised by the strike, and make tentative plans to have the election address delivered to the voters through the party's own distributive channels, although this would have been a costly operation in terms of the manpower resources being diverted from canvassing and other crucial tasks. As it turned out, however, the postal strike did not materialize, and the party did not need to implement its plan.

The major crisis for Labour in the 1964 campaign grew out of the issue of restrictions upon Commonwealth immigration. Although the proportion of colored immigrants in Barons Court was not as high as in some other places in London, they were a noticeable minority in the constituency, comprising as much as 5 to 9 per cent of the population in some districts. The influx of people whose color definitely marked them as immigrants into an area where adequate housing was at a premium exacerbated the difficulty and helped to stir up some resentment. The problem confronted many of Labour's partisans with a real dilemma. Many of them recognized the need for limited controls, so that the immigrants already on the scene could be absorbed more readily into the British community, but the mere thought of a "color bar" was anathema to them. Moreover, there was an important group of activists who were strongly opposed to any restrictions at all, except for medical checks and restraints upon the admission of criminals. The leaders of the Labour Party had long been aware of the fact that the problem of colored immigration was a disturbing one for many people, including their own supporters. In the early stages of the campaign, however, most of the party officials tended to play down the importance of the issue. They doubted that the question would significantly influence the outcome of the election, and they were extremely reluctant to anticipate the issue by making a public statement about Labour's position. They believed that such an action would only make matters worse by focusing undue attention upon a suppurative condition which was better left alone for long-term remedy. Mr. Richard was of the opinion that immigration would become an issue in the campaign, but he thought that they might get over it all right, and he wanted to avoid any electioneering on the question. As pointed out earlier, no reference was made to the issue in his election address.

Party workers, however, began to encounter the immigration question very early in the campaign. When it showed signs of dominating the Saturday street meetings, the official in charge of these gatherings reported the matter to the agent. After some discussion involving this official, the agent, and the candidate, it was agreed that the speaker should deal with the question the first time it was raised and then postpone further discussion until a set time later in the afternoon. This solution enabled the Saturday speakers to spend their time during the earlier part of their meetings discussing other questions.

Soon the canvassers began to report with increasing frequency that they were having to contend with the immigration issue on the doorsteps, and that some traditional Labour voters were expressing disenchantment with what they thought was the party's position, i.e., no or few restrictions upon those entering the country from the colored parts of the Commonwealth. (The Labour Party had come out for immigration controls in 1963.)

Party officials were understandably disturbed by these reports from canvasser visitation. Some of them urged that the candidate make a public statement challenging his Conservative opponent on the issue, and he did this in a limited way at a public meeting in Halford Ward—a speech that was reported in the local press. Other party leaders suggested that the candidate draft a special message to be distributed to the electorate, explaining his views and Labour's official position on immigration. Some members of the campaign team, however, indicated to the agent their opposition to such a written statement by the candidate. An action of this sort, they felt, would single out the colored population, when these people should really be treated as an integrated part of the electoral community. The agent himself hoped that the party would be able to sustain the displeasure of Labour supporters without taking any public action in the matter, since any public response from headquarters would merely draw more attention to the issue and the social undercurrents it represented. The agent, the candidate, and their colleagues discussed at great length the problem of how to deal with the issue fairly and effectively. At one point it was even suggested by some key workers (though the plan never reached Robert Owen House) that the campaign planning committee, which had gone out of existence several months earlier, be summoned to decide the appropriate strategy. The purpose of this idea was to spread responsibility for the decision so that no single leader could be unfairly blamed for any action taken. In the end, the people in charge of the campaign concluded that it would be best not to issue any local statement at all. Instead, the high points of Harold Wilson's speech on immigration—which he had delivered at Birmingham—were printed in leaflet form, and these were distributed on a limited scale in designated sectors of the constituency.[6] Party leaders, however, continued to keep a watchful eye on the situation, ordering a recanvass of selected streets from time to time in order to check on the degree of backsliding within Labour's ranks.

6. See above, p. 157.

In the 1964 campaign, the two issues that necessitated crisis decisions on the part of Conservative leaders in Barons Court were immigration and housing. Before the campaign had advanced very far, it had become unmistakably clear that the bulk of the wavering voters would be won over or lost on these two issues, the immigration question being a possible advantage to the Tories and the housing issue a distinct liability.

Of the two questions, immigration was potentially the most explosive issue, and one on which Conservative politicians could seize the initiative. As we have already observed, the greatest fear of uncontrolled immigration was probably exhibited by traditional Labour supporters from the working class, especially in those districts that had experienced an influx of colored immigrants. Indeed, many of these traditional Socialist voters had been concerned about Labour's opposition to immigration controls when the issue was being debated in parliament in 1961–1962. But for a Conservative to exploit the apprehensions of these Labour supporters, he would have to appeal to racial prejudice and paint vivid pictures of "exotic elements" alien to the native culture crowding into Britain's industrial centers, taking up housing space which might otherwise go to the home folk, and possibly threatening the jobs of Britishers sometime in the future. The exploitation of this issue in this way was something that Bill Carr could never bring himself to do; indeed, he would never even dream of discussing the issue in these terms.

In principle, Carr favored the integration of the colored immigrants with the rest of the British community, and on this premise he felt that there was a limited rate at which the country could absorb adult immigrants who adhered to different values and who generally had poorer educational backgrounds and lower levels of skill. In his view, some form of restriction was necessary if the influx of immigrants was to be kept within the limits set by the rate at which they could be absorbed.

Mr. Carr was as disgusted with Labour's policy on immigration as he was with Tory candidates who sought to exploit the issue irresponsibly. He considered that a policy calling for a set of negotiated agreements with the Commonwealth countries limiting entry into Britain was unrealistic, and he had persuaded himself that the leaders of the Labour Party knew this. In his opinion, Labour's official position on immigration was a dishonorable attempt to lessen the fears of their working-class supporters, while at the same time making an effort not to alienate those Labour activists who favored unrestricted immigration.

Thus, out of this complex issue there emerged a dramatic paradox for the Tories in Barons Court: a question upon which Mr. Carr held strong opinions and on which he personally was most put out with the Labour Party received virtually no attention during his formal campaign. His view that Labour's immigration policy was nothing more than a political shift to mollify their own supporters would win him few votes and might stir up the racial issue. So he chose to pay very little heed to it, even at the cost of victory.[7]

Although they devoted virtually no attention to immigration, the Conservatives were soon called upon to deal with the housing question, which was of concern to many voters and upon which they found themselves extremely vulnerable as the campaign advanced. This issue was not as passion-provoking as immigration, but it was almost as complex, and it evoked strong sentiments from nearly all types of Barons Court citizens. In November 1957, the Conservative Government had introduced into the House a rent bill which removed a large number of properties from rent control. This meant that landlords could charge what they considered to

7. Mr. Carr never made his complete position on the immigration question explicit to his supporters. More remarkable than the fact that there were Peter Griffiths who could defeat a prospective Labour Foreign Secretary in a Socialist stronghold is the fact that relatively few of the Conservative candidates sought to make use of the racial issue when it was to their political advantage to do so.

be a fair economic rent for their premises, and, since the supply was limited and the demand was high, the cost of rentals rose sharply. As it happened, 1964 was the year in which many tenants had to renegotiate their leases, and they were usually faced with sizable increases in their rents. Even if this had not been the case, however, the Rent Act would probably still have been an important issue in the campaign because the press had for several years been carrying stories of unscrupulous landlords who had badly abused the law. Moreover, the Labour Party had vigorously fought the Rent Act when it ran the hurdles of parliamentary debate, and the Labour struggle against it was carried forward into the 1964 campaign. We have observed that Labour promised to repeal the Rent Act and to restore security of tenure to tenants whose accommodations had been decontrolled.

In his indoor meetings and in his gatherings on the street corner, Mr. Carr encountered many questions on the housing issue, both from the hecklers and from people who were earnestly seeking information about the Conservative position. Invariably his response was that the only effective way to deal with the housing problem was to build more houses. The Rent Act, he argued, had encouraged and would continue to foster the construction of private homes, and this development, when added to an increased emphasis on public housing (which he favored), would hasten the day when London would no longer be plagued by a severe housing shortage.

But however sound they may appear to the experts, long-range solutions to social problems do not always win votes in the short run. Many electors who were suddenly faced with a sharp rise in their rents tended to see the Rent Act of the Conservatives as the major cause of their plight, and the propaganda of the Labour Party helped to reinforce this interpretation.

About halfway through the campaign, indications of the seriousness of this issue for the Conservatives began to arrive at 84A North End Road. The proportion of voters living in rented properties was very high even in the strong Tory areas, and they were obviously affected by the rise in private rentals. Experienced canvassers soon began to report that resentment over the Rent Act was running strong among voters who normally gave their allegiance to the Conservative Party. In the expensive flats in Avonmore Ward, for example, where the Tories had to turn out an overwhelming majority if they were to have any hope of winning the seat, residents were indicating dissatisfaction with the new round of rent increases. As they called upon voters who were action cases, both the candidate and his wife discovered the salience of the problem. A survey of canvass returns from Avonmore and other strong Tory districts revealed an abnormally high proportion of "doubtfuls" and "don't knows" in the electorate.[8]

Ten days before polling day the agent and the candidate discussed the possibility of getting out a "last-minute" leaflet. They agreed that the idea was a good one, but that it should focus upon a single issue rather than upon several. On Wednesday, October 7, just a week before polling day, Bill Snodgrass arrived at the agent's office to design the leaflet only to discover that the subject had not yet been decided upon. Since Mr. Carr's personal values and his analysis of the immigration issue ruled out this subject as the basis for a last-minute appeal to Barons Court voters, the attention of the leaders naturally shifted to the Rent Act. On this issue, of course, the Tories were on the defensive and could not expect to win converts from the Labour side by defending the Rent Act; the most they could expect out of such a position would be to keep Conservative voters from switching to Labour or from consciously abstaining. In a constituency in which the sitting M.P. was a Conservative,

8. The Rent Act may have been of greater consequence to the Conservatives in Barons Court than in other constituencies because of the low percentage of owner-occupiers and because a relatively high proportion of these owner-occupiers are probably traditional supporters of the Labour Party.

a strategy of this type—if it were completely successful—would probably be sufficient.

The last-minute leaflet, entitled "Rents and You. . . . A Message from Bill Carr," was written by the candidate and put in its final form by Mr. Snodgrass. In this message, Carr expressed concern that, since the passage of the Rent Act, increases in rents had been virtually automatic at the expiration of the lease periods, and he pledged himself to support any "measure designed to alleviate unnecessary or unfair burdens." The leaflet also called attention to the special commission which the Government had set up to study the problem of rented accommodations in the Greater London area, and it cited the pledge in the Conservative manifesto that ". . . additional safeguards for tenants will be provided if shown to be necessary by the inquiry into rented housing in London." The leaflet was mimeographed and delivered from door to door in the strong Conservative areas and to known Tory voters in other districts.

Although the immigration issue generated a sense of crisis in the Labour camp and the housing question created anxious moments for the Conservatives, both of these matters requiring high-level decisions by the respective party strategists, neither issue led to action and counteraction between the two organizations. Labour was worried about the potential effects of the immigration question upon its electoral fortunes, but the Conservatives did not take advantage of the issue. In the matter of housing, the Tories were on the defensive, but their response was not conditioned by any specific campaign strategy developed in Robert Owen House. Labour, to be sure, designed some selective appeals to disenchanted "Rent Act Tories" in places like Queens Club Gardens. But for the most part the two organizations passed by each other on the housing and immigration issues without interacting in each other's crises.

The 1966 election provided a much better example of how a local issue emerges in a parliamentary campaign and how one party seeks to exploit it and the other to counter its effect. The issue involved housing, but this time Labour was on the receiving end.

Council properties in the Borough of Hammersmith were losing about £167,000 a year. Some Tory members on the council, as they viewed the financial picture, anticipated that rents on council flats would have to be increased, and they saw that, according to the calendar of business, the announcement would not be made until the April meeting, after the general election was over. Here, then, was an issue that the Conservatives could exploit. When rents on private housing are increased, the landlord becomes a villain in the eyes of his tenants. When such increases are deemed necessary in council estates, the local council, as a special type of landlord, opens itself to biting criticism. In Hammersmith, the council was Labour-controlled.

As the formal campaign was about to commence, the leaders in Tory headquarters learned from one of their councillors that an increase in council rents would probably be levied. This information prompted them to design a special leaflet to be sent to all tenants in council properties. It warned them of the rent increase and blamed it on the Labour council. At an appropriate time the leaflets were enclosed in the envelopes that carried the election address to all registered voters residing in council flats. In some wards special canvassers, who had been thoroughly briefed on the rent issue, were sent into particular areas, each being responsible for all the canvassing in a designated block of flats.

About the time that the leaflets were being stuffed into the envelopes, the Tory cause was aided by wider circulation of news about the rent increase. When the borough council met to discuss the financial estimates for the coming year, the proceedings received ample space in the local press.[9] Rumors were quickly transformed into forecasts when the Labour chairman of the housing committee, in a letter to the editor of the local paper, reported that he was unable "to confirm or deny" that rents would be increased, since

9. For reports of the council meeting, see *Shepherds Bush Gazette* and the *Hammersmith Post*, March 24, 1966.

191

the committee had not yet brought in a recommendation and the council had not taken official action.[10]

Even before they learned about the Tory leaflet, Labour campaign officials knew that something was astir among their traditional supporters. Alarmed by rumors about the increase, many council tenants grumbled about the Socialist council. Before very long Labour canvassers began to report dissension on the doorsteps —a development that was soon reflected in the cumulative canvass returns. Already a few polling districts were straining to meet their targets, and the party was still some distance away from its goal of total promises. The competent canvassing officer had set up a system of bar graphs for each district, and, when the bar designating the number of "doubtful" and "against" voters began to edge closer to the target point than the bar for "supporters," he became perturbed. (That there was cause for concern was indicated by the fact that on the eve of polling day Labour was still 1,000 promises short of its goal.) His system of analysis, however, enabled him to tell at an instant what areas were in trouble, and he set about to discover what the trouble was.

After detailed study, including interviews with ward organizers and canvassers, the canvassing officer pinpointed three areas which accounted for more than half of the reduction in Labour pledges. The problem was largely one of dissatisfaction with local housing conditions, and the dissent took on renewed glow when the word went out about possible rent increases.

Signs of shifting loyalties on the housing question appeared first in Broadway Ward, which, as we have seen, contains a mixture of accommodations, including a number of council estates. When the ward organizer spotted trouble in council blocks under his supervision, he notified the authorities at Robert Owen House. In an effort to dampen the unrest in Labour's ranks, the candidate was sent to Broadway to visit thirty or forty voters who nursed grievances against the council. By this time the canvassing officer's bar

10. *West London Observer*, March 24, 1966.

graphs indicated that things were not going well in the ward, especially in polling district Jb and to a lesser extent in Jc. Shortly before polling day, the organizer of Broadway Ward revealed that the Labour promise was down about 2 per cent and that he would have great difficulty in meeting his targets. To offset the disproportionate rise of "against" and "doubtfuls" in what were normally Labour areas, party officials sent the candidate from door to door in several parts of the ward, and, as we shall soon note, they prepared a special letter for distribution among the council tenants.

Another lagging area was polling district Lb in Margravine Ward, strong Labour territory. When he saw the danger flag, the canvassing officer ordered a recanvass which was completed a week before polling day. In comparing the results with the promise and poll in previous elections, he identified the area of discontent as one made up of four roads. He found that the rent question was not so important in this district, although some residents were niggled at the Labour council on other grounds. Two roads consisted of owner-occupiers who were mostly displeased with the redevelopment program as a result of which they had been given notices to move. Apart from sending the candidate and experienced canvassers to visit the backsliders in this district, there was little more that could be done.

The third emergency area was polling district Mb in Gibbs Green Ward. Part of the lag in Labour pledges could be explained by the relatively large number of removals. But this was not the whole story. Party workers, during the third week in March, discovered shifts in loyalty in some council flats, and they listed the rent increase as the chief cause. Labour was in the process of plugging the holes in the Mb dike and was continuing to shore up its strength in other disaffected areas when a key worker discovered a copy of the Tory leaflet warning about the rent increase.

It was on Sunday morning, March 27—just four days before the election—when the Labour people found out that the Conservatives had distributed the rent leaflet in the council estates.[11] They brought the matter to the attention of Mr. Richard and some of his colleagues just as they were preparing to canvass in Grove Ward. Somewhat stunned by the Tory maneuver, they immediately notified the agent, who scheduled a "strategy session" at Robert Owen House that afternoon.

At this meeting the agent, the candidate, and several other campaign officials, including some borough councillors, discussed the question of what their response should be to the leaflet. They knew that the rent-increase issue, along with other housing problems, was likely to hurt them in the Labour strongholds. They sensed an undercurrent of uneasiness sweeping through the Labour camp, and they realized that they were going to have to be satisfied with fewer promises than they had originally hoped for. The distribution of a Tory leaflet among council tenants at this time would probably generate more unrest and make the situation even worse for Labour. But what, if anything, should be done about the leaflet? Some Labour leaders felt that the Tories had sent it out too soon for it to be very effective—that it might have had a more potent impact if it had appeared on the eve of poll. To prepare and distribute an answer, they suggested, would only call more attention to the issue. Most of the Labour officials agreed that a qualifying statement might be interpreted as a denial. This, they believed, would be unfair, since the Labour council would probably have to increase the rents for its tenants very soon (as proved to be the case). After a thorough discussion, the Labour strategists decided to send out a letter reminding the tenants that this was an election for the parliamentary seat, not a municipal election—that the time for arguing about the council's rent policy would come in the borough council election

11. The Conservatives in Fulham put out a leaflet of their own, but it was not as well done as the one in Barons Court. Obviously, on this maneuver no liaison existed between the Conservative parties in the two constituencies, although here was an opportunity for joint effort, since both organizations were attacking the same Labour council.

later. The candidate then drafted and signed a letter making this point, and it was distributed to council tenants, particularly in Broadway Ward, on the evening before the election. Having adopted this strategy, the Labour chieftains left the rent issue to the good sense of their traditional supporters and turned their attention to the campaign tasks that remained.

After this short excursion into the 1966 campaign, it is time for us to return to the 1964 encounter. The local issues in that campaign made the leaders on both sides visibly nervous. What would be the likely impact of these issues upon their respective clienteles? For Labour, the big question mark was immigration. For the Conservatives, it was the operation of the "Tory Rent Act," which had adversely affected their supporters through increased rents for private housing. Labour and Conservative officials alike could only guess at the potential effect of these issues and hope for the best. The answer would be forthcoming on polling day. As this important day approached, the leaders of the two parties set about with grim determination to put their polling-day machines into high gear in order to derive maximum benefit from the electioneering activities they had been conducting for so long.

CHAPTER 4

Mustering the Vote:
Polling Day

The tempo of political activities had noticeably heightened in both the Labour and Conservative camps during the last few days of the campaign. There was a last-minute push on canvassing, lists of pledges had to be prepared, and the eve-of-poll leaflets had to be drafted and distributed. By this time, of course, many of the procedures had become routinized, and as bands of outside volunteers began to show up with greater frequency, especially on the Labour side, more workers were carrying out the routine tasks without as much supervision as had been the case earlier. But by this time both of the organization machines were running relatively smoothly. The parts of each mechanism which were discovered to be malfunctioning had been repaired or replaced, and the friction-producing areas had been thoroughly lubricated. Both machines were now in such condition that they responded quite well to the increase in activity, and, as the two agents checked them over, each leader could be reasonably sure that his party organization could carry the load to the polling-day operation.

Advance Preparations

Effective and efficient committee rooms that are in close communication with the constituency headquarters, especially when the polling-day activities are fairly centralized, are the key to success on election day. On the Labour side, each ward had a main committee room from which the organizer had been directing the activities in his area. The campaign plan called for the establishment of other committee rooms in advance of polling day, in most instances one in each polling district to be located as near as possible to the polling stations. By polling day a total of eighteen Labour committee rooms were in operation, most of them in people's homes. In several wards, a number of committee rooms—in addition to the main one—had been in operation for some time, serving as headquarters for canvassing activities on a somewhat decentralized basis within the ward. In wards that had been directing their operations from a single committee room (as, for example, Broadway Ward), organizers and their helpers proceeded to disperse to outlying committee rooms on the eve of the poll, delivering the party records to these rooms from which the election-day activities in each polling district were to be carried out.

The Conservative polling-day organization was very similar to Labour's. It was even more decentralized, with twenty-two committee rooms having been set into operation. Two of these were almost completely manned by outsiders, and some of the key personnel in other committee rooms were not members of the Barons Court Association.

Mrs. Bowman had prepared mimeographed instruction sheets for the clerks in charge, clearly spelling out their duties. In addition to keeping the records and directing the activities of the knockers-up, the committee room staff was to provide transportation for those who would have difficulty in getting to the polls. In each committee room there was a board with envelopes attached—one envelope for each hour of the day—and the transportation request cards were placed in the appropriate envelopes. One could see at a glance about how many pickups would have to be made each hour. The responsibilities for transport were not heavy, because all removals who required transport were to be handled centrally.

The primary task of the people in each of these committee rooms, whether Labour or Conservative, is to keep an accurate record of their supporters who have already voted, and to direct the activities of those party workers who go from door to door to urge lagging supporters to get to the polling stations. In order to perform these tasks adequately, certain basic information has to be made available. The clerks in charge of a given committee room need to have a list in some form of the names and registration numbers of all the voters in the polling district who have promised the party their support, and a list of the names and addresses of voters who require transportation, as well as the time of day when transportation is requested. All of this information had to be assembled before the workers could go home on the night before the election.

The Labour system took notice only of potential Labour voters; electors who had been listed as doubtful, Liberal, or Conservative were by this time in the "against" file and were completely disregarded. Apart from the transportation requests, the clerks in a committee room had only two items to work with: (1) a huge sheet containing the registration numbers in sequence of all the electors who had given their firm promise to vote for the Labour candidate; and (2) a set of cards for each street in the polling district on which were typed or written the name, registration number, and home address of every Labour promise, all arranged in sequential order so that a party worker could take a card and go rapidly from door to door down one side of a street. The "knock-up cards" also had a space for remarks which facilitated the entry of information about particular voters who needed to have transportation provided for them.

The system employed by the Conservatives, though operating

on the same basic principle, was slightly more complicated. The Tories kept a record of both those "for" and those "against," with all those not listed as pledges being marked as "against." The long lists of registration numbers in each committee room were marked in blue to identify supporters and in red to designate all those against. In addition, every voter who had a postal or proxy vote was identified. An individual pledge card was prepared for each Conservative promise and arranged in order by street and house number.

Mechanics of the Polling-Day Operation

On the day of the election, each committee room was manned by two or three responsible people, one of whom was in complete charge. Activity in the committee room commenced shortly after the polling stations opened at 7:00 A.M. When a voter went to the polls, he encountered at the door at least two number-takers, or tellers, each wearing a rosette appropriate to his political affiliation. Although of questionable legality, he could refresh his memory on the name of his party's candidate by asking the number-taker outside the polling station. The elector then went inside to mark his ballot and placed it in the box. On the way out of the polling station he gave either his electoral registration card or the number on the card to one of the tellers, who then noted on a special form that this particular voter had gone to the polls. Each party, of course, had a number-taker at the door, and they cooperated in giving each other the registration numbers they had collected. After a teller had recorded a page of registration numbers and collected a batch of cards, he delivered them to a messenger—often the older child of a party member—who jumped on his bicycle and rushed the information to the committee room.

When the messenger arrived at the committee room with the list of registration numbers for people who had already voted, the clerks struck off the numbers from the master list. In addition, the name of the supporter was scratched in colored pencil from the knock-up card (Labour), or the pledge card was transferred from the "not voted" file to the "voted" file (Conservative). This meant that the records of these voters were now complete; these people were not vulnerable to any more contacts by any party workers during the rest of the day.

Periodically throughout the day—usually every hour or so, but more frequently after three o'clock—the clerk in the committee room would send in a report to central headquarters on the total number of people who had already voted in that polling district and also the number of party supporters who had been to the polls. In the case of the Conservatives, the reports included the number of "against" voters who had cast their ballots, as well as the total of party supporters.

The concern of every official and every worker in the two parties was to get their supporters to the polls as quickly and as efficiently as possible. Beginning shortly after the polls opened, some of the Labour and Conservative committee rooms began to process the requests for transportation, and this operation continued throughout the day, although the requests diminished in number toward evening, especially in the Labour camp. The drivers were supplied with cards indicating the time and place of pickup and the polling stations to which the voters were to be taken.

The two candidates were also preoccupied with the work of helping to round up their supporters. Early on polling day, each of the candidates and his wife began to visit their respective committee rooms to greet their workers and to help boost morale—a traditional feature of a candidate's activities on election day. But on the way from one committee room to the next, the candidates turned on their loudspeaking equipment to remind the people to vote. At various times during the morning and afternoon, the two men consulted with their respective ward organizers or other campaign officials and cruised with their loudspeakers through the streets where they expected heavy support, urging the voters to get to the polls and to mark their ballots in the "right place." As reports from the committee rooms began to flow into central headquarters, both the Labour and Conservative candidates started to devote more attention to streets where the polling had been slack.

What the British refer to as "knocking-up" is the final stage in the process of ferreting out voters who have been identified as party sympathizers but who have not yet made their way to the polling stations. The main objective of the resource expenditures in canvassing was to identify these supporters, and the door-knocking activity, which was carried out sporadically during the day and speeded up from later afternoon until the polls closed, aimed to capitalize on this information by urging the tardy voters to cast their ballots. The ordinary elector, of course, is not as keen about politics as the party activists, and in the comfort of his sitting room after a hard day at work, he may need a little gentle pressure to get him to exercise his franchise. This type of individual who might otherwise abstain is a clear target for the knockers-up. Without an effective polling-day organization designed to persuade a maximum number of these people to go to the polls, all of the effort which has gone into publicizing the candidate and which was spent in canvassing voter intent on the doorsteps runs the risk of being wasted.

These attempts to encourage a large turnout began fairly early in Barons Court. Shortly after ten in the morning, Labour volunteers scattered throughout sections of the constituency to distribute "Vote Labour—Vote Richard" leaflets to known supporters, using the knocking-up cards as distribution lists. They also embarked upon door-knocking activities on a limited scale until about five-thirty, when this work was undertaken with feverish intensity. By mid-morning the Conservatives, too, had instituted a more extensive house-to-house campaign to urge their supporters to vote early. Small squads of knockers-up operating out of each committee room took the marked canvass cards and proceeded to call upon people who were identified as Tories, reminding them of polling day and presenting them with a small card imprint with "CARR X."

Operating a complex polling-day machine obviously requires a heavy commitment of manpower. The assignment of committee room clerks, relays of number-takers working in one- or two-hour shifts, messengers, car donors and car drivers, and a veritable army of knockers-up involves the recruitment of hundreds of people.

In order to mobilize the necessary resources on the Labour side, the ward organizers were requested on the day before the election to estimate their needs and to report them to the agent, indicating the number of people in each job category who were available in the local district. With this information at hand, the agent allocated the outside workers among the various committee rooms on the basis of need. About a hundred volunteers from outside the constituency were used for knocking-up. Several cars were retained at Robert Owen House for the purpose of transporting these supplementary workers to their assignments.

In principle, the task was essentially the same for the Tories, although their problems were perhaps a bit more serious. The number of volunteers from outside the constituency on polling day was greater than those who reported into the Socialist camp. To employ these external recruits efficiently requires more time and effort than it does to handle loyal workers from the constituency organization who are familiar with the terrain and with the mechanics of the operation.

The pattern of centralized canvassing probably also made the establishment of committee rooms more difficult, because there were fewer intermediate ward committee rooms from which they had been operating. The agent had to be more directly involved in supervising the removal of records from central headquarets and in the establishment of the polling-district committee rooms. This is in sharp contrast with the Labour operation in which the establishment of the polling-district committee rooms was more of a ward responsibility.

A political lull settled over Barons Court on the eve of poll. The canvassers were off the streets, and the key workers were preparing for the committee room activities the next day. By 8:00 P.M. the twenty-two Conservative and eighteen Labour committee rooms were ready for action. A clerk in charge was at his post in each of them. He was responsible for directing the work of the squads of knockers-up, keeping the transportation moving to pick up voters at the times they had requested, and supervising the activities of tellers, runners, and the clerks who had to keep the records accurate and up to the minute throughout polling day.

From twenty-five to more than a hundred workers reported for duty at each committee room on polling day. It was impossible for one individual to keep track of all the committee rooms during the polling operation, but spot checks indicated that the Tories had well over 1,000 workers in Barons Court at one time or another during the day. If one considers the polling-day workers of all three parties—Labour, Conservative, and Liberal—it is likely that there was one polling-day worker in Barons Court for every sixteen to twenty votes cast. This gives us some idea of the effectiveness of the effort of the three groups to recruit manpower. It also gives us a notion of the problems of control and direction that faced Mrs. Bowman and Mr. Clarke on polling day.

A Polling-Day View from the Labour Side

Alan Clarke arrived at Robert Owen House shortly after sunrise, and after glancing at the final poll results in the *Daily Telegraph*, he made himself a cup of tea. He knew that his polling-day organization was set up on a decentralized basis and that its effectiveness would largely depend upon the performance of the leaders in the various committee rooms. He had trained them and briefed them for this responsibility, and now the outcome of the election depended upon them and the disposition of the voters in Barons Court.

Before very long the canvassing officer, the man in charge of allocating cars to the committee rooms, and a few other workers arrived on the scene to take their places in central headquarters. By 9:00 A.M. volunteers from outside the constituency began to show up, and the agent directed them to the committee rooms that were in most need of help. Soon the candidate and his wife drove up in front of headquarters, having already voted in Avonmore Ward. After a cheery word of greeting, Clarke instructed them to make the rounds of the committee rooms and to use the loud-speaker enroute.

By ten o'clock the agent began his hourly analysis of the polling reports which were telephoned into the information center at Robert Owen House. The figures enabled him to examine the rate of voter turnout in each polling district and the flow of Labour supporters to the balloting station in comparison with previous elections. He and the canvassing officer had to keep a sharp watch on these reports, because they would indicate whether any of the party units were in special need of help. If, for example, the per-centage of voter turnout appeared to be running low in strong Labour areas or if there was a relatively high proportion of Labour pledges who had not yet voted in certain districts, the agent could shift groups of knockers-up to the neighborhoods that appeared to be sagging.

As Clarke mused over some of the early reports, he realized that the Conservatives were in a better position than Labour to analyze the early figures on voter and promise turnout and to make the necessary shifts of personnel when certain strong areas showed signs of sluggishness. There was a very good reason why this was the case, and it was related to the differences in the voting habits of the two clienteles. Many of the Tory voters were able to get to the polls during the course of the day, and this enabled the high command at North End Road to determine how well the voters in their strongholds were turning out and whether they would need to exert an extra effort in certain districts later that evening.

But the pattern of Labour voting was markedly different. While some Labour supporters managed to make their way to the polling stations before going to work, a great many more postponed their trip to the polls until much later in the day. The prevailing pattern of the working man in Barons Court, as in other parts of London, was to come home from work in the late afternoon, wash up, eat a light meal, and then saunter to the polling station around seven or eight o'clock. If this election followed the general pattern, only slightly more than 40 per cent of the total Labour pledges would be redeemed by six o'clock. The agent shuddered at the possibility that the sun would shine brightly during the day while the Conservatives were garnering most of their votes, and then a downpour of rain around suppertime would discourage the Labour people from heading to the polling stations.

Mr. Clarke was aware of the fact that the voting habits of Labour supporters had important consequences for his organization on polling day. To begin with, his party workers had to round up nearly three-fifths of their pledges in a fleeting three-hour period between six o'clock and nine o'clock. Such a task naturally placed a heavy burden upon the organizational machinery. But he and his colleagues had learned to live with this situation, and he felt confident that, barring a great catastrophe, his organization could stand the strain on this particular polling day.

A more serious consequence of delayed Labour voting was this: the agent and his lieutenants were unable to tell with much precision during the morning and afternoon how well their support was holding up. In other words, the fact that so many Labour people would be voting after supper made it difficult for the officials to determine how many of the party's supporters had decided to sit this election out. About the only assessment that the Labour agent was in a position to make was whether the voter turnout in traditional Tory strongholds was inclined to be up, down, or relatively steady, as compared with past performances. When Labour voters started moving to the polls in massive numbers, there would hardly be sufficient time for the outlying committee rooms to relay information to Robert Owen House concerning the size of the turnout and the number of Labour supporters who were exercising their franchise. The committee room people would have all they could do to supervise the knockers-up. For this reason any sluggish areas would have to be detected by the ward and polling-district organizers, and if any transfer of resources became advisable, they for the most part would have to make the decision on the spot and order the diversion of manpower resources.

As the hours passed by, there were no signs of bottlenecks developing at central headquarters. The staff there were mostly engaged in directing outside workers and last-minute car donors to designated points throughout the constituency. There appeared to be just enough automobiles distributed among the committee rooms to handle transportation requirements without undue congestion. The main responsibility for avoiding obstructions and keeping the machinery running in the various districts had, of course, been delegated to the ward organizers and their assistants.

Toward the end of the afternoon, the Labour agent decided to make a tour of all the committee rooms to make sure that the machinery was ticking properly. As he drove his car through the streets of Barons Court, he began to wonder again whether his decentralized organization would hold up under the pressures that would be generated after six o'clock. He had turned over a great deal of responsibility to the ward organizers, most of whom, in consultation with him, had decentralized their operations further by delegating authority to other functionaries at the polling-district level. The party was fortunate, he felt, in that nearly all of the executive personnel in the polling-day organization at the various echelons had been under election fire in Barons Court many times before.

An examination of the work in the committee rooms revealed no major crises, only a few minor irritations. The organizers in one or two districts remarked that they could have used a few more knockers-up, while others indicated that they had never seen so many volunteers in previous electoral encounters. Such diverse comments suggested that the party had not achieved a "golden mean" in the distribution of its manpower resources, but no political organization operating under the heavy demands of polling day ever does. Some of the clerks in the committee rooms, intent upon keeping their master sheets and knocking-up cards in shape, became so preoccupied with this work that they complained about having to spend time in preparing their voter turnout reports for the central office.

One of the committee room organizers had accepted the challenge of squeezing out what few Labour votes there were in a heavily Tory district, and he was determined to get a vote out of *every* Labour promise. As the pressure mounted, he began to feel that some of his workers were not carrying out their assignments with sufficient zeal, and he proceeded to admonish them accordingly. This was a bit risky, since he had recently taken over the work in the district and was not well acquainted with the people under his jurisdiction. As he was urging his colleagues on to greater effort, a gentlemen entered the committee room to wait for his daughter, an election volunteer. Not knowing who the man was and unaware of the purpose of the visit, the organizer assumed that he was an election worker who should have been out on the doorstep. Hypnotized by the urge to get out the vote in this barren area, the organizer approached the gentlemen with a batch of knock-up cards and let him know in no uncertain terms that he should get off his posterior and out on the doorstep. He was later shocked to learn that he had, in a most unsubtle way, censured a titled member of the House of Lords.

One source of tension in some committee rooms was the relentless drive of the canvassing officer, who was conscientiously trying to get out the highest possible vote for the Labour candidate. His view was that a committee room with only two people in it is the most efficient, for this means that the rest of the personnel are presumably on the doorstep where the votes are to be won. He had warned party workers that he did not want to see any teacups in the committee rooms, nor would he tolerate people sitting around. According to his outlook, tea-drinking and comradely chatting would be appropriate activities on the day after the election. Some of his curt comments on polling day indicated that he meant what he said, and it took several days, together with an election victory, for the wounded sensitivities to be healed.

By five o'clock the staff at Robert Owen House had stopped analyzing the voting reports from the outlying committee rooms, and their activities were confined to the reception of workers from other constituencies and the assignment of these volunteers as supplementary knockers-up in polling districts that might be in need of help. At this point in the polling day operation, the attention of the agent and his colleagues was centered almost exclusively upon the organization of the knockers-up, since such a large number of the Labour promises had not yet registered their votes. Alan Clarke knew that his Labour partisans had a huge assignment to perform during the next three hours; he munched on a sandwich as the operation got under way.[1] A look of concern soon appeared on his face as a light rain began to fall. Heavy rains after 6:00 P.M. can dissolve the best of Labour's vote-getting efforts.

Each Labour committee room had a corps of knockers-up varying from six to more than two dozen, depending upon the size of the area and the strength of Labour support. Before sending the knock-up teams to their assigned streets, the clerk in charge of the committee room, who had in most cases been selected because he was knowledgeable about the area, checked the street cards to make sure that they were in sequence and were complete with the latest strike-offs (red pencil marks indicating that people had voted).

1. The knocking-up procedures were essentially the same in both the Labour and Conservative camps. However, we shall describe this activity from the Labour side, since that party was probably behind at this stage and faced a greater challenge.

The knockers-up then took the cards and dashed off on foot or by car to the designated streets. At the residence of every voter on his list, the party worker followed his instructions and addressed his respondent in this way: "I am from the Labour Party, and Mr. Richard is our candidate. I note that you have not as yet voted. Can you please come and do so now?" Usually the response was favorable, and the voter would put on his coat and head down the street. But if the Labour supporter indicated his intention of waiting for a time and going to the polling station a bit later, he could expect to be called upon again before the evening was over. Indeed, the Labour plan called for the blanketing of the constituency with knockers-up three times between five-thirty and the closing of the polls. Teams operating some distance from the polling stations were usually equipped with automobiles so that they could offer rides to the lagging voters.

As a rule it was considered better to send out two or three knockers-up, each carrying a few cards, to work about a hundred houses in two roads. This procedure made it possible for the polling-district organization to spread its workers throughout the area and to cover it in about half an hour on the first go-around. Such a tactic, the party leaders felt, was good for morale and presented the image of a well-organized campaign, with Labour people appearing everywhere at the same time. In addition to this advantage, the returns for the entire polling district tended to come back to the committee room very quickly.

Liaison between the knocking-up teams and the committee rooms in the polling districts was maintained by having messengers on bikes and scooters bring fresh cards to the knockers-up and carry the completed ones back to the committee rooms. In this way the workers were able to remain in the field the whole time. Whenever possible, car drivers were used to run a shuttle service between the teams in the streets and the polling stations.

A special type of knocking-up organization was set up in Broadway Ward, which was the largest in the constituency in terms of land area, embracing eight polling districts when Fc and Fd in Starch Green were added to the responsibility of the organizer. Although it was possible to set up Labour committee rooms in each of these districts, it would have been a strain on the manpower availability of people who were capable of supervising election-day activities at all of these points. For this reason, the ward organizer decided to command the strongest Labour sections himself from the main ward committee room, where he could give them his personal supervision. Two subcommittee rooms had been established on the eve of poll in other parts of the ward, each of them operating in several polling districts under delegated authority from the organizer. Each polling district, however, had an organizer of its own who was thoroughly familiar with his area and with the knocking-up system. Between 4:30 and 5:00 P.M., each polling-district organizer positioned himself outside a prearranged telephone kiosk, the number of which was known in the ward committee room and the two subcommittee rooms, and he remained at his post until 9:00 P.M. The public telephone made it possible for the ward organizer to get in touch with his lieutenant concerning any instructions that might be needed, and for the polling-district organizer to communicate with the ward organizer and the two subcommittee rooms when matters required special attention. The organizer was supplied with messengers who carried the knocking-up cards back and forth. He also had several teams of knockers-up at his disposal, as well as a number of cars so that he could provide lifts to the polls. All of the knockers-up who were assigned to the polling-district organizer were expected to remain with him unless he received instructions from the ward organizer to transfer them to a different area, in which case he would dispatch them in one of his cars. By effectively decentralizing the knocking-up procedures in this way, the ward organizer was able to keep his committee rooms free of people dashing in and out, and his clerks could thus get on with the task of scratching off without interference the names of people who had already voted. Moreover, the organizer had enough time to check the work in all eight polling districts, to transfer knockers-up to the sluggish areas, and to make his periodic reports to Robert Owen House.

When the door-knocking by Labour workers was commenced on a mass scale, the council flats were usually the first residences to be hit. The rationale for this was that Labour voters were likely to be most numerous in the council blocks and the easiest to contact. It was an amazing sight to see swarms of energetic knockers-up emerge upon a council estate like a colony of ants driven from their habitat by a foursome of beginning golfers. After this phase of the operation was completed, the knockers-up were distributed throughout a given polling district, going over it two or three times to contact people who were not at home or who did not respond on the first visit. Then, at about eight-thirty—just half an hour before the pools closed—the knockers-up began to move in closer to the polling stations, gearing their efforts to distance and time. So long as they could get a voter to put one foot in the door by nine, that voter was permitted to cast his ballot. At one of the polling-district committee rooms, two of the clerks left their clerical assignments ten minutes before the polls closed, taking some of the scattered knocking-up cards with them. "We can't do any more good here," they shouted, "and we might be able to get three or four more of our supporters to the polling stations!"

A Polling-Day View from the Conservative Side

Mrs. Bowman's directives to the clerks in charge were explicit. All committee rooms were to be opened by at least 6:45 A.M., fifteen minutes before the polls opened. The agent, of course, expected to be at her post at central headquarters well ahead of her key workers, and on polling day she was driving across London before sunup, and was hard at work at her desk before the voting began. There was little doubt that she was concerned about the polling-day operation. The organization she had set up would not work smoothly unless the twenty-four clerks in charge carried through to the letter on every detail. An efficient polling-day machine also needed knowledgeable, hard-working people in central headquarters. In an organization that was hastily revamped after having run for months without a regular agent, were the people she had appointed on the basis of limited information qualified to carry out the responsibilities? Would the outsiders she had brought in and assigned to some of the committee rooms be able to overcome their lack of familiarity with the area and with the organization? As these questions ran through her mind, Mrs. Bowman seemed to be anticipating problems. She did not have to wait very long before they began to emerge.

Trouble broke out at headquarters about the time the polls opened, and the source was not unanticipated. Much of the transport was to be handled centrally, including many of the early morning pickups, all internal removals, and many external removals. The transportation officer arrived early enough and set himself up in the main room next to the agent's office. But few automobiles arrived as early; in fact, not enough to meet the demands for pickups in the period from seven to eight. By scurrying around and calling upon workers who had come for other tasks, the transportation officer and other members of the staff could solve the problem of too few cars. But the sudden appearance of too many automobiles led to chaos.

Conservatives responded to their party's call for autos—after 9:00 A.M., that is—in the same way that the cabbies of Paris responded to Gallieni's call for transport to move troops to the Marne. By midmorning the central committee rooms were swamped with drivers from all over West London (and even further) who were prepared to carry the party faithful to the polls. Every parking space for blocks around 84A was taken up. Every five or ten minutes a frantic female would charge up to the transportation officer (ignoring the queue), and cry, "Quick! Tell me where to go—I'm double parked!" But there was little hope of a quick dispatch. Since few drivers were familiar with the area, most of them had to be given detailed and time-consuming instructions on how to reach a specified address. Finally, when so many drivers packed the committee rooms that they began to use the agent's office as a lobby, Mrs. Bowman intervened: "Disperse them among the committee rooms." They were then ordered, in blocks of four and five, to bolster the outlying forces. In this way the congestion was cleared, but only for a short period. Within half an hour the drivers began to return with the news that they were not needed at the committee rooms. Again the agent intervened: "Tell the committee room clerks to use drivers as knockers-up!" This information, however, should have been given to the clerks in charge of the outlying committee rooms. For some reason most of the drivers did not relish the suggestion that they park their cars and turn to the task of knocking on Conservative doors. A sizable number of them never found their way back to committee rooms.

In the midst of the confusion, a telephone call came for the agent. Since Mrs. Bowman was trying to organize the first voting reports from the committee rooms, was helping to solve the drivers' dilemma, and was dealing with many *ad hoc* requests, she was reluctant to take the phone. The caller, however, insisted that a committee room was facing an emergency. With her face drawn and signs of weariness from the relentless campaign beginning to show on her face, the agent took the phone. Slowly a broad smile broke through. "Well . . . get a lady—a respectable, middle-aged matron—to accompany her the rest of the day—every minute, that is!" It seems that a lady of questionable reputation had volunteered her services as a Conservative knocker-up, and in her quest for Tory votes—or Tory voters, as the case may be—was seen to disappear behind a door for almost an hour.

At this point Mrs. Bowman decided to tour the committee rooms to make sure that they were in good working order. At her first stop there was an air of efficiency and effectiveness in the polling-district headquarters. The clerks were going about their work with industry and calm, and squads of knockers-up were already out in the streets. Indeed, this was one of the few instances in which Mrs. Bowman was apparently successful in getting knockers-up who were working from canvass cards out in the morning. One of the clerks explained to Mrs. Bowman that she had gone carefully through the cards and had put a tick in front of the name of every Socialist voter in order to alert the knockers-up. On the other side of the room another clerk sat near the door, and she explained to the agent that she was doling out the cards to the knockers-up and instructing them to contact only those voters who had pencil marks in front of their names. The look of puzzlement on Mrs. Bowman's face turned to consternation and then alarm. She called across the room to the first clerk. "I say, whose names are you ticking off?" "Why, all the Socialists, of course," came the quick reply. Then the agent turned to the clerk at the door. "Whom are you instructing the knockers-up to call upon?" she asked. The look of horror on the face of the clerk was a sufficient answer. All of the people in the committee room suddenly stopped their work, and alarm spread over their faces as they realized that they had been expending their resources to get out the Labour vote.

Nothing quite so dramatic was turned up at the other committee rooms. Most of them were operating smoothly and getting their work done with dispatch. In a few rooms, however, the intense pressure tended to provoke personality conflicts among a few workers, especially those from outside the constituency, and these minor difficulties began to show signs of cutting down the efficiency of committee room operations.

The agent's tour of the committee rooms consumed nearly two hours, and, as the trip drew to a close, Mrs. Bowman had to content herself with just a short visit with the workers in the two committee rooms in Avonmore Ward because she was most anxious to get back to the main headquarters at North End Road.

Upon returning to her office, the agent began to check the

reports on voter turnout which had been sent in by the organizers in each of the committee rooms. These reports were cause for some concern. But, considering what she had just observed in one or two of the outlying committee rooms, she decided to get the official "percentage of poll" (the proportion of the electorate which had already voted) from each of the polling places. At 3:00 P.M., she began her tour of the polling stations in order to collect this information. After looking at the results during the next hour, Mrs. Bowman perceived the situation to be serious. While the size of the poll in district Ic was a respectable 42.6 per cent at 3:00 P.M., it was only 33.4 per cent in polling district Kb of Avonmore Ward and 30 per cent in polling districts Fc (Starch Green) and Ma (Gibbs Green). On the other hand, the strong Labour districts in Grove Ward had turned out about 24 per cent of the electorate, and in district Jb (Broadway Ward) and in district Na (Halford Ward) the size of the poll was 28 per cent. In light of these figures, Mrs. Bowman realized that if the Conservatives were to have a chance of winning, they should have a 15 to 20 per cent higher turnout than Labour by six o'clock.

Thus it appeared, from these preliminary returns, that Conservative voters were abstaining in sizable numbers, while there was a relatively good turnout in the Labour districts even this early in the day. Obviously something had to be done, especially in Avonmore Ward, where the Tory vote should have been much higher. Mrs. Bowman pointed her "mini" toward the Avonmore committee rooms with the determination of Nelson on the Bridge of Victory. Barons Court, however, was not to be a Conservative Trafalgar.

Despair and frustration permeated the atmosphere in the Avonmore committee rooms. Through no fault of the committee room workers, their records were proving to be unreliable. Under the election law, the returning officer is responsible for providing a separate polling station for every polling district. In Avonmore Ward, however, two separate buildings could not be found, even though the Conservative agent and the candidate had assisted the returning officer in his search. They finally decided upon Avonmore Primary School as the polling place for both of the polling districts, Ka and Kb. Efforts were made to insure that voters from the two districts would enter the building on opposite sides and would mark their ballots in different sections of the school. It was also understood that a barricade would be erected between the two voting places so that people would have to leave the building through the same door they had entered. The barricade, however, was never set up. This meant that after the voters had cast their ballots, they could leave the polling station through either exit. Hence, some Ka voters departed through the Kb door and vice versa. The tellers standing by their respective doorways were not aware of what was happening. They were unknowingly collecting registration numbers indiscriminately from voters in both polling districts and returning them to the committee rooms as if the numbers were from only one polling district. The clerks in both the Ka and Kb committee rooms were likewise unaware of the problem and were diligently checking off the names of their pledges. But, because of this mix-up, the records they were keeping so diligently were most inaccurate.[2]

The size of the electorate in Ka was slightly larger than in Kb, and it was not until midafternoon that the clerks in Kb began to receive numbers that were higher than any listed on their register. Then they suddenly realized that something was seriously wrong. Upon arriving at the Kb committee room, Mrs. Bowman immediately recognized that unless something was done quickly, there could be no selective knocking-up. Every Tory promise in Avonmore Ward would have to be contacted within the four hours remaining before the polls closed!

2. The Tory information problem was further complicated by the fact that the voters in Barons Keep, a Conservative stronghold in Avonmore Ward, had not received their poll cards from the returning officer. While this oversight did not prevent them from voting, it meant that they did not have number cards to turn over to the tellers after they had cast their ballots.

An emergency task of such proportion required manpower, and Mrs. Bowman, perhaps entertaining the vision of a multitude of car drivers waiting for their assignments, telephoned central headquarters for help. Unfortunately, however, the surplus of workers was no longer available. Some of them had already been dismissed; others, after having tried to make themselves useful without much success, had simply left. Plans were then made to recruit for work in Avonmore Ward the new volunteers who would be appearing for duty in the evening after their regular employment, and in the meantime to transfer workers from other wards. But there was a limit to the number of knockers-up who could be processed through two committee rooms in two or three hours. Hence, in the fourth and seventh most populous polling districts in the constituency, where the Tories had to run up a big majority, the inability of the party's workers to discriminate between those who had voted and those who had not made it virtually impossible for them to carry out an efficient knocking-up campaign. But they made a valiant attempt. After six o'clock knockers-up poured into Avonmore. Special leaflets, which had been prepared in advance for general distribution, were rushed into the ward. Some had the face of a clock printed on them with the hour approaching nine. The message implored the Tories to vote before it was too late. Other leaflets took the form of a facsimile telegram with a cryptic message expressing concern about the lateness of the hour. At the time it was designed, no one dreamed how appropriate it would be.

The polls closed promptly at nine. A minute later, the people in charge of the committee rooms began to collect the knocking-up cards and other records which were lying on the tables and put them in boxes to be analysed and stored later. While the policemen were sealing the ballot boxes at the polling stations preparatory to delivering them to the returning office at the Fulham Town Hall, the ward leaders and other key workers who had been lucky enough to obtain entry permits and had signed the oath of secrecy proceeded to the Town Hall to observe the "count."

The Count

In preparation for this important event, the custodians at the Town Hall had removed the chairs from the main auditorium and had set up tables to form a large *U* around the walls, with two lines of tables inside the *U*. On one side of each table sat two official counters, and positioned on the other side were the poll watchers—one from each party—whose job it was to scrutinize the ballots and the counting.

The officers and key workers from each political organization were listed as "visitors," watching the proceedings from the large stage. One or two of them had managed to get small transistor radios into the building, and, as they listened and reported to their friends the returns from other constituencies, occasional shouts of joy could be heard from the rival groups, depending upon the nature of the result. On the floor Mr. and Mrs. Carr, Mr. and Mrs. Richard, and Mr. Knott paced nervously up and down the aisles, stopping occasionally to chat with their party friends and less occasionally with each other. His worship, the mayor of the borough, who was wearing his chain of office, added a touch of dignity to the proceedings over which he presided. He was assisted by the town clerk who, adorned with the traditional wig, made the necessary administrative decisions sternly and impartially.

Each team of counters was handed a stack of ballots which were quickly separated into four piles—one each for the three candidates and one for the spoiled ballots. The counters then proceeded to count the ballots in the four piles. When the town clerk's assistant was satisfied that the total number of ballots in the four piles was equal to the number of ballots in the original stack, he recorded the results, tied the ballots together with a bright red ribbon, and placed them on a table in the center of the auditorium. As the counting neared completion, the mayor, the town clerk, and the candidates and their agents grouped themselves around a small table to make a judicious disposition of the ballots that had been designated as spoiled.

In a little more than an hour, the ballot-counting was over, and the mayor summoned the interested parties to the center of the auditorium to inform them of the results. Then, as a hushed silence settled over the assembly, the mayor, with the three candidates at his side, solemnly announced the outcome of the election: With 72.9 per cent of the electorate voting, the results were—Mr. William Compton Carr, 14,800; Mr. Simon H. J. A. Knott, 2,821; Mr. Ivor Seward Richard, 15,966.

Tumult and cheering instantaneously broke out among the Labour partisans, and the mayor had to restore order so that the remainder of the traditional ceremony could be completed. Mr. Richard, as the victor, was called upon to say a few words, and, after thanking his workers for their successful effort, he moved a vote of appreciation to the civic authorities for having conducted the count so efficiently and carefully. Although the runner-up is usually called upon to respond to the speech of the winner, this time the mayor handed the microphone to Mr. Knott, who made a few brief comments. Mr. Carr had fought a vigorous campaign, and now he listened to the results and the speeches of his opponents in silence—a tragedian denied by the ritual in Barons Court the opportunity to deliver a closing soliloquy. Only the close observer could detect slight signs of dampness in his eyes.

After the announcement of the result and the ceremonial genuflections to courtesy and good sportsmanship had been completed, the mayor adjusted his chain of office and stepped up to the microphone. "Now that a new member of parliament has been duly elected, I hereby declare that the count is now concluded!" With this announcement he brought down the curtain on the Battle of Barons Court, 1964.

CHAPTER 5

Putting the Pieces Together:
An Overall Assessment

W

hen the final curtain is drawn upon a theatrical performance, reviewers, commentators, and critics quickly move into focus to appraise the work. The purpose of this chapter is to present our review and analysis of the Battle of Barons Court.

In the narrative of the campaign, we have centered our attention upon the constituency party as an organization which plans and wages a political struggle within a given social, economic, and political setting. We have observed certain organizational, strategic, and tactical differences in the campaigns that were carried out by the Conservative and Labour parties in Barons Court. Were any of these differences crucial to the outcome of the election? One is even tempted to ask the question: Does local organization make any difference at all to the voting result? Although it is an enticing subject for inquiry, the latter question cannot be dealt with adequately without additional data gathered in other constituencies. But the first query—whether any of the differences between the two parties explain the victory of one organization over the other—lies within the boundary of our concern. In seeking to answer it, we can start by asking whether there were any significant differences in the effectiveness and efficiency of the Tory and Labour campaign machines.

Effectiveness and Efficiency

The significance of answers to question about effectiveness and efficiency depends upon how the two qualities are measured. The measurement problem, however, creates difficulty for the analysis of any political organization. We have attempted to evaluate the effectiveness and efficiency of the Conservative and Labour organizations in Barons Court on the basis of four different types of data. While none of these bases of assessment is adequate—they are crude measures at best—they do suggest leads for additional empirical studies and further theoretical development.

Voting Strength

Effectiveness in a political campaign must be related somehow to the number of votes a party gets—the more votes it gathers in, the more effective is the party organization. The difficulty with this gauge is that many other factors besides organization are operating to affect the number of votes that a given candidate receives. With all of these factors at work, it is difficult to isolate them in such a way as to measure the influence of organization per se upon voting outcome on the basis of a case study of one constituency. It is possible, however, to compare the result in Barons Court with the outcome in other constituencies, and this exercise might provide some clues for subsequent analysis.

Table 5.1 presents comparative data for Barons Court and three different groupings of constituencies with respect to voter turnout in 1964, the percentage of increase or decrease in the size of the poll compared with 1959, and the "swing" to Labour between the 1959 and the 1964 elections.[1]

Perhaps the most refined "norm" against which to examine Barons Court is that established by the London marginal constituencies with sitting Tory M.P.s. The first thing that strikes the eye is the comparatively lower turnout in Barons Court, which is in fifth place out of a possible eighth. Nor was the 1964 election idiosyncratic in this regard, for Barons Court was in sixth place in the same grouping of constituencies in the 1959 and 1955 elections. The fact that, compared with other districts with a similar political history, the size of the poll in Barons Court tends to be lower would suggest several possibilities: (1) that this constituency has a disproportionately high number of "removals" and "deads" on the voting register; (2) that there is a relatively high number of deliberate or disinterested nonvoters in the area; or (3) that a com-

Table 5.1—Voter Turnout and Size of Swing to Labour

(in percentages)

Area	Voter Turnout, 1964	Increase/ Decrease in Size of Poll, 1959–1964	Swing to Labour, 1959–1964
England	77.0	—1.9	3.0
County of London	64.7	—5.4	4.3
Conservative Marginals in London*	74.0	—4.5	5.6
Barons Court	72.9	—3.4	2.9

* A constituency is arbitrarily defined as "marginal" when the majority is 2,500 or less. The "Conservative Marginals" in this group include Battersea South; Camberwell, Dulwich; Holborn and St. Pancras South; Wandsworth Central; and Wandsworth, Clapham.

1. The basic data used in the preparation of this table have been taken from D. E. Butler and Anthony King, *The British General Election of 1964* (New York: St. Martin's Press, 1965), especially Appendix I; and *The Times House of Commons 1964* (London: The Times Office, 1965).

bination of both of these factors is at work in Barons Court. We have no information on these matters for the other Tory marginals, but we do know that Barons Court is a highly mobile area, and there is some evidence to indicate that deliberate abstentions were to be found among both Labour and Conservative voters, although more among the latter than the former.

Despite the comparatively smaller poll, however, the decline in voter turnout, compared with 1959, was significantly less in Barons Court, the second smallest decrease in the group. This might mean that, with a decline in turnout generally, the Barons Court voters were, relatively speaking, more highly motivated on their own, or were more highly mobilized by one or both of the major parties. Moreover, the swing to Labour in Barons Court was much lower than in any of the other Tory marginals, 2.9 per cent compared with 5.6 per cent for the rest of the group as a whole. The low rate of the swing can be partly accounted for by an increase in the Liberal vote of 1,055, a larger figure than the third-party increments in the other marginals. But even if this increase in Liberal votes had been distributed between the Labour and Tory parties at the ratio of two to one, the swing to Labour would still have been lower than the swing in the other constituencies.

The relatively low swing to Labour in Barons Court suggests several possibilities:

1. That the Barons Court Tories had developed an organization that was able to resist the adverse electoral tide better than were the Tory organizations in the other districts.
2. That the Labour organization in Barons Court was less able than its counterparts in other marginal constituencies to push the tide against the Conservatives.
3. That a higher proportion of the "removals/deads" in Barons Court were normal Labour voters than was the case in the other districts.

4. That a higher proportion of the Labour voters in Barons Court abstained than was the situation in the rest of the Tory marginals.

5. That the socio-economic composition of the constituency had changed in favor of the Tories, more than was the case in comparable constituencies, and/or

6. That the Conservative candidate in Barons Court, who had developed a reputation for being an excellent "constituency man," was able to extend his appeal into the ranks of the working class more effectively than Tory candidates elsewhere.

In considering these potential explanations, our research would definitely rule out the weakness of the Barons Court Labour Party as one possibility. The regional agent ranked the organization as among the best in the area. It also seems unlikely that a higher proportion of the "removals/deads" were normal Labour voters than in the other London marginals, although this conclusion is more intuitive, because we do not have a basis for comparing Barons Court with other London marginals. In light of these considerations, points (2) and (3) above do not seem to be reasonable interpretations.

A comparison of the election outcome in Barons Court with other marginal constituencies, however, is not a very fruitful line of inquiry. For one thing, the huge population turnover in Barons Court makes comparisons over a five-year period (1959 to 1964) questionable; and it is most unlikely that the qualitative changes in the electorate were duplicated in the other constituencies. By the same token, the rate of nonvoting—a choice that is open to the electors but which is not taken into account by the swing—is not likely to be uniform at successive elections or among constituencies, and thus can "distort" the swing. It may be, too, that the socio-economic composition of the electorate in Barons Court was significantly different from that in the other constituencies, and was for this reason more vulnerable to certain issues. The relative paucity of homeowners even in strong Tory districts, for example, and, conversely, the high number of voters in rented property, made the area susceptible to rental increases, and this may have occasioned a disproportionately large number of Tory voters to abstain, to vote Liberal, or possibly even in some cases to shift over to Labour. The comparison is also rendered more difficult owing to the personal popularity of the Tory candidate, who enjoyed the advantages of incumbency in 1964 and who had sunk deep personal roots in his constituency.

Identification of Supporters by Canvassing Returns

Some of these disadvantages could be overcome if, as a measure of effectiveness, we could gauge the outcome in terms of the stated objectives of the two Barons Court parties. The basic strategy of the Labour and Conservative camps was, as we have seen, very similar: each organization desired to identify its supporters in advance, and then to make sure that these people voted on polling day. With this objective in mind, both parties looked upon canvassing as their most important activity, and they poured a large proportion of their resources into this type of effort.

Although party organizers usually place great stock in canvassing reports, many journalists and political analysts are inclined to doubt their accuracy and to regard them as an unreliable predictor of what the voters will do when they get into the polling booths. A typical comment is that expressed by Professor Richard Rose:

> Canvassers tend to let their zeal bias the records, and show less skill than market research interviewers in allocating "don't knows." In a marginal seat, the number of uncertain voters in canvass returns is usually larger than the margin of victory. Furthermore, canvass returns are not likely to cover the whole constituency, and if they do, a

fair proportion may have been assembled from three to six months before the campaign.[2]

Because of the enormous commitment of resources by both parties to the canvass of voter intent, it is important to assess the accuracy of the information that is produced by this activity. To make this assessment, one would ideally select a sample from the voting register, check the information gathered from these registered voters by both Conservative and Labour canvassers, and then send out a professional interviewer, preferably just a day or two before the election, to secure an independent appraisal. Unfortunately, we did not have the necessary resources to carry out the analysis of canvassing in this way. As an alternative we selected a total of sixty-five canvass cards from among the Conservative records. These cards were chosen at random among polling districts, but the respondents within the polling districts were not selected randomly. The cards contained the names, addresses, and electoral numbers of 4,022 registered voters in eighteen of the twenty-four polling districts, as well as the information which the Tory canvassers had gleaned from these individuals. Identifying these voters only by polling district and electoral number, we then collected the information which the Labour canvassers had received from each of these 4,022 registered voters.

Not all of these voters, understandably enough, were contacted by both the Conservative and Labour organizations. The Tories established contact with 409 individuals for whom we found no markings on the Labour cards, and the Labour canvassers had markings for 555 voters on whom the Conservatives had no information. A total of 912 people listed on the canvass cards were not contacted by the canvassing teams of either party. The sampling of cards gave us a total of 2,146 individuals who had responded to the canvassers of both parties. By assuming that the information in the hands of each organization was correct when the registered

2. *New Society*, October 15, 1964, p. 5.

voter gave identical responses to both the Labour canvasser and the Tory canvasser, we have a measure of accuracy of the canvass. The degree of congruence can be seen in Table 5.2.

In interpreting this table, we should keep several points in mind. First, each Tory canvasser had five major categories from which he could choose in making his mark on the card: (1) Conservative; (2) Labour; (3) Liberal; (4) Doubtful (don't know, won't say); (5) Dead, Removal, Postal Vote, etc. The Labour cards gave each canvasser four major options: (1) For Labour; (2) Against Labour; (3) Doubtful (don't know, won't say); (4) Dead, Removal, Postal Vote, etc. Thus the probability that there would be congruence of response from any given registered voter if only chance were

Table 5.2—Overall Breakdown of Dual Responses

Areas of Congruence:

1. Listed as Labour by both parties	622
2. Listed as Tory or Liberal by Conservatives and "Against" by Labour	477
3. Listed as Removal, Dead, or Postal Vote by both	201
4. Listed as "Doubtful" by both	52
Total no. of Congruent Cases	1,352 (63.0%)

Areas of Non-Congruence:

1. Listed as Tory by Conservatives and as Labour by Labour	268
2. Listed as "Doubtful" by Conservatives and as Labour by Labour	219
3. Listed as Tory by Conservatives and as "Doubtful" by Labour	68
4. Listed as Tory by Conservatives and as Removal by Labour	27
5. Miscellaneous*	212
Total no. of Non-Congruent Cases	794 (37.0%)
Total no. of Dual Responses	2,146 (100.0%)

*This includes a variety of combinations, all of which had ten cases or less.

operating was 0.25. Each party organization, in addition, usually identified from its office records each of its dues-paying members and noted this information on the cards. Second, the Conservatives used about 400 different canvassers at various times, and the Socialists used slightly over 100. Third, the individual voters in our sample were probably contacted at different times. All of the information gathered from the Conservative cards was the result of canvassing activity during a three-week period before the election, but some of the Labour markings had been made in the previous summer. However, we have no way of knowing the time interval between one party's contact with a registered voter and the contact made with that voter by the other party.

In light of these three points, we find the degree of congruence amazingly high. Of the 706 registered voters listed by the Tories as being for Labour, the Labour canvassers gave the same appraisal on 622—88.1 per cent—of the cases. The Labour people listed 610 voters as being against them, and the Tory canvassers agreed with them in 447 of the appraisals (73.3 per cent). The degree of correspondence was not as high when each party attempted to identify its own supporters. The relevant information is presented in Tables 5.3 and 5.4.

Of the 1,138 registered voters whom the Labour canvassers

Table 5.3—Distribution of Labour-Designated Supporters

Total No. of Labour-Designated Supporters	1,138	100.0%
Area of Congruence:		
1. Listed as Labour by both parties	622	54.7%
Areas of Noncongruence:		
1. Listed as Tories by Conservatives	268	23.6%
2. Listed as "Doubtful" by Conservatives	219	19.2%
3. Miscellaneous	29	2.5%

identified as Labour supporters, 622 (54.7 per cent) were listed as Labour voters by the Tories. The Tories marked 783 voters as Conservative or Liberal, and the Labour canvassers identified 447 (57.1 per cent) as being "Against Labour." While at first glance these figures suggest that the canvassing was accurate in identifying supporters in only slightly more than half of the cases, further reflection gives them additional meaning. On polling day the two parties "knock-up" only those voters who are listed as supporters on their own records. Our comparison reveals that 268 of the 2,146 people in the sample—12.5 per cent—were listed as Tory voters by the Tory canvassers and as Labour supporters by the Labour canvassers. Although these 268 cases indicate the existence of error on one side or the other, they were all potential targets for "knocking-up" by both parties. We shall return to these disputed voters in a moment.

A different interpretation has to be made when one side lists an elector as one of its supporters and the other side lists him as doubtful. A total of 219 Labour-designated voters were marked as doubtful by the Tories, and 68 Labour doubtfuls were claimed by the Conservatives as supporters. We detected a tendency on the part of some voters to give affirmative support to the party of their

Table 5.4—Distribution of Tory-Designated Supporters

Total No. of Tory-Designated Supporters, and Liberals*	783	100.0%
Area of Congruence:		
1. Listed as "Against" by Labour	447	57.1%
Areas of Non-Congruence:		
1. Listed as Labour by Labour	268	34.2%
2. Listed as "Doubtful" by Labour	68	8.7%

* This includes those voters (46) listed as Liberal by the Tory canvassers. These have to be included in this category, since the Labour people did not distinguish between Conservatives and Liberals, listing them all as "against."

real choice, while indicating to the canvassers from the other side that they were doubtful. This seemed to be particularly true of working-class Labour supporters who were responding to middle-class canvassers from the Tory organization. It is not unreasonable to suppose that a high percentage of the Labour-designated supporters who were listed as "doubtful" by the Tories were in fact potential Labour voters, and vice versa. Assuming this to be the case, we could argue that of the 1,138 Labour-designated supporters, 841 (73.9 per cent) were likely Labour supporters, and that of the 783 Conservative-designated Tories and Liberals, 515 (65.8 per cent) probably favored either the Conservatives or the Liberals. If we assume that the Tories were accurate in picking up Liberal voters (46 were so identified in our sample), we could state that 469 of the 737 (63.6 per cent) Conservative-identified supporters probably favored the Tory candidate.

But let us make one further assumption. If we assume that the 268 registered voters who were listed as supporters by both parties were in fact either Labour or Tory, and that the errors were distributed equally on each side, then we could conclude that 134 of these voters supported Labour and that 134 of them supported the Conservatives. We could then argue that 975 of the 1,138 Labour-identified supporters probably supported Labour (85.7 per cent), and that 603 of the 737 Tory-identified supporters in fact supported the Tories (81.8 per cent). This analysis leads us to the conclusion that about 83 per cent of the Barons Court voters who were identified by the canvass as supporters of one or the other party were probably actual supporters of those parties. In other words, out of every twenty registered voters identified as supporters, about seventeen were probably in this category.

While the statement that the canvass was about 83 per cent accurate in identifying supporters has been based upon several assumptions, other aspects of our analysis of the canvass cards also suggest a high degree of accuracy. If the canvass was in fact very inaccurate, with many cards being checked in the comfort of a neighborhood pub rather than on the doorstep, we would still expect to find a certain degree of congruence between the two sets of cards. Indeed, if nothing but chance were operating, there would still be a 25 per cent agreement between Labour and Conservative markings. But if this were the case, every type of divergence would show up in equal numbers. However, our analysis shows that certain types of "wild" disagreement were virtually absent. For example, a registered voter listed by the Labour organization as being a member of the party was never listed by the Tory canvassers as being a Tory supporter, a leaning Tory, or in need of a postal vote. Similarly, the Labour canvassers rarely marked those voters who were members of the Conservative Association as being Labour-inclined, as needing a postal vote, or as "not likely to vote."

The most significant lack of agreement between the two sets of cards shows up when we analyze the "doubtful" category. But because of the tendency of supporters of one party to tell canvassers of another party that they are "doubtful," we would not expect much congruence on this item, and we would question the accuracy of the doubtful categories in the records of both parties. This lack of accuracy, however, is of little consequence, because it is only in exceptional circumstances that this information is used as a basis for action by either party.

The evidence from the 1964 canvass in Barons Court prompts us to register disagreement with those political analysts who contend that political canvassing is not worth the effort because the results are grossly inaccurate. But the justification requires another assumption: that a significant number of a party's supporters will not vote in the election unless they are "knocked-up" by the party's workers. Both the Conservative and Labour parties make this assumption; they operate in the belief that it is too risky to suppose that their supporters will go to the polls entirely on their own initiative. This is the next problem we must investigate.

Getting Party Supporters to the Polls

The total vote in the Barons Court election is not a good measure of how effective the two parties were in getting their supporters to the polling stations, because a significant number of the people who voted had not been canvassed by the party of their choice. For our purpose, we are more interested in the percentage of each party's pledges who actually cast their ballots. By comparing the Conservative and Labour parties in terms of the proportion of promises redeemed, we shall have a rough index of the relative effectiveness of the knocking-up operation of the two organizations.

After polling day each party analyzed the committee room records and calculated the totals of its pledges who were known to have voted. Unfortunately, comparable data for the two parties are not complete in every polling district. For the reason given in Chapter 4, the records in polling districts Ka and Kb are useless for our analysis, and for a variety of reasons one party or the other was unable to supply the figures in eight other polling districts. We do, however, have comparable data for fourteen of the twenty-four polling districts. These are reported in Table 5.5.

These fourteen polling districts contained 24,221 registered voters (a little over half of the 46,048 persons listed on the register in all of Barons Court), of whom 16,642 actually cast their ballots. The size of the poll in these districts was 68.7 per cent, slightly less than the 72.9 per cent who voted in the constituency as a whole. Of the 24,221 registered voters, 10,138 were marked as Labour pledges (41.9 per cent) and 7,193 were recorded as Tory promises (29.7 per cent). Out of its 10,138 pledges, the Labour Party managed to get 7,859 to the polls (77.5 per cent), while on the Tory side 5,608 of their 7,193 pledges actually voted (78.0 per cent). Thus, if we take as a measure the proportion of promises who voted, the polling-day operation of the two parties was equal in effectiveness.

An accurate interpretation of these comparisons, however, must take into account three points:

1. The Labour Party had conducted a more complete canvass and had accumulated more pledges; in order to equal the proportion of Tory pledges who voted, the Labour workers had to rout out nearly 3,000 more supporters than did their oppositon.
2. Working-class voters are less likely to go to the polls without prodding than are middle-class voters.
3. A higher proportion of working-class voters cast their ballots after six o'clock in the evening, thus forcing the Labour Party to cram its knocking-up operation into a shorter time period. Thus, even though the Labour people faced a much more difficult task, they succeeded in equaling the Tory percentage record in rounding up their supporters on polling day.

An examination of the subtotals in Table 5.5 shows that the two parties performed equally well in their strong polling districts, with Labour redeeming 84.8 per cent of its pledges and the Conservatives getting 85.1 per cent of their promises to the polls. The Tories, however, were more successful in the "leaning Tory" districts than Labour was in the "leaning Labour" areas—82.7 per cent, compared with 74.7 per cent. The Conservatives also produced better results in marginal district Mb. On the other hand, the Labour performance was better in the strong Tory districts than the Conservative record in the strong Labour territories.

Other available data provide an even more interesting assessment of the relative effectiveness of the two organizations. Labour received a total of 15,966 votes in the election. After polling day the committee room clerks were able to account for 14,287 Labour pledges who actually cast their ballots. This is not an exact figure, owing to the mixup in Ka and Kb and the fact that no analysis was made of the voting in one small polling district (Ja). However, the statistics suggest that only about 1,700 voters—slightly more than 10 per cent of the total—could not be accounted for from Labour's

Table 5.5—Effectiveness

POLLING DISTRICT*	ELEC- TORATE	TOTAL NUMBER VOTING		LABOUR PROMISES	
		Number	Percent of Electorate	Number	Percent of Electorate
Strong Labour:					
Lb	—	—	—	—	—
Gc	1,407	944	67.1	737	52.4
Na	—	—	—	—	—
Jb	2,312	1,751	75.7	1,408	60.9
Ga	3,393	2,381	70.2	1,759	51.8
Total:	7,112	5,076	71.4	3,904	54.9
Strong Tory:					
Ic	1,351	907	67.1	208	15.4
Kb	—	—	—	—	—
Fd	1,117	807	72.2	321	28.7
Fc	938	577	61.5	207	22.1
Ka	—	—	—	—	—
Total:	3,406	2,291	67.3	736	21.6
Leaning Labour:					
La	—	—	—	—	—
Jc	1,296	960	74.1	690	53.2
Oa	—	—	—	—	—
Gb	2,406	1,665	69.2	1,130	47.0
Hb	3,009	1,890	62.8	1,244	41.3
Total:	6,711	4,515	67.3	3,064	45.7
Leaning Tory:					
Je	622	465	74.8	217	34.9
Ma	2,669	1,800	67.4	955	35.8
Jd	499	375	75.2	196	39.3
Mc	—	—	—	—	—
Jf	501	366	73.1	156	31.1
Total:	4,291	3,006	70.1	1,524	35.5
Marginal:					
Nb	—	—	—	—	—
Nc	—	—	—	—	—
Mb	2,701	1,754	64.9	910	33.7
GRAND TOTAL:	24,221	16,642	68.7	10,138	41.9

* See Chapter 1 for a discussion of how the polling districts were classified. Polling district Ja is not included, since neither party was able to get an accurate assessment of its support because of the mobility of the electorate.

| TORY PROMISES† | | LABOUR PROMISES POLLED | | TORY PROMISES POLLED | |
Number	Percent of Electorate	Number	Percent of Total Promises	Number	Percent of Total Promises
—	—	—	—	—	—
354	25.2	685	92.9	255	72.0
—	—	—	—	—	—
490	21.2	1,094	77.7	376	76.7
744	21.9	1,531	87.0	466	62.6
1,588	22.3	3,310	84.8	1,097	69.1
640	47.4	157	75.5	522	81.6
—	—	—	—	—	—
468	41.9	263	81.9	392	83.8
316	33.7	164	79.2	298	94.3
—	—	—	—	—	—
1,424	41.8	584	79.3	1,212	85.1
—	—	—	—	—	—
315	24.3	503	72.9	230	73.0
—	—	—	—	—	—
692	28.8	905	80.1	515	74.4
719	23.9	882	70.9	490	68.2
1,726	25.7	2,290	74.7	1,235	71.6
244	39.2	187	86.2	229	93.9
1,082	40.5	646	67.6	825	76.2
184	36.9	146	74.5	179	97.3
—	—	—	—	—	—
191	38.1	124	79.5	173	90.6
1,701	39.6	1,103	72.4	1,406	82.7
—	—	—	—	—	—
—	—	—	—	—	—
754	27.9	572	62.9	658	87.3
7,193	29.7	7,859	77.5	5,608	78.0

† The number of Tory pledges listed here is greater than the number shown in the final canvassing report because additional promises were added from a previous canvass.

pledge lists. Although the Conservative records are not as complete, it is possible for us to make some estimates. It was noted in Table 5.5 that the number of Tory pledges listed for knocking-up purposes was slightly higher than that reported in the final canvassing returns. What happened was this: several days before the election each committee room added to the list of pledges drawn up from the autumn canvass the voters who had expressed support for the Conservatives during the summer canvass. If we assume that all committee rooms added names in roughly the same proportion as those on which we have information, the Tories entered polling day with 13,968 pledges. If all committee rooms redeemed an average of 78 per cent of their promises, the Conservatives would have been able to identify 10,895 of the 14,800 votes they received. This means that there were "in the woodwork" many Tory voters who were not discovered by the canvassers. Our analysis indicates that, whereas 77.7 per cent of the registered voters who were pledged either Labour or Conservative went to the polls, the comparable figure for unpledged registered voters was only 46.1 per cent.[3] Some of the difference can be explained by unlocated removals, but this category probably accounts for only about 10 per cent of the discrepancy. Hence, we are forced to conclude that canvassing and knocking-up activities pay important dividends.

The Tory Party's failure to carry out a more thorough canvass damaged its campaign. Our analysis suggests that approximately 3,900 registered voters who were not on the Conservative pledge lists nevertheless voted for the Conservative candidate. Many of these, of course, would have been picked up by a more complete

3. These figures are based upon an analysis of the data from the fourteen polling districts in which *both* parties compiled information on the number of pledges who actually voted. By combining the number of pledged voters in the two parties, we can account for 77.7 per cent of the total number of electors who actually voted in these fourteen polling districts. By comparing the number of registered voters with the number of actual voters who were not pledged to either party, we arrive at the figure of 46.1 per cent of the nonpledged registered voters who actually cast their ballots.

canvass. This, however, was not sufficient to produce a victory. But if the Tories had been able to increase their canvass by 11,000, they would probably have gained an additional 4,000 promises. If we assume that 1,500 of these people would have voted Conservative even though they were not recorded as pledges, the additional 4,000 pledges might have resulted in a net gain of 2,500 Tory-inclined voters who did not go to the polls in 1964. If these 2,500 pledges were redeemed at the rate of 78 per cent, the Tories could, theoretically speaking, have won Barons Court. In other words, if the Tories had managed to obtain a canvass of 87 per cent instead of 63 per cent, and had there been no mix-up in Ka and Kb, they might have achieved victory.[4] A canvass of 87 per cent would have required prodigious effort, and only the best of political organizations could reach such a high target. To do this, the Barons Court Tories would have had to develop a better organization than Labour's. This study indicates, however, that it was neither as effective nor as efficient. This judgment does not fault the Conservatives as much as it compliments Labour. In other words, if some of the problems we observed in the Tory camp had arisen on the Labour side and if Labour's canvass had been only 63 per cent complete, the Conservatives might have been able to hold the seat with an organization only marginally more effective than it was. This is to suggest that if an exceptionally strong Tory organization had encountered a mediocre Labour organization in Barons Court,

4. This task, to be sure, would have been difficult, but by this time canvassing had become somewhat less complicated for the Tories. We must remember that, although they contacted 5,000 fewer voters than Labour did, they were able to identify virtually the same number of removals, "deads," etc. This was possible because the Conservatives had concentrated upon the postal vote during the summer. All of the information from this early canvass was transferred to the fresh cards which were used during the autumn canvass. In other words, the Tory canvassers had knowledge about a high proportion of the removals; hence, their effort to contact a greater number of voters on the doorstep would not have been hampered by having to deal with the names of registered voters who were no longer in residence.

the election outcome could have been reversed. But this was not the case. According to our analysis, the most significant difference between the two parties is seen in the fact that the Labour organization, with fewer workers, was able to complete a 76 per cent canvass, clearly outdistancing the opposition and thereby gaining a decisive advantage.

Evaluation on Qualitative Grounds

There are other bases, more qualitative in nature, upon which we might assess the relative effectiveness of the two organizations. For example, the Labour Party by and large seemed to perceive its problems more quickly and to make the adjustments needed to cope with them. Although early in the campaign most of the Labour leaders misjudged the importance of the immigration issue and, under pressure from the printers, made a quick decision to ignore it in their election address, the organization nevertheless soon picked up the salience of the question and made a strategic response. The party also experimented with different ways of organizing the canvass, and when its plan for the establishment of units below the polling district level proved to be unworkable, the organization quickly abandoned it.

The Conservatives, on the other hand, did not perceive some of their problems as quickly, and their organization appeared to be less flexible in meeting these problems. The Tories, for example, were somewhat slower in picking up the widespread dissatisfaction that was associated with the Rent Act, and their response to the issue was not commensurate with the magnitude of the problem. By the last week of the campaign, there was a clear recognition by all directly involved with the circus that this enterprise was not a smashing success; yet it appeared to be too difficult to change the pattern, and no one tried to figure out a way to shift manpower resources from the circus to squads of doorstep workers who might tackle the problem of winning back Tory voters disenchanted by the operation of the Rent Act. Again, when the Conservatives encountered problems in organizing their canvass, it proved to be difficult for them to institute significant changes.

In addition, certain weaknesses appeared in the Conservative organization which were not encountered on the Labour side. The mix-up in transportation on polling day is one illustration of break-down in the machinery. Even more important was the inability of one of the wards that was responsible for its own canvassing to mobilize the manpower needed for the task. As a result, a group of canvassing cards was simply laid aside and never sent out—a development that was not uncovered by central headquarters until after polling day. Without knowledge of what was happening, the agent could not shift additional manpower into the ward. We have no evidence of similar breakdowns in the Labour organization.

Summary

The evaluation from these imprecise "measures" leads us to conclude that in Barons Court the Labour organization was, on the whole, more effective and more efficient than the Conservative. The reasons for this judgment can be seen from an assessment of specific operations in the campaign. The Labour canvass was more complete and more efficiently conducted. The organization perceived its problems more quickly and responded to them more flexibly. The Labour organization on polling day worked more smoothly. In this evaluation, a special point should be made about the *relative efficiency* of the two campaign machines. Compared with its opposition, the Labour Party was able to do more and do it more effectively with fewer manpower inputs and with identical financial inputs.

This conclusion with respect to the two party organizations and their relative performance, however, is difficult to relate directly to the actual voting result. It is impossible for us to say, for example, to what degree Labour's victory was tied to the more effective and more efficient campaign organization which the party was able to put into the field. Labour might possibly have won the election even if its machine had been inferior to that of the Conservatives. An evaluation of the role of organization in producing electoral victory cannot be made in the kind of study we have undertaken. However, it is possible for us to examine some of the factors that help to explain the differences in performance between the two parties.

Differences in Party Performance

When we speak of the Labour organization as being more effective and more efficient, it must be clearly understood that we are using the language of comparison. We do not mean to imply that the Labour organization was "good" and that the Conservative organization was "poor." On the contrary, from interviews we have had with regional and local party organizers on both sides of the political fence, both of these parties, when compared with other constituency parties in and around London, had *good* campaign organizations. But we are saying that, in relative terms, the Socialist organization was marginally more effective and more efficient. Such an evaluation naturally invites a further question: Why?

The Agents

In inquiring about some of the possible reasons for the differences in performance between the Labour and Conservative parties in Barons Court, one obvious explanation may be dismissed without much discussion. As one converses with professional organizers in Britain about organization matters, it is easy to reach the conclusion that most of the variation in the effectiveness of party organizations can be traced directly to the agent. Competent agents tend to develop good party machines; the agents with lesser skills or those who are employed only on a part-time basis generally have organizations that are less effective.

In our view, however, this generalization does not help us in analyzing differences in Barons Court. Both Mrs. Bowman and Mr. Clarke would be ranked among the finest professional agents in the country. In Mr. Clarke's case, the evidence is to be found in the portions of this study where the Labour Party is treated. Taking over an organization that had been weakened by internecine rifts, he welded it into a smooth-running machine which was able to win the 1964 contest and increase its majority in 1966.

While documentation of Mrs. Bowman's competence is to be found throughout the pages of this study, there is additional evidence to support the point. Although she lost the battle in Barons Court in 1964, we must not forget that she won the marginal seat in Holborn and St. Pancras South in 1959—a victory that brought Mr. Geoffrey Johnson-Smith into the House of Commons. Moreover, after leaving Barons Court, she did an outstanding job of organizing Hendon North. She became the agent in that constituency in 1965, less than a year before the 1966 election. In about ten months (with time out to have a baby), she built an organization that was able to protect a Tory seat which had a margin of only 1,124 votes. In an election in which some Conservative margins of more than 3,000 crumbled under the avalanche of Labour votes, Hendon North was saved for the Tories by a 600-vote majority, the swing to Labour being only 0.6 per cent, contrasted with a swing of 3.1 per cent in the London area. That this marginal seat was maintained as a Tory outpost appears to have been due to the organizational skills of Mrs. Bowman, as well as to the weakness of the opposition machine. Thus, it would seem that Barons Court in 1964 had two highly competent agents, and this factor on its own can hardly explain the performance differences between the two organizations.

Centralized vs. Decentralized Organization

If the talents of the two agents do not account for differences in organizational effectiveness, we must look elsewhere for an answer to the question we are posing. Let us turn first to that sphere in which the differential effectiveness is most clearly visible—the management of the canvass.

As we have noted, Labour clearly outdistanced the Conservatives by completing a 76 per cent canvass and obtaining a total of 19,248 pledges, while the Conservatives canvassed only 63 per cent of the electorate, garnering 11,529 promises for their party. As we perceive the matter, much of the difference in achievement may be accounted for by the inefficiencies of the centralized pattern of organization which the Tories were forced to employ. It is not our contention that centralization is inefficient per se; in fact, there are certain types of problems that are more easily resolved through a centralized structure. Much of the advantage that the Conservatives gained over the Socialists in processing the postal vote, for example, may be attributed to the effectiveness of their centralized operation. In order for us to make the argument pointedly, we must show why centralization appears to be beneficial for certain kinds of activities and a disadvantage in others.

To do this, we must first discuss the canvass as an informational problem, for it is, after all, merely a device for gathering certain types of needed information. In running an effective campaign, both aggregated and disaggregated information are necessary if the results of the canvass are to be of maximum utility. But these two types of information become the basis for different kinds of decisions which have to be made at different levels of organization. At the polling-district echelon, for example, disaggregated information is the most important. On election day, the polling-district committee room must have available the name, address, polling place, and registration number of every voter who has promised to support the party. At this level of organization, none of the basic decisions which have to be made depend upon aggregate information (such as the *total number* of pledges).

By contrast, the central headquarters makes little use of disaggregated information in its basic operations; it follows the progress of the canvassing primarily through the analysis of gross figures. If an examination of cumulative reports reveals that the canvass is lagging in a particular ward, the party leaders can direct more manpower into that area. Apart from those occasions when an individual voter desires to meet with the candidate, or when voters requiring transportation have to be identified so that their requests can be handled from the center, none of the staff at the main headquarters needs such specific information as the names and addresses of individual pledges.

Thus, under ordinary circumstances there are no significant informational advantages to be gained through a system of centralized canvassing. On the other hand, as has been pointed out in this study, a centralized operation does involve heavy costs. While their late start probably impaired the Tory effort to realize their canvassing objectives, the fact that they did less canvassing with more manpower can to some extent be attributed to the time waste incurred in processing the canvassers through central headquarters.

It must be emphasized, however, that in those cases where it is beneficial for the people at the center to have disaggregate information available to them, the Conservative machine showed up to excellent advantage. The most notable example of this was in the processing of the postal vote. The Tory system of "priority" postal votes and centralized registration of the postal voters required that disaggregated information be channeled to the main headquarters, and for this reason the party could derive advantage from centralizing the entire operation.

If the centralized management of canvassing activities was one reason why the Tory canvass was less efficient than Labour's, why did the Conservatives decide to adopt this system? It was certainly not because the agent favoured the centralized pattern; indeed, she preferred exactly the opposite. But, just as Mr. Clarke could not have employed centralized methods even if he had wanted to, Mrs. Bowman had little option but to reject decentralization. The reason for this was because of the weakness of several ward organizations. The Conservative agent simply could not run the risk of turning the important job of canvassing over to some of the outlying units. Had she been the agent in Barons Court for eighteen or twenty months prior to the election, she would have had more time to build up these ward organizations to a position of strength so that they would have been able to undertake more of the campaign tasks. (The wards were in a healthier condition by 1966, and the canvassing activities were more decentralized.)

All of the difficulties encountered by the Conservatives, however, cannot be attributed to the fact that the party was without an agent on a continuing basis for such a long time. A comparison of the two political organizations reveals two other differences which appear to have far-reaching consequences:

1. The flexibility of the agent in assigning tasks to the key workers in the campaign.
2. The capacity of the agent to maintain surveillance over functional units within the organization, particularly those that operated outside of central headquarters.

Flexibility in Assigning Personnel and the Problem of Surveillance

One of the striking differences between the two organizations lies in the larger number of full-time, or virtually full-time, workers in the Tory camp. Gladys Hendon was employed full-time to handle the postal vote. Pat O'Brian volunteered to work with the circus throughout the day, and he often did other chores in the evening; the circus, in addition, required the services of a regular, daytime driver. Mrs. Draper, the clerk-in-charge of the central committee room, was more than an evening volunteer. Whenever a visitor dropped in on the King Street committee room, he invariably encountered Mrs. d'Anton, who was supervising the canvassing and the distribution of literature in three polling districts. Besides these people, there were several local party activists who kept committee rooms operating during the day, and throughout most of the campaign a corps of enthusiasts from South Kensington were working on virtually a full-time basis. The chairman of the association appeared for duty on some mornings and on many afternoons, helping with the postal vote early in the campaign and turning to other jobs later on. Several ladies from the women's organization also put in long hours, some in clerical tasks and others in canvassing activities from midmorning until early evening.

Compared with this crew of Tory workers who made a heavy time commitment and were able to keep the campaign machine running at a fast clip throughout the daylight hours, the Labour organization appeared to be pitifully undermanned. Most of the key workers, including the ward organizers, had regular jobs which occupied them during the day, and, except on Saturdays and Sundays, they appeared for duty each evening after eating an early supper. The only full-time political workers at Robert Owen House were Russell Lowe, who was sent by his trade union to work in the campaign, spending most of his time on removals, and Sydney Ainsworth, the candidate's aide, who took a leave from his regular job. The canvassing officer was able to adjust his hours of employment so that he could appear at Robert Owen House when he was needed.

But while Mrs. Bowman had many more full-time workers at her disposal, she tended to be restricted in the assignment and reassignment of campaign personnel. This was noticeable, for example, in the crucial canvassing operation, which suffered from inadequate management and supervision. John Markham, the canvassing officer, was an experienced agent in his own right and had all the skills necessary to do a superb job, but he was able to work only in the evenings. When he appeared for duty, most of his time was spent in distributing and collecting the canvass cards—a task that would have gone more smoothly if the arrangement to have a good assistant assigned to him had worked out well. Since the Conservatives recognized canvassing to be the single most important job in the campaign, one wonders why Mrs. Bowman did not shift some of her full-time workers to help Markham with its supervision. After a week of circus tours indicated that this activity was not a smashing success, why did the agent not attempt to diminish the resources invested in the circus and reassign them, for example, to the job of identifying the "Rent Act Tories" in Avonmore Ward so that at least some of them could be brought back into the fold? Although Mrs. Bowman was very much aware of the difficulties, it was virtually impossible for her to make the necessary shifts in executive personnel in order to cope with these problems. In a real sense she lacked flexibility in reassigning her workers so that she could deal effectively with problem situations which emerged as the campaign unfolded.

Even though Mr. Clarke was operating under tighter manpower constraints, he seems to have had greater flexibility in assigning key personnel both before and during the campaign. Take canvassing, for example. Carlyle Thomas, like his opposite number in the Tory camp, was not able to work full-time. But when he was assigned to the job, it was known that he could adjust his employment schedule so as to be on tap on a fairly regular basis. By working the night shift from time to time and thus by piling up hours to his credit, he was able to spend half-days and occasionally a full day at Robert Owen House. It is important to note that, although Clarke had at his command very few people who could devote large blocks of time to the campaign, he saw to it that one of these activists was assigned to the crucial role of supervising the canvass.

The fact that the canvassing was handled on a decentralized

basis also made the job of the Labour canvassing officer somewhat easier. It was not necessary for him to spend time passing out canvass cards; he could devote his attention to directing the effort and to analyzing the returns. Moreover, the decentralized pattern of operation in the Labour campaign afforded a measure of organizational flexibility. If the work in a ward showed signs of lagging, the agent could move in supplementary aid from other wards or from headquarters, or transfer responsibility for a given task from a ward to central headquarters. Individuals who were assigned to one task could be subtly shifted to another job if the need arose. Mr. Wallace Franklin was a good illustration of this flexibility. A borough councillor in Fulham, he was selected as meetings officer by the campaign committee. He had made all the necessary arrangements for the public meetings well in advance of the campaign, and, once it was underway, he was called upon to handle only routine matters. Early in the campaign proper, the work in his home ward was behind schedule, and Franklin shifted his attention to this area, assuming major responsibility for organizing it. He directed some of the canvassing, he went out on the doorstep himself to deal with difficult cases, and on polling day he supervised the operation of one of the committee rooms. By the same token, when the agent saw that continuity of performance was needed in the job of addressing envelopes for special appeals to certain groups of voters, he consulted with the candidate's aide—a full-time worker—who took over much of this responsibility.

Before addressing ourselves to the reasons why the Labour organization had greater flexibility in the assignment of key personnel than the Conservatives, let us examine a closely related problem. While the decentralized pattern of organization adopted by Mr. Clarke has many advantages, all of which were recognized by Mrs. Bowman, it does create a major problem which does not arise in a centralized structure. It is far more difficult to maintain surveillance over a set of activities that are operated from five or six different centers than it is in a centralized organization where authority is concentrated, even though it may have smaller sub-centers.

While Labour had a more difficult surveillance problem, the party was able to handle it more effectively than the opposition. The agent and his colleagues working out of Robert Owen House picked up the salience of the immigration issue early in the campaign, despite the fact that no canvassing in the most affected areas was done from the center. Mr. Clarke also learned of weakness in some of the ward organizations and of the difficulties they were encountering in time to take corrective action before the effectiveness of the campaign was seriously impaired.

The Tory headquarters, by contrast, was slow to pick up the extent of the disaffection of the "Rent Act Tories." Knowledge about the undermanning in one of the wards and the consequent failure to canvass some of the territory did not reach the central authorities until after polling day, when the unused canvass cards were discovered. The postmortem after the election also revealed some canvass cards on which all the electors were recorded as "doubtful," with neat little check marks which looked as though they had been made in the comfort of a pub rather than on the doorstep.[5] It is significant for our analysis that in all three of these instances the canvassing was being done from an outlying committee room. The fact that these problems emerged in the wards where the canvassing was decentralized provides adequate reason for Mrs. Bowman's decision to centralize her campaign operation in spite of the costs involved. Where the work was decentralized, she was not in a position to maintain adequate surveillance over what was going on and thus lacked the information necessary to deal with the problems which arose.

We have identified three important and interrelated differences between the Labour and Conservative organizations which help

5. Some of the "suspicious-looking" cards were discovered before polling day, and a recanvass was conducted.

to explain why the Labour campaign was run somewhat more efficiently and effectively.

1. The Tories had more workers who contributed a good part of the working day to the campaign, but most of them came from Conservative associations outside of the constituency, and hence had no regular affiliation with Barons Court.
2. Although Mrs. Bowman had more executive personnel available on a full-time basis, she had less flexibility in assigning them to crucial campaign tasks.
3. While the Labour Party, with its decentralized structure had a more difficult surveillance problem and had fewer resources to cope with it, the antennae of the organization were more sensitive to difficulties in the outlying areas, making the necessary information available to the leaders at the center.

Mrs. Bowman's problems of achieving sufficient flexibility in personnel assignments and of maintaining surveillance over the units of the organization were directly related to the fact that most of the full-time Tory workers came from outside the constituency. Some of these people were personally committed to Mrs. Bowman, who had recruited them for a specific executive task, which in many instances they had carried out in previous campaigns. Other workers had been sent out from the Central Office, and here again Mrs. Bowman usually moved them into a specific assignment. From whatever outside source they came, however, a certain period of time was needed to "break them in" and to enable them to become acquainted with the members of the local association with whom they would be working closely. These outside people could hardly be expected to have detailed knowledge about Barons Court as a constituency or about the idiosyncracies of the local party organization. Quite apart from the fact that the agent felt an obligation to keep these outside workers in the posts for which some of them had specifically volunteered, she was concerned about the time that would be lost if she reassigned them—a reshuffling that would require them to go through another "break-in period."

Shifting personnel about during a three-week campaign can only be effective if the persons concerned can begin to function effectively in their new jobs right away; but the outsiders who came to Barons Court were not equipped to shift gears that quickly. The Barons Court Tories were unable to find enough local people who could devote sufficient time to the campaign. Veterans of previous elections, the outside people had made a time commitment to the Conservative Party and not necessarily to Barons Court. In other words, they had a larger option than would ordinarily be the case; if they could not do in Barons Court what they wanted to do, they were free to go into some other marginal constituency where their desires would be met. Mrs. Bowman knew what each of these key workers could do well, and she recruited each individual for a special purpose. Thus, each worker had an advance understanding with the agent as to what his responsibilities were to be. For this reason the agent was understandably hesitant about making any shifts in assignments; she did not want to impose duties upon any worker that she knew the individual might object to.

Even if they were willing and able to be reassigned, the people from outside the local party could not be assigned to surveillance tasks. In a voluntary organization, where interpersonal relationships are delicate, as well as important, effective surveillance can be carried out only by persons who are well known and respected in the organization and who have good rapport with the activities in charge of the outlying committee rooms. A stranger who is unknown to the ward worker would probably be percieved as a Pinkerton detective, and the local people might take steps to hide rather than to reveal the problems that were being encountered.

The point we are making will become even clearer if we examine, by way of contrast, the operation in the Labour camp at

Shepherds Bush Road. With one exception, the workers who carried the main burden of the Labour campaign were Barons Court people who were deeply absorbed in the affairs of the local party. Furthermore, most of them were longtime "professionals" in the politics of the district. For example, more than three-fourths of the personnel to whom administrative responsibility was delegated were borough councillors. In this capacity they had had direct contact with the voters in Barons Court in previous elections, they were thoroughly familiar with local problems, and, especially in the case of ward organizers, they not only had an intimate knowledge of the streets and polling districts under their supervision, but they were personally acquainted with the active workers in their wards.

The lines of authority between Robert Owen House and the committee rooms were very similar to those that existed normally. This meant that the volunteers who were working in their local bailiwicks knew the chain of command. They had grown accustomed to work with their ward organizers, and they respected the central officials who were supervising the committee rooms, often very subtly, from the main headquarters.

Although Mr. Clarke had confidence in his ward organizers and was usually in daily contact with them, he did not have to rely entirely upon their good intentions to keep himself informed about what was going on. The canvassing officer, not tied down every night by the need to distribute cards, kept his eye on the committee rooms, discussed the canvassing results with the ward secretaries, and studied the returns as they were reported. In this way he was able to detect areas that showed signs of falling away from Labour. Then, too, the social intermingling at the two meetings of the key workers resulted in a sharing of information which helped the agent to assess his organizational strength. In addition, the candidate and his wife went canvassing regularly, each time from a different committee room. This not only helped to bolster the morale of the workers in the wards, but it also gave them an opportunity to talk with workers and to observe the situation in different locales. With this experience, the candidate was able to give his impressions to the agent. When canvassers working out of a number of committee rooms began to pick up the salience of the immigration issue from their conversations on the doorsteps, the agent knew about it almost immediately, and he was in a position at once to discuss the matter with his colleagues and to plan remedial action.

If the Labour Party was more flexible than the Tory organization and was able to resolve the surveillance problem more effectively, largely because its active workers were better equipped to perform the necessary campaign tasks, we are confronted with another set of questions which cry for answers. Why did this happen? Why was the Labour Party in Barons Court able to recruit such a high percentage of its active workers from its own ranks, while the Conservative organization was not? Why did great numbers of Tories come pouring into Barons Court from the safe constituencies to engage the Socialists in battle, while activists from safe Labour districts were relatively inconspicuous at Robert Owen House and the outlying committee rooms? In order to answer these questions, we must first address ourselves to a more fundamental query: Why were so many workers in both parties willing to throw themselves actively into the campaign, often at considerable personal cost? An answer to this question should help us to understand the differences in the kinds of people who were involved in the Labour and Conservative campaigns in Barons Court.

In pursuing this inquiry, we shall not only use information collected in Barons Court, but we shall also draw upon interviews and observations made in other constituencies in the London area. We make no claim that we have systematically sampled the London constituencies, and hence we cannot be certain about how generalizable our findings are. The patterns we report here do exist; how typical they are is a question that can be answered only by additional studies.

Incentives for Party Activists

Our organizational approach to the study of political parties leads us to hypothesize that there is an incentive system operating in both the Labour and Conservative organizations. Since the local party in a political campaign is a voluntary association and cannot effectively employ negative sanctions to stimulate its workers to greater and more effective activity, the basic incentive system must involve primarily a set of "rewards" which many of the most active members seek. To the extent that a political organization can manipulate this incentive system, bestowing rewards upon those who work the hardest, while denying such rewards to those who fail to carry their share of the load, it is likely to improve the effectiveness and efficiency of its operation.

The incentive system, of course, functions over a long time period (not just during the campaign), and thus it affects the size and quality of the talent pool from which the executive officials in a political campaign will be recruited. If this analysis has any validity, we should be able to demonstrate that the Labour Party in Barons Court was relatively "rich" in rewards sought by its hard-working volunteers, while the Conservative Party was relatively "poor" in the rewards available to its workers. But we shall attempt to go a step even beyond this, although our evidence is not complete enough for solid generalization. We have seen that the Conservatives sent many more workers into Barons Court from the outside than the Socialists did. While the difference between the two parties in the number of outside workers mobilized may not be typical, we strongly suspect that the Tories in the London area tend to be more effective than Labour in encouraging their strong constituencies to pour mutual aid into the marginal areas during an election campaign. If this estimate of the situation is accurate, then we would hypothesize that the Conservative organization has a more effective incentive system operating *above* the constituency level, and is therefore able to dispense rewards to people who are willing to work hard for the cause outside of their own local districts.

Rungs on the Ladder to a Parliamentary Career

Among the Tory workers who made the greatest expenditure of time in both the 1964 and 1966 campaigns, no fewer than nine had hopes of someday winning a seat in parliament. The two most active volunteers in each of these contests were anticipating that they would be selected as candidates in winnable constituencies in the near future. But the Conservative organization in Barons Court was not atypical in having such hardworking parliamentary aspirants who were willing to devote long hours to the election struggle. As one visits Tory headquarters in other London constituencies, he frequently discovers that those men (but not women) who are spending the most time on a campaign will confess a desire to have their names placed on the candidate list, or, if they are already on the approved list, to be selected as prospective candidates. A good illustration of this phenomenon is provided by one London constituency where the chairman of the association and the agent have reputations for being extremely effective campaigners. Young men who want support in their efforts to get a seat, as well as experience under seasoned leadership, flock into this district to work on election campaigns.

In the Barons Court Labour Party, there were at least six activists in the two campaigns who were either seeking a parliamentary constituency or who expressed at least a mild interest in this as an eventual objective, some of them indicating that they had only faint hopes of ever getting into the House of Commons. Two of the most active workers in 1964 were parliamentary aspirants. Other constituency Labour parties in the London area have active campaign workers who are interested in parliamentary careers. But the Labour aspirants do not constitute so large a proportion of the activists as they do in the Conservative Party, and they are more likely to be working in their home constituencies.

254

If the pursuit of a parliamentary career is one factor that motivates some highly involved workers to engage in political activity, is the party organization able to take advantage of this fact and help to deliver the "prizes" to the most industrious of its adherents? To some extent this appears to be the case in the Conservative Party. Perceptive Tory agents in the London area recognize that a volunteer who has visions of getting into the House can be of good use in a campaign, especially if he is at the stage of trying to get on the candidate list at the Central Office, or has just recently been placed on the list. In speaking about this matter, one London agent pointed to a young gentlemen who was dashing through the door on his way to carry out a campaign assignment: "That young man wants to get on the candidate list, and I can flog him half to death! I doubt that he has much of a chance of being selected by a constituency party. But I can't worry about that now. I need a reliable person who will be available most of the time to do important chores, and he is always at my beck and call!"

In the case of the Conservatives, many parliamentary aspirants seem to perceive that active participation in a campaign is likely to improve their chances of getting on the list and of eventually being selected as a candidate. On the other side of the coin, some Tory agents recognize these people as a fruitful source of executive manpower for their campaign battles, and they are eager to recruit them. But does the Conservative Party actually manipulate the access to candidacy as a way to reward activists for their hard work in political campaigns?

The answer to this question appears to be both yes and no. When an individual applies to the Central Office for placement on the candidate list, the vice-chairman of the party organization and his colleagues who make this decision scrutinize the prospect's record of political activity. If he is young, does not come from distinguished Conservative lineage, and has not done much political work, he may be told to get more political experience by attaching himself to a local association and by working in some election campaigns, and to apply again a few years hence. But if the applicant is middle-aged, is well established in business, comes from a long line of officeholding Tories but has had little political experience, he may be placed on the approved list.

The Central Office attempts to maintain a record of the political activity of parliamentary aspirants who are being considered for placement on the candidate list, as well as those who are already on the list but who are anxious to be presented to a constituency so that they can have a crack at selection. The Central Office agent is the individual responsible for reporting on the political performance of these candidature-seekers. After a campaign in a regular election or in a by-election, he may contact the agent in the constituency where an individual has been working, requesting an evaluation of him as a prospective candidate. The Tory candidate in the constituency may also be contacted for this appraisal, though this is rare. While the aspirant may request the agent or the candidate to write a letter to the Central Office in his behalf— or they may volunteer to do so—the Central Office tends to give less weight to these recommendations than to the inquiries it initiates.

This assessment of campaign performance by the Central Office generates the impression among many aspirants that a young man who works diligently and effectively for the party and who meets other specifications may be "rewarded" by being placed on the candidate list. "Reward" is, of course, a tricky "careerist" term, and very few aspirants and not many more agents would deign to use it, though some of the latter would recognize its appropriateness when it was suggested to them. Among the people with parliamentary ambitions there were reports—some of them apparently apocryphal—of the otherwise promising young man who did not take his organizational and campaign work seriously and who was not placed on the candidate list. These serve to indicate how some aspirants perceive the consequences of their political activity.

Whether exceptional service during election campaigns helps a parliamentary hopeful who is already on the list to win a candidacy is another matter. That the Central Office has enough influence over the selection process to be able to reward an aspirant for superior party work is clear enough. When a constituency party is looking for a candidate, the Central Office, when asked for advice, may respond in different ways. It typically sends a list of all potential candidates who are looking for a constituency of the type making the request. However, a high official in the Conservative organization informed us that if the Central Office has a few men whom it particularly wants to place, it may recommend from three to five people and supply background information on each of them. Since recommendation by the Central Office is generally recognized as improving one's chances of being selected, the recommendation itself could be used as a "reward." In some cases, however, the Central Office can go much farther than this. When asked whether one member of the recommended group might be singled out for particular support, a highly placed Tory official, who for obvious reasons must remain anonymous, replied in words to this effect: "Never in writing. But if there is a man we would especially like to see chosen, I will have a personal chat with the chairman of the selection committee (who is usually the chairman of the association), and indicate our choice. Normally this is enough to get the right man through the selection committee. Sometimes, however, one of the other aspirants—usually a local man—may have the chairman of the committee in his pocket. Then I might take the chairman of that association aside and remind him that association chairmen whose work is appreciated by Central Office are sometimes placed on the Honours List. Rarely does this fail to accomplish our objective." But such a technique cannot be used in some constituencies, and, in any case, is employed only in exceptional circumstances.

Thus it is apparent that the Conservative Central Office could use its recommendations to selection committees as a reward for faithful campaign service to the party. One must recognize, however, that so many factors other than his record of political activity enter into decisions to support an individual that the Central Office would be defeating its own purpose if it placed too much weight upon party activism. Moreover, most of the people who are so high on the candidate list as to be recommended selectively by the Central Office have records of party accomplishment, and the differences are not likely to be very discriminating. But when a newcomer among the Conservative activists manages to be selected as the Tory candidate in a winnable seat—with or without the involvement of the Central Office—the willingness of the hard-working activists on the approved list to sacrifice themselves for the party cause is dampened.

In 1965 a safe Tory constituency adopted a middle-aged candidate whose greatest claim to distinction appears to have been his well-established business and a line of ancestors who had had persistent, if not distinguished, careers in the House of Commons. His active political work was apparently limited to delivering one speech and hosting one tea. While his credentials were strong enough, even without an active political record, to win approval from the Central Office, it is important to point out that some other older parliamentary aspirants (who did not aspire to the safe seat we are referring to) were virtually inactive in the 1966 campaign, although they had driven themselves very hard in the 1964 encounter. When asked about this sudden change in behavior, their replies were simple and direct: their efforts were apparently not appreciated, and, in any case, were not necessary in order for them to achieve their goals. The younger aspirants, however, could not be so cavalier in their approach to the problem.

Before we can determine whether the Labour Party can assist an activist with a good organizational record to get on the trail toward parliament, it will be useful to see what is involved in getting on the list of approved candidates. The situation is complicated by the fact that there are two lists:

1. List A, which is a register of people who have been placed on the parliamentary "panels" of most of the trade unions, who have been initially approved by the National Executive Committee (the subcommittee on organization is the group that makes the de facto decision), and who will be "sponsored" and financed by their trade unions if they are selected.
2. List B, which is a roster of "unsponsored" aspirants who have had the preliminary approval of the NEC—people whose names have been sent forward as a result of action by the local General Management Committee or by some affiliated organization.

This means that the politically aspiring trade unionist has two routes available to him, and he need not be entirely dependent upon his local party for preferment. However, the individual who has not been active enough in trade union work to gain recognition has to focus his efforts upon getting on the B List, and this does involve a connection with his local party.

The usual procedure for an individual who desires to bid for a place on the B List is to be nominated by one of the ward organizations, preferably his own. He then appears before a meeting of the GMC of the constituency party, where he makes a statement about his background and qualifications and then answers questions put to him by the delegates. If the GMC votes approval, his name is submitted to the National Executive Committee, and he is requested to fill out an application form and to provide the names of two "referees" who are "well-known members of the Labour Party." Subsequently he is supposed to be called before some members of the organization subcommittee for an interview to determine his "suitability" as a potential candidate.

The important question for our purposes is whether industrious effort in behalf of the party is a strategic factor in helping an individual to get on List B or in keeping him off, and whether the aspirant perceives this to be the case. To begin with the local party, where the initial steps are taken, the agent is not usually expected to give his appraisal of the qualifications of the applicants, and the Labour agent in Barons Court did not do so. The wards sometimes consider whether the aspirant has carried his fair share of party work in the unit, but the rejection rate on these grounds is extremely small. By the same token, the delegates to the GMC may occasionally embarrass an applicant who wants to get on List B by asking him why he has ignored some of the "heat and burden of Labour toil" in his own bailiwick, but in the overwhelming number of cases they end up approving him anyway. When his name goes forward for preliminary consideration by the National Executive Committee, the people in charge of the screening are primarily concerned about any extremist political views that he might have, and in rare instances they have been known to deny approval on this ground, though they never disclose the reasons for their action. But if the aspirant appears to be suitable candidate material on the "paper record," they may not even call him in for an interview. If they do hold a personal confrontation, the national officials may ask him when he last attended a meeting of his trade union branch and of his ward party. If they discover that the applicant has done little or no party work, they are likely to raise their eyebrows, but as a rule they will accept the recommendation of the local constituency party.

What is more crucial for our research is the fact that the Labour people who are inclined toward careers in parliament do not usually think that failure to work hard in the organization and in a campaign will be a serious impediment in getting their names on List B. They do recognize, however, that active work in party affairs may give them valuable political experience. They get more used to expressing their views on political issues, they become better known throughout the party, and they develop a political base in their respective wards, which usually make the initial nominations for B List entries.

But, once an individual has his name included on this list, does his record of party work significantly influence his chances of getting a candidature? The answer seems to be that it may, but that in most instances it likely will not—and this is probably how a great many of the Labour aspirants for a seat in the House see the matter. We shall tackle the problem first by examining how a good record of party activity might be of some assistance, especially for the neophyte candidate who is looking for a constituency party to adopt him.

When a local constituency party is authorized by the National Executive Committee to begin the search for a candidate, one or more of the wards which are entitled to nominate individuals for consideration by the selection conference may wish to support a local activist, and they are not likely to give preference to a local man who has not been deeply involved in party affairs. Again, some of the people in a ward may be drawn to a particular outside candidate who has become known to them through his work in an adjacent constituency or in a marginal constituency during a by-election. For example, it was through his political activities in South Kensington, especially his propaganda work at street-corner meetings, that the name of Ivor Richard commanded the attention of some members in Grove Ward, and as a result this group gave him a nomination. Then, too, when a local party man has rendered outstanding service to his party, it is possible that the agent may contact their colleagues in other constituency parties to let them know that a potentially good candidate is available, although he must be careful, for this can have an adverse effect. It is also possible that the agent may informally give the regional organizer some information about the candidate talent in his district. When a constituency party begins the search for a standard-bearer, the leaders ask for advice from the regional agent, and occasionally he is able to suggest a few names so that the party's range of choice will be broadened. However, the cases in which the regional organizer has been able to influence selection as a result of his personal relations with the officials of a local party are rare, since the local organizations jealously guard their autonomy in the choice of their parliamentary candidates.

When an individual's performance in the party's "donkey work" may have some effect is when the Executive Committee begins to pare down the group of nominees to a "short list" of six or eight people. Some members of the Executive may be suspicious of an individual who has not spent much time or effort in political work, and they may be prompted to exclude him from the list of finalists on this score. But it is doubtful that very many of the aspiring Labour neophytes view the problem in terms of these probabilities and set about in a calculating way to structure their behavior accordingly.

There are, on the other hand, a number of more realistic reasons why a commendable record of party service at the grass roots may not be of much help to an aspirant who is looking for a candidacy. In the first place, Transport House does not recommend a small group of names to a constituency party as the Conservative Central Office may. If a local party decides to request names from the national headquarters—and it is not required to do so—the officials send along the entire list, whether it is List A, List B, or both. Thus, there is not the same opportunity for preferment in individual cases. The National Executive Committee, however, is given more authority over the selection of parliamentary candidates in by-elections, and instances can be cited in which the national authorities made changes in the short lists and in other ways attempted to influence selection.[6] But even in by-elections, Transport

6. See Austin Ranney, *Pathways to Parliament: Candidate Selection in Britain* (Madison, Wisc.: University of Wisconsin Press, 1965), especially pp. 146–150. This work is a careful and thorough study of candidate selection in the Conservative, Labour, and Liberal parties.

House is able to act only in an advisory capacity, with the final decision resting in the hands of the local party. Even more than is true of the Conservatives, the local Labour people are suspicious of any attempts from Smith Square to influence their choice of candidates unduly. Moreover, any efforts on the part of the national organization to secure a by-election candidature for a hardworking neophyte are limited by the need to find seats for former M.P.s and to secure trade union cooperation by running a sponsored candidate from List A.

By the time an aspirant gets to a Labour selection conference, his party record is less likely to undergo careful scrutiny than is the case with the Conservatives. To be sure, he may have to field a question or two about it, and, if his work on the doorsteps has been good, he may try to score a point over one of his intellectual opponents by pointing out that, although he has published no articles in the capitalist press, he has worn out several pairs of shoes by trudging along the pavement in Labour's behalf. But, unlike the Tory selection process, the delegates to the selection conference proceed to the voting without discussing the individual qualifications of the various nominees. Thus, while one or two of the delegates may be sensitive to deficiencies in political activism, they have no real opportunity to press this point upon their colleagues. As a rule, a selection conference is more likely to be persuaded by how well the speakers perform, and this becomes a much more important criterion for assessing their qualifications as candidates. Moreover, since the Labour Party is an ideological movement which has been an arena of struggle between partisans of the "right" and the "left," the delegates who are about to make a final choice are usually, at this stage in the process, much more concerned about whether the aspirant will support or attack the national party leaders than about his failure to put in enough time canvassing.

Several tentative conclusions can be drawn from this analysis of how and to what extent control over parliamentary candidacies may be manipulated as part of the incentive system as it is applied to party activists. First, in a general election a significant portion of the most involved Tory activists are interested in becoming parliamentary candidates. The proportion is noticeably lower in the Labour Party, and the parliamentary aspirants tend to come from the party's middle-class adherents. This tendency for Labour "hopefuls" to be drawn from the middle-class segment of the activists is supported by a study conducted in 1961–1962.[7] Of the thirty-seven members on the Labour General Management Committee in an upper-class residential district, sixteen of them (43 per cent) aspired to become M.P.s. If occupation is used as an index of social class, all of these people would qualify as members of the middle class. By contrast, only 8.5 per cent (five out of thirty-nine) of the GMC members in a working-class constituency in South London listed a parliamentary career as one of their political objectives, and all of these people were either in middle-class occupations, had higher educational attainments than was the norm for that type of district, or were trade union activists who thought they might be able to get on the candidates' panel from their unions. Similarly, in a marginal constituency in West London where 32.6 per cent of the GMC members (fifteen out of forty-six) were interested in getting into parliament, further analysis revealed that all were in middle-class occupations except one, and he was an active trade unionist. From these data, it seems reasonable to conclude that some of the difference between the two parties in the proportion of parliamentary aspirants to be found among the campaign activists is simply a reflection of the differing social composition of the two organizations.

Second, the younger parliamentary hopefuls in the Tory Party feel that distinctive political work will help them to get on the candidate list. Enough applicants have been turned down by the Central Office, presumably because of the absence of party activity

7. John E. Turner, *Doorstep Politics: Organization and Leadership in Three Local Labour Parties* (Minneapolis: University of Minnesota Press, forthcoming).

on their records, to support the perception of these young aspirants. At the local level, the most important person evaluating party work is the agent, but the effective decision is made in the Central Office. When he sends to the Central Office agent a strong, favorable report concerning a young man's campaign effort, this action can certainly be looked upon as a "reward" for service to the party. The agent can therefore use his position to "stimulate" certain people to work as hard as possible during a campaign.

The situation is quite different in the Labour Party. Except for the right of veto, rarely exercised by Transport House, the effective decision for placing an individual's name on the B List is made through the local party organization. Although the ward or GMC may withhold the endorsement of a person because of dissatisfaction with his party work, this seldom happens, and is not a part of the norms of expectation. In any event, the agent usually plays an inconsequential role in getting his workers on the candidates' list, and hence he is not in the same position as his Tory counterpart to use this as a carrot to urge the young aspirants on to great effort.

Third, once an individual has had his name entered on the approved list in either party, the selection committees have to take so many other factors into account that effective campaign work in the past tends to become an unimportant consideration. The Conservative Party, however, is the only one that is organized in such a way as to make candidate selection a possible reward for party work.

Fourth, and in summary, we conclude that the Conservatives are able to use their control over the lower rungs of the parliamentary ladder more effectively than Labour as a basis for rewarding certain party activists. This stems from the fact that a parliamentary career is more appealing to and/or is a more realistic goal for members of the middle class. Moreover, the agent in a Tory association is in a position to wield greater influence when it comes to making recommendations for the list of approved candidates. In comparing the two parties on this dimension, we should also point out that, because the effective decision on entry to the B List is in the hands of the local Labour Party, the young Labour aspirant is well advised to work hard in his local bailiwick, unless he is joined by many of his fellows in an excursion to the outside. On the Conservative side, however, the choice is made by the Central Office, taking into account the reports of the local agents the hopeful has worked for. It makes little difference to the Central Office whether a man works in his own constituency during a campaign, or whether he performs service elsewhere. Indeed, the people in the Central Office prefer to have additional resources poured into the marginals. For this reason the young Tory activist will have no hesitation—on solely career grounds—in leaving his own constituency for work in a marginal district, since his departure will not have an adverse effect upon his chances of getting on the candidate list.

This analysis indicates how one of the rewards to campaign activists may operate differentially in the two parties, and it helps to explain two things:

1. Why parliamentary aspirants show up with greater frequency in Conservative than in Labour campaigns.
2. Why campaign activists in the Tory organization in a marginal constituency are less likely to be local people.

Membership in "Local Parliaments"

While the United Kingdom has only one parliament, a large number of elected legislative bodies are responsible for governing the various units of local government, and these councils in several respects mimic the form and practice of the House of Commons. The London County Council and the borough councils are examples of these "local parliaments." Britain has a long tradition of service in the units of local government, which even today provide no regular compensation for people in elective posts.

In this study we have already noted that a large number of

266

Labour members on the borough councils occupied executive positions in the campaign. The Tories, of course, had fewer people on the councils, and, although one or two of them surfaced for the campaign, by and large they were much less active than their Labour colleagues. In addition to the active Labour councillors, a number of other people involved in the Socialist campaign revealed in their interviews that they were interested in getting into council work at some future time. Similar levels of interest were not to be found among the hardest working activists in the Barons Court Conservative Party. Only one of them expressed a keen interest in winning a seat on the local council. Indeed, interviews with Tory councillors, association officers, and the agent indicated that the Conservative organization often experienced difficulty in securing qualified candidates to stand for the borough councils.

It is no exaggeration to state that many Labour activists would look upon an opportunity to run for the borough council as very desirable, while most Tory activists would tend to regard it as a somewhat onerous duty. This situation immediately raises two questions. Why do many of the activists in the Barons Court Labour Party (and some Labour people in other marginal districts) relish the opportunity to stand for the borough council, while most of the Tory activists seek to avoid such a fate? Can the Socialist organization take advantage of this desire on the part of Labour stalwarts and build it into the incentive system?

The first question seems to be partially related to the social class base of the two parties. In the three-constituency study referred to earlier, 43.6 per cent of the GMC members in the "butler and brandy" constituency desired election to the borough council or the London County Council, or were already serving on one of these bodies.[8] In the Labour Party located in the working-class area, 71.2 per cent of the GMC members already held local legislative posts or expressed a desire to do so. In the marginal constituency, the comparable figure was 65.2 per cent.

The evidence suggests that, in the London area, service on

8. Turner, *Doorstep Politics*.

local councils is more attractive to members of the working class who are active in politics than to members of the middle class. On the surface, this may seem like a strange twist in British local government and politics. The typical textbook usually calls attention to the sense of responsibility for local government and civic affairs that characterizes local Tory dignitaries. While this situation may still prevail in the rural areas and in some safe Conservative districts in urban centers, it does not appear to be true of the marginal constituencies in London.

It may be that the Tories find other outlets for their energies, and derive satisfaction and acclaim for other kinds of community service. Perhaps, too, the political climate in the marginal constituencies makes it difficult for the Conservatives to render the type of service in local government that they were able to perform in the past.

Although Barons Court is a marginal *parliamentary* constituency, it was in 1964 located in two boroughs where Labour commanded a strong majority. Indeed, the councils in Hammersmith and Fulham were dominated by the Socialists for many years. The important point is this: in a district that has moved from the Conservative column into the marginal category in parliamentary elections, Labour is likely to have won control of the Labour council already or will have made significant inroads into it. In other words, barring an adverse national swing or the emergence of a local issue, the Labour Party tends to run stronger in local than in parliamentary contests. This means that the Labour Party, for local government purposes, has certain safe wards under its control and has a stronger hold over other wards that are not so firmly in the Labour camp when it comes to electing a member of parliament.

Under these circumstances, candidacies for local council seats grow less attractive to the activists in the Conservative Party. The organization is able to offer fewer safe wards to its enthusiasts, who are forced to spend their time on harder campaigns in marginal wards. And even if they win, they often find their organization in a hopeless minority position on the council. Thus, not only do they lose control over policy, but they no longer have access to the important committee assignments and committee chairmanships which are appealing to individuals who seriously engage in local politics.

When Labour manages to secure a grip on the borough council, the party is in a position to offer preferment to more of its activists, who, as we have seen, tend to be more interested in borough politics than their opponents. This preferment may be in the form of seats in safe wards, winnable seats in marginal wards, desirable committee assignments, and important offices, such as leader of the Group, chairman of the Finance Committee, or chairman of the Housing Committee. The decision as to who shall stand in the safe wards and who shall occupy the important posts on the council is in effect made by the local party. Hence, for the purposes of this study, the basic question is whether or not the local party organization is able to use these choice candidacies and council positions as "rewards" for its hardworking activists.

Our impression is that in many cases a local Labour party probably does. We have heard criticism from time to time of councillors who fail to attend ward and GMC meetings regularly, or who are not sufficiently active during parliamentary campaigns. In some constituency parties, instances can be cited of councillors who have been dropped from the candidate list for "neglecting" their party responsibilities, or who have been forced to fight local elections in marginal wards because they have been denied re-adoption by the local party in the safe wards. When this happens, the organization is, in effect, applying negative sanctions against individuals who have fallen below the expectations of their colleagues. For every vacancy that is created in this manner, the party has an opportunity to reward another of its activists.

There are other ways, too, in which the local party can express its appreciation for loyal service. One of the best examples of reward for good organization effort is through appointment to the aldermanic bench, which in most instances is bestowed by the local party. Sometimes people who have worked hard in a local election only to sustain a defeat are rewarded for their effort by being appointed to these archaic positions.

For many people, the crown jewel of local government is the position of mayor, which is filled by the party in control of the borough council. Elected by the council for a one-year term, the mayor is the ceremonial "monarch" of the borough. During his tour of pleasant duty, he severs his overt ties with the party so that he can preside with nonpartisan spirit over the colorful civic functions of the community. During his year in office, he does everything from gracing charity bazaars with his presence to greeting members of the royal family if one of them makes an official visit to the borough. In spite of the fact that the person selected as mayor may suffer financial loss because he has to take a leave from work and because the cost of official entertainment often exceeds his expense allowance, we have encountered no instances of the post being refused. More important for our purposes, rarely does one find a mayor in a Labour-controlled borough who has not had a long and distinguished record in his local party and on the council.

A lively Labour Party in a London marginal can and often does effectively use the various positions in local government as a means for "rewarding" its competent activists. When we observed so many Labour councillors pouring their energies into the campaign to elect Ivor Richard, it took us a while to realize that they were also indirectly helping to preserve their own political careers in local government. By contrast, the Tory councillors, who were relatively inactive in the campaign, were not faulted by their party colleagues. Indeed, most Tories excused them from work in the campaign on the ground that they were already doing a difficult job for the party as minority members of the council, and, if anything, should be rewarded in some special way for performing in that toilsome role.

The Holding of Party Offices

If any of the offices in a political party are perceived as being desirable, whether for reasons of prestige or as a means of re-inforcing an ideological position, then it is possible that these posts might be considered, in an analytical sense, to be "rewards" that are even more directly under the control of the organization. Our interviews suggested that in Barons Court the holding of ordinary party office in the Tory camp was not much of an inducement; indeed, except for party leaders who have parliamentary ambitions, very few would regard a seat on the Finance and General Purposes Committee as a "reward" for party service, and the organization experienced some difficulty in recruiting people to act as ward leaders and to take other executive positions. On the Labour side, however, the situation is much more complicated and in some respects unclear. For this reason we need to give it brief examination, and within a wider context than just Barons Court.

More than is the case with the Conservatives, the Labour Party is an ideological movement, and the people who gravitate toward it usually display a keen interest in policy issues. While most party people do not actively seek ward offices or posts at the constituency level and in some instances have to be pressed into service, many of them desire to get on the General Management Committee. When asked why they like to be GMC delegates, they point out that they are interested in having a voice in the running of the local party and that they enjoy discussing policy matters. The GMC, they indicate, is the place where the decisions on party affairs and policy stands are hammered out; this is where the action and excitement are. They also point out that this is the only body where party workers have contact with their colleagues in the rest of the constituency.

In some wards in a Labour constituency party, there may be no competition for the GMC delegateships, and everyone who seeks membership in the group is able to get it. On the other hand, competition for these posts frequently breaks out in some wards in the constituency. When an issue controversy is rocking the party, an individual's stand on the issue may determine whether he will be elected or defeated. But as a rule whether or not a person will be chosen as a GMC delegate will be decided on the basis of how effectively he has worked for the ward party and how willing he has been to perform the routine, thankless tasks. A number of Labour Party activists sense that there is a relationship between how hard they work and their security of tenure on the GMC. This research uncovered the case of one individual who moved into a larger ward which needed help in organization so that he could take over some of the official responsibility and thus get on the GMC more easily.

In some constituency parties, the activists who are keen to get on the GMC are extremely reluctant to take over the responsibilities of office in the ward organization or in the central party itself. In many places the recruitment of ward officers especially poses a serious problem. On the other hand, in some districts the position of ward chairman is considered to be prestigious, without all of the work that is attached to the post of secretary, and this office may be contested. In other areas, the secretaryship is regarded as a desirable post, and open contests are held to determine who will fill it. In either case, when competition does emerge, the election is likely to go to the individual who is perceived to be the best qualified as evidenced by his party record, unless the ideological factor intervenes to influence the result. As one Labour agent in London expressed it, those who take the initiative usually rise very quickly.

Sometimes people are willing to stand for the office of ward secretary because this post entitles them to exofficio membership on the GMC. One also encounters ward secretaries who did not seek the post initially, but, after being entrusted with it, they come to look upon it as a challenge and grow deeply involved in carrying out the responsibilities of the office. This was the case with several people in the Barons Court organization; some preferred to remain as ward administrators rather than to try for a seat on the local council. But in most well-organized parties, whether a ward

secretary has actively sought the position or has had to be persuaded to take it over, he is not likely to hold the post for a long
period of time if his performance does not live up to expectations.
The reshuffling of ward secretaries in some constituency parties
that are attempting to strengthen their organizations provides
support for this observation.

As has been suggested above, ideological disagreements may
have a substantial impact upon how the executive offices within a
constituency party are contested and what sorts of people are able
to win them. When a party tends to be issue-oriented, groups within
the organization soon grow interested in winning control of the
machinery so that it can be used to further the policy stands they
espouse. Under these circumstances, what people hold which offices
becomes a matter of considerable concern, since it is generally
recognized that a party chairman, for example, who feels very
strongly about a point of view can be expected to emphasize that
view and to work hard in support of it during his term in office.

But how can this ideological factor be fitted into an analysis
which deals with a system of incentives to encourage those who
work the hardest? In attempting to show a relationship, let us
assume that the Labour activists in a marginal constituency can be
roughly classified into three fairly distinct groups:

1. Those who are usually on the "left" side of the political
   spectrum on policy matters.
2. Those who are to be found at the opposite pole—the
   "right."
3. A group of activists at the "center" who are loyal to the
   broad goals of the party but are not committed to any
   particular policy stand; these people are much more
   oriented toward the *party as an organization* and the concrete tasks that have to be performed.

This simple typology, it might be added, is not entirely divorced
from reality.

The activists on either the left or the right will be able to maximize their influence and advance their respective policy positions if they can win the key posts in the ward organizations and gain a majority on the General Management Committee. But if neither the left nor the right has enough strength to become dominant, the people in the center, who have somewhat less concern about a given issue than they have about the general health of the organization, will in effect make the decision as to which individuals will win election to the party's important offices. And the people in the center will be the most prone to support those activists—whether from the left or the right—who have demonstrably turned in the best records of untiring service to the party. That this may be a factor in the distribution of party offices is suggested by the remark of more than one stalwart from the central wing of the party to the effect that "those who do the most talking about issues are sometimes the people who do the least work in a campaign!"

The argument boils down to this: If it is necessary to control the major party offices in order to reinforce a given ideological position, and if, in order to win office, it is necessary to demonstrate effective party work not only for a particular wing but for the organization as a whole, then the people who desire to control the party are required to work hard. Their "reward" is accession to office.

Nuances of Distinction: Symbols after the Surname

Local government positions and party offices cannot be used effectively as rewards in the Conservative Party, because, as we have indicated, they are not sought after by enough people. To many activists, these amount more to a chore than a reward. But there is one symbol of prestige that still commands magical deference throughout most of British society and is coveted by some middle-class adherents of the Conservative Party—identification with the exclusive social group whose members have been placed on the

"Honours List." Although Honours may be revered by a few members of the working class, most of them regard the list as far beyond their level of realistic aspiration. The middle-class supporters of the Labour Party tend to be critical of the superficial outgrowths of the monarchy, and they identify the Honours List as a hangover from the past which should be curtailed, if not abolished, in an effort to create a more equalitarian social order.

Thus, the basic question is whether the Conservative Party uses the Honours List to reward its activists for their successful efforts. When the Tories are in control at No. 10 Downing Street, it is a common occurrence—particularly evident under Harold Macmillan—for a number of chairmen of constituency associations to be awarded the Order of the British Empire or some other distinguished citation when Honours are announced on New Year's Day and on the monarch's birthday. We must, however, pause to sound a special note of caution. It would be a serious mistake to create the impression that the possibility of getting on the Honours List is the central concern of the Tory officials in a local constituency organization. Indeed, in our attempts to detect the operation of a reward system, we spent several weeks interviewing people who held or had held positions in local Conservative parties, and none mentioned the Honours List. But when it was suggested to them, they immediately placed it at the very top of the reward structure. It was not that they were trying to hide something; the list simply did not occur to them, because it is such a subtle part of the political landscape.

In fact, the first clear indication that the Honours List might be used to reward faithful party officers came from the rank-and-file workers in the organization. In an evening during the campaign, it was a usual part of our regimen for us to walk door to door with different canvassers. While walking between buildings, while standing in front of a door waiting for the voter to appear, or, more especially, while chatting with local party people in the nearby pub after the canvass cards had been turned in, we talked at great length with these "rank and filers" about their perceptions of party organization and campaign problems. The Tory workers recognized and appreciated the long hours which the association officers were forced to put in and the serious difficulties they had to cope with. When they were asked how the party might reward these officials for their effort, the immediate and frequent response was that the party might see to it that they were awarded Honours. According to the outlook of many of them, Honours up to a knighthood would be justified.

Among the officers of the local associations, however, the Honours List is rarely mentioned. A conversation we had with a gentleman who had been the association chairman in a marginal constituency for about seven years and had served as a ward chairman for a much longer time provides an illustration of how the subject might be obliquely introduced:

Q. Percy, you have been chairman of this Association for almost seven years now. You have worked very hard, and your achievements have been great. I hear that you are considering giving up the job. If the party wanted to reward you, is there anything that it could do?

A. I don't want any reward, Bob. I will admit that I've worked many long hours on this job and have had lots of problems to solve. But I believe in the principles of the Conservative Party, and I am afraid of the control and regimentation that may come with too many years of Socialist government. I am not looking for any reward for my work here.

Q. I know you're not looking for anything, Percy. But the party surely recognizes how hard you've worked. If it wanted to, is there anything that it could do?

A. Well, after Reginald resigned as chairman in 1959, they gave him an O.B.E. But, of course, he won the seat for the candidate in the 1959 election.

While this was the most explicit reference, the comments from other association officers in a number of London constituencies suggest that the hope for Honours, however faint, at least hovers in the back of their minds, and they realize that effective election performance—especially the winning of seats in marginal or Labour areas—is the best way for them to get on the list.

For officials in the Central Office and those in the Parliamentary Party who have an interest in organizational problems, the Honours List is clearly conceived as one device for rewarding the faithful, the hardworking, and the electorally successful officials who are responsible for their constituency organizations. One high party official, who has a great deal to do with national organization, perceived a clear relationship between the Honours List and the recruitment of the necessary volunteers to man the important party posts. In fact, he exhibited some concern about the party being out of power and being deprived access to the Honours List; he indicated that thought was being given to the establishment of some alternative. This official was the one who most clearly recognized that commitment to the party and its principles was not enough to hold an organization together. Some system of rewards had to be available, and these rewards had to be valued by the local people whom the party desired to have undertake the volunteer positions of responsibility.

While the Honours List *is* involved in the reward system of the Conservative Party, let us be clear about how we think it operates. We are *not* trying to imply that a young man joins the Conservative Party, works in his ward and at the association level, and then finally accepts the responsibilities and tasks of the chairmanship *because* he has had his eye on an O.B.E. from the beginning. This is obviously not the case. It seems more likely that an individual may join the party for any number of reasons, and "apolitical" social motivations may be as important as the political. However, after growing involved in party work and holding office for whatever reason, the person who displays a talent for organization may be considered for the chairmanship. By this time, many of the rewards that were available to him for previous activity have begun to lose their efficacy. It is at this point in his career that the Honours List may begin to look attractive, especially if he is engaged in professional or business employment, where honorific symbols after the surname are often expected.

It should be noted that the Honours List has very limited application as a "reward" in a single constituency. Since the awards are relatively few and there is a large number of good Conservative parties which must be given recognition, the most that can be expected (for political reasons) is for one party activist from a marginal constituency to be placed on the list only about every seven to ten years.

Among Conservatives, this treatment of the Honours List as a reward for party activity will be the most controversial section of the book. Some well-informed agents will go so far as to say that the main political use of Honours is not as a reward but as a technique for "buying off" a long-tenured but ineffectual chairman in an effort to infuse the organization with new blood. In other words, Honours may occasionally be granted "on condition that" the recipient resign his post. Obviously, most association officers who have given years of devoted service to the party would be greatly insulted if anyone implied that they worked hard largely because they desired to get on the Honours List. They would be even more insulted if they felt that Honours were given as a bribe to get rid of the ineffectual rather than as a reward for real achievement. We underline the fact that in our discussion of the Honours system we have made neither of these claims. Our evidence that the Honours List provides an efficacious reward for a limited number of party stalwarts comes primarily from comments volunteered by rank-and-file Tories who perceive it as such and justify its use, and from responses by high Conservative officials who recognize the reward potential of the list and have made use of it in this way.[9]

While the middle-class Labour activist may not covet an O.B.E., he is not completely immune from the desire to have some symbolic inscription after his name. For some people, an appointment as a justice of the peace may bring a certain satisfaction. Justices of the Peace occupy an ancient and honored place in English history, but their present significance may perhaps be judged less by history than by the cynical pundits who designate the position as a "poor man's baronetcy." One occasionally encounters Labour activists who would like to become J.P.s, especially professional and business people who are able to make adjustments in their work schedules so that they can serve several times a week in their official capacity. When the Labour Party is in power at the local level, an appointment as a justice of the peace is one way in which the local party organization can help to provide recognition for an individual who has given outstanding service to his party and to the community. We found no activists in the Conservative Party who indicated any desire to become a J.P. The Labour people, when interested, seem to prefer initials that are something more than honorific, while Tories seem inclined to the view that the more honorific the symbol, the better. In either case, however, the two parties have managed to build parts of an incentive system around what at least some of their members desire.

9. Might we add a personal comment on the Honours List? We venture to say that it might be useful if the United States had a similar device for rewarding dedicated workers in political parties. The granting of Honours is a much more innocent type of patronage than is ordinarily employed in this country. Political parties are fundamental institutions in a democratic society; dedicated service to a party is, in fact, a valuable community service. Even greater use of the Honours List as a reward for political leadership can easily be justified. Instead of being disparaging or cynical, we compliment the Tories for having adapted an archaic practice to the support of an important institution in modern society.

Political Activity and Social Rewards

An individual who serves as a borough councillor, as mayor, or even as a local party official gains a certain amount of *prestige* in the special "community orbit" within which the position is operative. This prestige is associated with the office and not with the characteristics of the particular individual who occupies it. The individual officeholder, however, might also enjoy a high measure of personal *esteem* which derives from the appraisal of him as an individual, quite apart from the formal office he holds. It is important to keep this distinction between prestige and esteem in mind as we deal with the subtle ways in which social rewards may be bestowed for political activity in a Conservative association.

The social life of many Conservatives tends to be closely linked with their political organization. The women's group, the "Young Marrieds," and the Young Conservatives—groups from which the association recruits much of its volunteer help at election time— are as much social as political organizations. In some associations, the tie is even more pronounced because of the existence of a Conservative social club which is organized as a parallel to the political association. The type of social activities in which the members engage is illustrated by a London constituency where the ward annual dinner-dance is a "white tie" affair.

Many Conservatives aspire to positions of social prominence and leadership in their communities. When politically astute leaders are in charge of a local association, they can increase the effectiveness of their political organization by bestowing positions of social leadership upon those who are diligent and successful in their political activities. Because the Barons Court Association lacked the social life and cohesion that are to be found in many other constituency organizations, we did not have an opportunity to examine in detail the way in which that party dispenses social rewards for effective political activity. We can, however, provide some examples from other constituencies.

In one Tory bastion in the London area, the local political party, far from being as moribund as the political science literature predicts, is strong and vibrant, keeping up a large membership and providing an avalanche of support for Tory parties in the adjacent marginals. One reason why the party remains strong, even though it has no one to spar with locally, is because a considerable amount of social life has been organized around the Conservative association. For example, for a number of years the chairman of one of the wards was a high-placed, wealthy businessman. Although he left routine matters in the hands of the secretary, he made it a point to attend the ward meetings and to take an active interest in its affairs. Rank-and-file workers flocked to his ward and competed for the lesser offices in the organization. Through this party work, they were able to bask in the esteem of the chairman and to establish contact with a segment of British society which probably would otherwise have been closed to them. The ward chairman asked for outstanding political service, and he provided "social rewards" for those who delivered. While the specific features of this example are not typical, they nevertheless illustrate the general way in which an esteemed personality with political interests can manipulate social rewards for political purposes.

Note that we began this discussion with the observation that *where the politically astute are in control, social rewards can be used effectively*. But there are grave risks involved when the wrong people get into control and make the political organization merely a vehicle for the social life of its members. The dangers derive from the fact that there are some incompatibilities between social and political organizations. For a political organization to be effective in a democratic society, it must be open to people from many walks of life. Individuals in the organization should be judged by their fellows largely on the basis of their contribution to the party's goals. What a person does in the organization and how well he does it should be more important than who he is.

Social organizations, by contrast, thrive on a certain degree of exclusiveness. They are often attractive because they restrict their membership. Who a person is, where he lives, and what kind of friends he has are usually more important than how well he performs in the organization.

If people whose intersts are primarily social move into positions of political control, the organization is likely to restrict its membership in subtle ways—perhaps by effectively excluding certain ethnic minorities—and the social leaders will hold on to their political positions in order to promote social rather than political objectives. One does not have to travel far in the London area to find an association where social dilettantes have controlled the main offices in the ward organizations for years, and where the Conservative social club will not admit Jews to membership. In this district, a sizable middle-class Jewish population, whose economic interests lie with the Tories, have good reason for voting for the Labour candidate. One can easily imagine the possible course of events if politically motivated individuals were to move into positions of control, open the club to Jewish membership, and let the Jewish people rise to certain positions of social leadership as a reward for having done their political chores successfully. We caught a glimpse of the effectiveness of such a strategy when a new agent moved into the constituency and introduced the necessary changes. There was a dramatic increase in the dynamism of the association, and it won an impressive political victory.

To make our argument as clear as possible, let us put it in the boldest terms. In a society marked by sharp social distinctions, effective work for a political party can become a ladder of social mobility. If people who have personal esteem and whose concerns are primarily political are in control of the organization, and if the political mobility ladder is recognized by the social elite as an appropriate instrument for climbing, then social rewards can serve as a powerful incentive for effective political activity.

As one might anticipate, social rewards of this type are not as important a motivation in a local Labour party. The Women's Section of the party is usually quite small, and the interested members are for the most part ladies in the higher age brackets. Attempts to recruit younger women through neighborhood coffee and sherry parties have met with only spotted success. No separate organization for young married couples exists. The Young Socialist appendage of the local party is also very small, and, far from being preoccupied with the social side, it is often engaged in struggles over controversial issues, usually on the side of the "left," but sometimes, as in the case of Barons Court, on the "right."

The counterpart to the Tory social club is the "workingman's club," but its links with a political organization are not strong. In fact, one frequently encounters Labour activists in the London area who have not graced the entrance of such a club for years. Unlike some of the Conservative organizations, a local Labour party usually does not draw its ward and constituency officers from the community's social elite, and hence there is little opportunity for rank-and-file workers to derive pleasure from associating with people of this sort.

A local Labour party will, of course, organize occasional social gatherings for its activists. Some of the ward organizations sponsor a "get together" from time to time, and the GMC delegates may have an annual dinner, an occasional theater party, or a Sunday afternoon ramble. The Young Socialists, too, carry out a schedule of social activities, sometimes in collaboration with sister organizations in neighboring constituencies. But this type of "fellowship" is not even a pale imitation of what the Conservatives do. Even more important for our analysis, it is doubtful that this mild form of social reward helps to discriminate between the more active and less active workers. In each of the campaigns in Barons Court, for example, the party sponsored an informal social gathering, and in each instance some of the people who were making the greatest time commitment to the campaign did not attend.

Summary Analysis of the Party Incentive Systems

In the Labour Party at the constituency level, access to the B List of parliamentary candidates, positions in local government, party offices, and, to a lesser extent, semihonorific posts like the justices of the peace constitute the major "rewards" that the party can, in various and subtle ways, hold open for its activists who make a significant contribution to the organization, especially in its political campaigns. Here an important observation is in order: it is the ward organization or the General Management Committee, or both, that wield effective power in allocating these rewards differentially. In effect, those workers who are most actively involved are the ones who pass judgment on the effectiveness of an individual's efforts. In the distribution of the rewards Transport House plays an almost inconsequential role, and the agent becomes involved only if he opts to exert his leadership at the ward level or in the GMC meetings.

Access to the list of candidates, the Honours List, and what we have called "social rewards" are the most important elements in the incentive system of the Tory constituency association. In the first two components of the reward structure, the agent and the Central Office are crucially important, while the "social rewards" are dispensed largely through the association officers and/or by the ward members and the auxiliary groups.

This important difference in the reward systems of the two parties helps to account for one of the major points of variance we observed between the Conservative and the Labour organizations in Barons Court. Since the central authorities play such an important part in the dispensation of rewards among Tory activists, an individual does not suffer when he leaves his own constituency for campaign work in a marginal district. The agent can appraise his performance in a report to Central Office, and the latter can act as it sees fit. When large numbers of Tory workers move as a group from their home base into marginal territory for a campaign effort, their system of social rewards can continue to operate. The Labour incentive system, on the other hand, is deeply rooted in the ward structure of the local constituency. Moreover, the kinds of skills developed by the ward leaders who are active in local government and politics are far more appropriate and more useful in their own bailiwicks than in some strange constituency.

The difference between the Conservative and Labour incentive structures, then, helps to explain why so many Tory workers poured into Barons Court from other constituencies. But thus far we have not accounted for the fact that the Conservative organization in Barons Court seemed to have so few local members working on a full-time basis in executive campaign roles—a characteristic that distinguished it, not only from the Labour camp, but also from most Conservative associations in other marginal constituencies.

When the agent and the old hands in the Barons Court association, all of whom were familiar with Conservative parties in other constituencies, were asked how their organization differed from those elsewhere, nearly always they immediately responded that it was much less of a social organization. Barons Court, split between two boroughs and embracing a heavily transient population, is not a "natural" community. There is little reason for social life to be organized in terms of an artificial boundary that delineates a parliamentary constituency. Under these circumstances, the Barons Court association had few social rewards to dispense. This situation, we would argue, helps to account for the relative paucity of local workers devoting large blocks of time to the Tory campaign. The fact that the man who served as chairman of the association was not a resident of the constituency tends to suggest the degree to which social life and political life were separated.

It will be recalled that we began this treatment of the two incentive systems in an attempt to explain why Mrs. Bowman, even though she had more full-time workers under her command, had restricted flexibility in the assignment of campaign tasks and had fewer people to whom she could delegate responsibility for surveillance. Our analysis relates these phenomena directly to the kinds of incentives that are most salient in Conservative associations. In the absence of a social setting in Barons Court, the Tory organization there did not have available to it the only effective rewards that are distributed entirely at the local level, On the Labour side, the absence of mutual aid from other constituencies on such a massive scale as the Tories had appears to us to be a function of an incentive system in which the most significant rewards are dispensed locally on the basis of local contributions to the local cause.

Ideological Commitment and Personal Satisfactions

The Labour or Tory activist who has struggled through the book thus far may be a trifle unhappy with the picture we have drawn of the incentive systems in the two organizations. Nowhere have we mentioned devotion to the cause and commitment to the goals and purposes of the respective parties. So far we have not referred to the altruism of those activists who unselfishly contribute their time and energy because they are convinced that their efforts will help a crusade in which they believe.

Anyone who has had an opportunity to observe the volunteers in a well-run political organization cannot fail to be impressed by the devotion and loyalty which they exhibit virtually every day in the campaign. But students of political parties who place their subject matter under the microscope quickly recognize that these characteristics of party workers are not very helpful in discriminating between those who are very active and those who are less so. We, in fact, began to investigate the motivation of party activists and their level of participation in the campaign effort on the hypothesis that levels of activity were related to ideological commitment. It seemed reasonable that those who work the hardest for the longest hours are likely to have the greatest devotion to the principles and goals of their chosen party. But, as we interviewed the activists who worked in Barons Court, we found little support for this proposition. While ideological commitment may differentiate the campaign activists from the people who exhibit no interest whatever in political matters, and while it may help to explain why the activists select one party over another, it does not distinguish clearly between party workers who are extremely active and those who are not so active.

After some interviewing and a little reflection, we discovered that the personal costs involved in the amount of time devoted to party activity vary greatly from one individual to another. Even though an employee paid by the hour reveals a strong identification with his party's goals, he finds it extremely costly to take off a few days from his job to work in the campaign. By the same token, a woman with a brood of small children may find it impossible to leave her home no matter how deep her ideological commitment may be. On the other hand, a trade union official, the business executive, the individual who is self-employed, and the housewife with no small children or with the financial means to hire a "nanny" may find that campaign effort involves little direct personal cost. The only decision these people have to make is whether to use their time in working for the party or to spend it on some other form of activity.

Correlations between ideological commitment and level of campaign participation would not be very meaningful unless some method were devised to hold personal costs constant. Our research, however, suggest that even this is not a promising path to follow if one is trying to differentiate the "highly involved" from the "merely involved." We picked up no patterned differences in the expressions of ideological commitment between the man or woman who was devoting half-time or full-time to party activity and the casual canvasser who was spending two evenings a week on the campaign. They all appeared to exhibit a fairly high degree of commitment to the policies and ideals of their party.

Nor did we find significant differences in the way in which the highly involved activists and those who were not so involved articulated their ideological concerns. A Tory who was working on the campaign seven or eight hours each day, when asked why he (or she) was a Conservative, might answer, "Because I love my country," "Because Winston Churchill won the war!" or "Because nationalization is ruining the economy!" Another Conservative might present a detailed, perceptive analysis of "welfare capitalism," contrasting with striking effectiveness the fundamental programmatic differences between the Tory and Socialist parties. In the opposite camp, the Labour worker who was appearing for duty every day might indicate that he (or she) was giving time to the party because "I hate injustice, and I want to reform this class-ridden society!" But this answer was not essentially different from the expressions enunciated by the less-involved activists: "Because I believe in more opportunity under Socialism!" "I want to get rid of the bomb!" or "I want more housing for the people and a better Health Service!" Hence, by analyzing the type or the intensity of the response given to questions which were designed to probe ideological commitment, one could not predict very accurately the amount of time that the respondent was spending upon the campaign.

We must also recognize that, in addition to any ideological commitment or the kinds of "rewards" which a party may be able to distribute among its most energetic activists, some individuals in the local organization undoubtedly derive personal satisfaction from assuming executive responsibility for political work in their districts. These people, to be sure, probably gravitated toward one camp or the other as a result of ideological inclination, but, once involved in party work, the personal satisfaction they receive operates independently of ideological commitment. While we made no attempt to study the "psychology" of participation in campaign affairs, we did uncover cases where this type of personal reward appeared to be influential.

In the Conservative Party, for example, one finds a significant number of middle-class women who are well-educated and have organizational talent but who are not engaged in regular employment. People of this type often find an outlet for their unused talents in political participation, and the party is the beneficiary of their efforts.

This factor, however, seems to be operating on a wider scale among some of the male activists in the Labour camp. This is probably to be expected in a political movement that is strongly protesting against the existing class structure. In interviewing highly involved Labour workers in some London constituencies, one frequently encounters intelligent individuals whose formal education was restricted by the "eleven-plus" system or who, for economic reasons, were forced to leave school at a premature age in order to take jobs that offer little or no challenge to their administrative talents. Many of these people are bored by the humdrum tasks of the assembly line, the workshop, or even the insurance office, and their workaday world takes on new meaning when they arrive at the committee room after supper to take over executive responsibility which may involve intricate, supervisory tasks. As one ward organizer expressed it, "At the big office where I am a clerk-typist, I am nothing more than a cog in a machine. So every night I work for the party in a task I enjoy, and occasionally I take a day off from my regular job to put the ward records in order." Another activist who occupied a high administrative post in his party pointed out that he could carry out his daytime job "standing on his head," and that the organizational work of the party was a real challenge to him. On the other hand, his young wife—also a Labour activist—worked as an administrator in her regular job, organizing all day long, and she was less inclined to take on executive responsibility in the party.

While the personal satisfactions derived from party activity must be recognized—and to the activists these may appear to be of major consequence—the student of political parties is forced to view the matter from a different vantage point. In a pluralistic society there are literally dozens of organizations that an individual may join. In almost any of these organizations, a person who needs an outlet for administrative skills (or some other talent) can find a position that will bring him personal satisfaction. This is another way of saying that the satisfaction a person may derive from performing a role in the party organization does not explain why he is working so hard on that job when he could be doing similar work and could be receiving similar satisfaction in a nonpolitical voluntary organization.

The incentive systems we have identified do discriminate between the political parties that have a certain type of reward structure and other organizations that cannot dispense the same rewards. If we were to pursue our analysis on a psychological level, we would inquire about the sorts of people who seek the particular kinds of rewards that the political party alone can distribute. But, unfortunately, we had neither the time nor the resources needed to pursue this interesting question.

Maintaining Morale under Campaign Pressures

If our description of the campaign in Barons Court falls short of the mark, it is largely because we cannot adequately depict with mere prose the pressures, the drive, and the resulting tensions that were a part of the political scene for nearly three weeks. Some activists were pegging away at their assigned tasks for ten, twelve, or even fourteen hours a day. Often the day's work was not wrapped up until 2:00 A.M., and the next round would begin only six hours later. Keeping up such a hectic pace, campaign workers grow tired and more "edgy," and in such an atmosphere little mistakes and slight misunderstandings tend to become magnified.

In the tense and trying situations of a campaign, when the personal costs of the struggle are clearly marked for each individual, the rewards he may anticipate seem to be a long way off. In fact, none of the rewards that we have considered is likely to be dispensed very soon after a single election campaign; the campaign is merely an interval in a longer period of expected service, and the "reward lag" is usually several years.

In light of this fact, we began to wonder whether there are any "rewards" that can be distributed to workers for noteworthy effort *during* the campaign—recompense which helps to minimize interpersonal conflict and to reduce the tension level. Our research suggests that the answer to this question is yes. In searching for this answer, we found some clues in the literature of social psychology. In their analysis of small groups, for example, Professors Thibaut and Kelley draw a distinction between a "task leader" and a "maintenance leader," and they describe the kinds of sanctions that each leader controls.[10]

According to their analysis, a social group that is confronted by a particular task or problem requires a "task leader" who initiates the "task-related interactions," which usually involve increased personal costs to the individual members of the collectivity. Unless the task assignment "quickly brings compensating rewards," the group members begin to evaluate the relationship as unsatisfactory to them—a perception that encourages them to direct their resentment against the task leader who issued the cost-incurring orders in the first place. If the situation continues to deteriorate, the ratio of costs to rewards becomes so imbalanced that the group may fall apart. It is at this point that the maintenance leader enters the picture. "His contribution is to increase the rewards to members, by warm supportive behavior toward them, and/or to reduce their costs, by such behavior as making jokes that release tension and, in general, by reducing their anxieties."

Thibaut and Kelley hypothesize that it is better for the two roles to be performed by different people. They require different abilities with which one individual is not likely to be blessed.

10. John W. Thibaut and Harold H. Kelley, *The Social Psychology of Groups* (New York: John Wiley & Sons, 1959), pp. 278–286.

Moreover, the roles tend to be incompatible, since one urges the members to get moving on the job and the other prompts them to be a bit more relaxed about their work. Then, too, the task leader is inclined to generate some hostility, while the maintenance leader attracts positive feelings of support; hence, if one individual were to occupy both roles, the group members would probably be ambivalent toward him, and his effectiveness in one or both of the roles would be diminished.

To return now to Barons Court. About five months after the 1964 election, Mrs. Bowman was asked how she conceived of the ideal role of the agent and the candidate during the campaign period. She had obviously given matter a great deal of thought, and her reply came immediately:

> The agent directs the campaign, issues instructions to the key workers, coordinates the activities of the subordinate units, and makes the necessary contacts with outside agencies. The job of the candidate is to help maintain the morale of the organization. To be effective, the agent has to issue orders—to tell people what to do and when. The candidate should mingle with the workers, visit the committee rooms, and cheer up the canvassers.

She went on to explain that when the candidate did not perform the function she was outlining, some of the effectiveness of the agent was sacrificed. This meant that the agent had to undertake some of the morale-building function, and perhaps could not drive the organization as hard as he would otherwise like to.

Mrs. Bowman's view of the respective roles of agent and candidate corresponds closely with Thibaut's and Kelley's concept of task leader and maintenance leader. The agent is primarily the task leader, who initiates "the largest number of task relevant interactions." The candidate, on the other hand, is the maintenance leader, providing a special type of reward to workers during the hard, driving weeks of the campaign. While an election victory may be reward enough for all, there are nevertheless some tiring, frustrating moments during a grueling campaign when additional support becomes necessary.

Mr. Carr's concept of the role of the candidate was quite different. When asked what he regarded as the most important job of the candidate in the campaign organization, he responded in this way: first, to identify himself with the issues which are important locally; and, second, to set a good example for the organization by working very hard—harder than anybody else. He did not like to interact too much with the volunteer workers, and he particularly rejected the idea of having the candidate make the rounds of the committee rooms or join in a mass canvass. Such activities, he felt, tend to weaken the organization.

We are in no position to judge which of these views of the proper role of the candidate is right. But the fact that Mrs. Bowman placed such emphasis upon the role of the candidate as a maintenance leader and Mr. Carr rejected this role meant that no leader in the Tory campaign specialized in this task. Yet the large number of outsiders in the campaign was bound to create some tensions, as strangers were thrown together without sufficient time to work out an accommodation among personalities before the trying problems of the campaign began to emerge. As we have indicated, the agent devoted some time to the smoothing of ruffled feathers and to the establishment of a modus vivendi among people who were experiencing difficulty in getting along with each other. Although she was very adroit at this task, it robbed her of some of the time that she could have spent in doing other, more valuable work. Even more important, there were some occasions when she felt that she would be able to push the organization harder if someone else were engaged in bolstering the morale of the workers while she was adding to the personal costs of their involvement in the short run.

While Mrs. Bowman could deal with those maintenance

problems that were brought to her attention, she simply did not have sufficient time to chase around hunting for them. Agents cannot join with canvassers in a mass canvass, and they cannot interact with the workers in a committee room. Even if they could, their efforts in this direction can hardly be as effective as those of the candidates, particularly if the latter hold credentials as sitting members of parliament.

Although we have no direct evidence to support the case, our research suggests that morale problems were of consequence in the Conservative organization—due in part to the fact that no one emerged as a real maintenance leader in the Tory organization.

Maintenance problems were handled much better on the Labour side, though not in accordance with the division of labor articulated by Mrs. Bowman. The agent, Alan Clarke, was certainly the task leader in that he initiated "the largest number of task-relevant interactions." But, as we have seen, he delegated some of the authority to organize activities and issue orders to a group of executive officials who were given relatively free rein and who, from the point of view of the workers, were the immediate task leaders. When the canvassing officer drove the party workers hard, any potential feelings of hostility were directed toward him and not the agent. This enabled Mr. Clarke to play the role of maintenance leader in his own right because the workers did not perceive him to be the leader who was driving them into the activities that involved high personal costs. As people came into his office, he jollied them along, sympathized with their problems, and encouraged them in their work, frequently complimenting them on the way in which they were handling their assignments. On his trips to the outlying committee rooms, he was instrumental in helping to bolster morale within his campaign organization.

Mr. Richard also built a large component of maintenance leadership into the role he played in the campaign, especially in 1964. When he appeared at Robert Owen House, he usually made it a point to have a cup of tea and a short chat with the ladies who were stuffing envelopes in the basement, thanking them for their work as he waved good-bye. Moreover, he spent a lot of his time in canvassing activities, usually in a different section of the constituency each day. This meant that he had to spend time in each committee room in order to get the canvass cards and to check them in again. Thus, he had plenty of opportunity to interact with the key campaign officials, as well as with the rank-and-file workers who were carrying out clerical and doorstep assignments. His campaign work indicated to these workers that he was willing to go door-to-door and to do the same sort of jobs that they were being called upon to undertake.

The level of interaction between Mr. Richard and the Labour activists leads us to suspect that, owing to the socio-economic composition of the organization, a Labour candidate may be potentially able to perform more effectively in a maintenance role than his Tory counterpart. Many Labour enthusiasts derive considerable satisfaction from having *their* member of parliament represent the constituency. They enjoy close association with an M.P. whom they know well and consider to be their personal friend. In their conversations at the pub or through his reports to the GMC, they like to hear about what is really going on at Westminster—the happenings and nuances that are never treated in the press. This means a great deal to an ordinary Labour enthusiast who lives in a fairly narrow social setting. Intimate contact with an M.P. widens his horizon a bit and gives him a link with a larger world. Since this type of personal association is attractive to many Labour activists, the Labour M.P. is in an execellent position to occupy the role of maintenance leader.

Although close association with an M.P. may be attractive to some Tory workers in much the same way, it is probably a much less significant influence in the Conservative Party. Many Tory activists are affiliated with clubs and other social organizations where they learn the "inside dope" on happenings in the House of Commons. Moreover, social interaction in the course of their normal business affairs is likely to satisfy their "informational needs" and may even bring them into contact with members of the House. Thus, the Tory activists are not so dependent upon intimate association with a single M.P. from their own constituency—a situation that makes it somewhat less easy for a Conservative candidate to step into a "natural" maintenance leader role.

Summary

On the few objective measures of efficiency and effectiveness presented at the beginning of this chapter, the Labour organization in Barons Court scored better in the 1964 campaign than the Conservative machine. Labour's canvass was more complete, and, when allowance is made for the fact that the party had many more pledges to redeem and enlisted supporters who were less likely to vote without prodding, the organization performed better on the knock-up. However, so far as we can judge, the two canvasses appear to have been about equal in accuracy, an interesting finding in view of the general criticisms which British observers have made of canvassing activities.

Labour's greater efficiency can be partly explained by its more decentralized organization, operating in a task environment in which significant advantages accrued to decentralization. Only on the gathering of postal votes—a campaign task in which centralization is an advantage—was the Conservative performance superior. The Conservative agent, of course, did not centralize the operation because she preferred this form of organization; she had no real alternative owing to conditions in the ward branches and her lack of experience in the constituency.

Another organizational difference related to the relative effectiveness of the two parties can be seen in the greater flexibility of the Labour agent in assigning executive personnel to their jobs. The Labour agent was also able to maintain better surveillance over his decentralized operation. Compared with the opposition, he picked up weaknesses in the organization more quickly, making the necessary adjustments to correct them, and he was quicker to discover the salience of issues that might hurt the party and to develop strategies to counteract their impact.

This difference, in turn, is closely related to the type of active workers who were at the disposal of the two agents. The Tories recruited most of their more-than-evening workers from outside the local organization. This can be explained by the contrasting reward systems in the two parties. In the Conservative Party, more of the rewards are controlled *above* the constituency level, i.e., distributed by the Central Office. This means that deeply involved campaign workers feel free to move from their home base into other constituencies during a campaign. A young Tory activist who wishes to get his name on the candidate's list knows that the decision will be made in Central Office, which consults with the agents who are familiar with his work. Hence, he may perceive advantages to be gained by throwing himself into a campaign in a marginal district, where the need for workers is more crucial than in his home territory.

The Labour reward system, on the other hand, operates almost entirely at the local level. For the relatively few workers who nurture parliamentary ambitions, the decisions of the ward organizations and the General Management Committee are important in getting their names on the B List. They are likely, therefore, to find it more advantageous to remain in their local bailiwicks. More important for the Labour activist than for his Tory counterpart are offices in local government and in the local party— positions that are distributed locally and can be used to reward loyal service to the political organization.

The most significant rewards that a local Conservative association has to dispense for political activity are social ones. But for these to be efficacious, social life in the community must be centered to a significant extent within the boundaries of the parliamentary

297

constituency. This was not the case in Barons Court, and the local Conservative association was unable to utilize the reward that in most Tory organizations appears to be the most salient locally.

These contrasting patterns of rewards in the Barons Court parties help to account for two observable characteristics of the campaign:

1. The major administrative load was carried by "outsiders" in the Conservative headquarters and by "insiders" in the Labour camp.
2. The kinds of people recruited for executive responsibility in the Tory organization tended to limit the agent's flexibility in assigning workers to particular tasks and to prevent the agent from handling the surveillance problem effectively.

Another noticeable difference between the two parties—though the evidence here is more intuitive—lies in the morale factor. As we followed the campaign in both camps, it appeared to us that morale was higher among Labour workers than among the Conservatives. The fact that the Tories lacked an active maintenance leader, while the Socialists had both the agent and the candidate performing in this role, may account for the difference.

One of the questions we asked at the beginning of this chapter was whether organizational factors make any difference in the outcome of an election. We cannot, of course, answer this question in generalized terms. But our research strongly suggests that organization was an important influence in the 1964 election in Barons Court. We cannot ignore the fact that the Conservatives were unable to make a thorough canvass, ending the campaign with only a little more than half the number of pledges that Labour had compiled. In attempting to explain the outcome, we conclude that this was the single most important difference between the two organizations. The difficulties the Conservatives encountered in meeting their canvassing targets were, in turn, related to some of the problems already discussed—overcentralization, lack of flexibility in the assignment of key personnel, and the inability to exercise adequate supervision over outlying units. In the Barons Court election in 1964, an exceptionally effective Labour organization confronted a good Tory machine. Had the levels of effectiveness been reversed, Barons Court might have moved against the national tide and remained a Conservative seat.

Epilogue

T his book has ended on a cold, analytical note which reflects our concern to use the data collected in Barons Court and a few other districts in London to broaden our knowledge about the local constituency party as an organization. While this suits our intellectual purposes—we designed the project with this objective in mind—it conceals to some extent the intensely personal nature of the interactions that were so fruitful as we carried out the study. In the role of participating observers, we conducted an inquiry that turned out to be a most enjoyable experience, and we have come to regard many of the people who are treated as actors in this drama as personal friends for whom we have great respect and affection. For this reason it has not always been easy for us to put their behavior under the microscope of scholarly analysis; close examination of this sort requires that the actions of leaders be dissected and that their diagnoses of the political situation, usually made in an atmosphere of emergency, be carefully scrutinized (with the benefit of hindsight) in light of knowledge which appeared later but which may not have been available to campaign leaders when crucial decisions had to be made. This means that, after weighing the evidence, we have sometimes had to be critical, but this could not be avoided if we were to present an accurate picture of the constituency party as an organization.

We were most fortunate in having two excellent and cooperative agents to work with. We became closely attached to these people, and we extend to them our best wishes as they go about their fascinating job of developing effective political organizations at the constituency level. It is regrettable that one side had to lose in Barons Court, but we quickly realized that we were observing the best in competitive organizations. Mrs. Bowman and Mr. Clarke will continue to serve their respective parties with distinction.

The Battle of Barons Court in 1964 saw the emergence of a new young Labour M.P. who soon began to make a name for himself in the House of Commons, where he is recognized as an influential speaker on defense policy and foreign affairs. He serves as Parliamentary Private Secretary to the Minister of Defense, and he is a member of Britain's delegation to the Consultative Assembly of the Council of Europe and to the Assembly of the Western European Union. It is likely that Mr. Richard will enjoy a long and successful political career, and that he will make an impact upon the Labour Party.

As the defeated candidate, Mr. Carr's political future is more in doubt. The constituency of Barons Court was fortunate in having two first-class candidates as competitors, but it was unfortunate that only one of them could be elected. A man with Carr's talents and policy preferences deserves a place at Westminster. On such policy matters as education and social welfare, he is one of the most knowledgeable people in the Conservative Party. As Edward Heath, the new leader, proceeds to streamline his organization and to remold the Tory program to fit Britain's needs, the party can use Carr's expertise both in its councils and in the House of Commons. We sincerely hope that very shortly he will be able to make a political comeback.

Appendix

Voter Turnout by Time Periods, 1964 and 1966 Elections*

(in percentages)

CATEGORIES OF POLLING DISTRICTS		NUMBER OF ELECTORS	TOTAL VOTER TURNOUT	VOTING FROM 7–8
1964 Election				
Constituency		46,048	72.9	3.0
Strong Labour	PDs	12,047	72.7	2.9
Strong Tory	PDs	8,756	69.8	3.2
Leaning Labour	PDs	10,501	70.0	3.3
Leaning Tory	PDs	6,520	71.6	3.5
Marginal	PDs	6,993	69.1	2.1
1966 Election				
Constituency		43,830	75.2	3.4
Strong Labour	PDs	11,247	75.5	3.4
Strong Tory	PDs	8,861	72.6	3.9
Leaning Labour	PDs	10,501	75.6	3.2
Leaning Tory	PDs	6,520	56.7	4.4
Marginal	PDs	6,993	73.2	2.3

* This Table does not include polling district Ja, whose idiosyncrasies do not permit classification into these categories. The political complexion of the polling districts is based upon Labour and Conservative canvassing reports for the two elections. The hourly voting figures have been obtained from the returning officer. The categorization of polling districts is as follows:

1. Strong Labour: Ga, Gc, Jb, Lb, Na
2. Strong Tory: Fc, Fd, Ic, Ka, Kb
3. Leaning Labour: Gb, Hb, Jc, La, Oa
4. Leaning Tory: Jd, Je, Jf, Ma, Mc
5. Marginal: Mb, Nb, Nc

VOTING FROM 8–11	VOTING FROM 11–1	VOTING FROM 1–4	VOTING FROM 4–6	VOTING FROM 6–9
17.2	11.1	13.7	15.4	39.1
12.7	9.8	13.8	17.2	43.6
25.4	12.2	13.5	13.3	32.2
15.1	11.5	14.4	16.0	39.6
21.8	12.2	13.4	14.7	34.5
14.3	10.8	13.4	15.1	44.4
17.8	11.2	12.8	15.8	37.7
13.3	10.5	13.0	16.7	43.0
25.6	12.5	12.7	13.9	31.4
15.2	11.4	13.1	17.5	38.1
24.1	11.6	12.0	15.2	32.6
14.6	11.2	13.5	15.9	42.4

Index

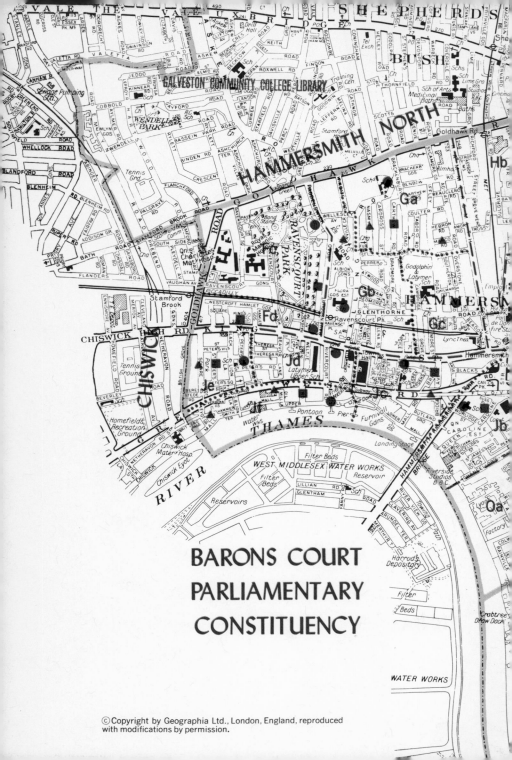

BARONS COURT
PARLIAMENTARY
CONSTITUENCY